Cooking for the Senses

VEGAN NEUROGASTRONOMY

*Jennifer Peace Rhind
and Gregor Law*

D1345465

LONDON AND PHILADELPHIA

First published in 2018
by Singing Dragon
an imprint of Jessica Kingsley Publishers
73 Collier Street
London N1 9BE, UK
and
400 Market Street, Suite 400
Philadelphia, PA 19106, USA

www.singingdragon.com

All photography and food styling by Gregor Law.
Cover and interior designed by Adam Peacock.

Library of Congress Cataloging in Publication Data
Names: Rhind, Jennifer, author. | Law, Gregor, author.
Title: Cooking for the senses : vegan neurogastronomy / Jennifer Peace Rhind and Gregor Law.
Description: London ; Philadelphia : Singing Dragon, [2018] | Includes index.
Identifiers: LCCN 2017031597 | ISBN 9781848193000 (alk. paper)
Subjects: LCSH: Food--Sensory evaluation. | Flavor. | Vegan cooking. | LCGFT: Cookbooks.
Classification: LCC TX546 .R54 2018 | DDC 641.5/636--dc23 LC record available at https://lccn.loc.gov/2017031597

British Library Cataloguing in Publication Data
A CIP catalogue record for this book is available from the British Library

ISBN 978 1 84819 300 0
eISBN 978 0 85701 251 7

Printed and bound in China

*For Derek and Gertie,
with love*
Jen

For my wife, Alison
Greg

Contents

Preface

Neurogastronomy introduces an alternative and inspiring way of looking at food and flavour, and changes the way we might perceive plant-based cuisine – perhaps breaking a few prejudices along the way. We look at the science behind the senses, which helps us understand our individual likes and dislikes, and introduce some kitchen science, which helps us understand how to maximise flavour. A wide range of ingredients from the plant kingdom are explored from the flavour perspective, and we present recipes that reflect neurogastronomy in action. But we hope that this is not a 'dry' read; in the spirit of neurogastronomy, we have seasoned it with tales of our own culinary experiences, from the sublime to the ridiculous – such is the human palate!

You may well ask why this is a book about plant ingredients and cuisine...and so here is some insight.

According to my mother, I began to reject meat and poultry when I was a toddler. I think that this was because I did not enjoy the texture of flesh in my mouth. As a child, I dreaded the visits to the local butcher's shop, where the sights and smells nauseated me. My first determined foray into the world of vegetarianism was when I was a teenager in the late 1960s to early 1970s, and my father (rather unfairly) blamed Pink Floyd and my musical heroes for this worrying development – probably because they represented the counterculture of the era. My mother gamely prepared lentil roasts, and eventually my father

became a pescatarian! However, like most of us who are interested in good food, I experimented with my palate, and a world of exciting flavours was revealed – at least within my self-imposed limits (poultry was never ever on the menu!). For decades, I lived as a flexible vegetarian and an occasional fish and seafood eater. So, why did I become vegan? The rise of the internet and freely accessible information about how our food is produced was making it difficult for me to reconcile my eating habits with my conscience. A vegan friend, Joe Bergin, posted an image on Facebook. It was a close up of a pig's eye, with the mirrored reflection of the horror of his surroundings...and then one of a cow with tears streaming down her face. They are all exactly the same as us, in that they are sentient beings; they have families, social bonds, feelings, emotions. And that, for me, was it. I literally 'became a vegan' in that instant. I stopped making excuses for the sake of my palate, and I began to follow a vegan lifestyle. When I told family and friends about my choice, there were mixed reactions, the most common being 'Oh my goodness, what on earth can you eat?' However, any time I was asked to explain myself, the most common responses were 'each to their own' or 'you do yours, I do mine' (i.e. please don't lecture me on my lifestyle choices!), or 'I don't have issues, but...' (followed by gentle jibes and/or justifications), or 'I hope you will not be vegan when you come over for dinner' (yes, really), or 'I admire you but I couldn't...' Then, of course, there were those who assumed it was for the good of my health, and somehow that made it acceptable, or, conversely, that I would be missing out on vital nutrients and, of course, protein, and then there were those who went down the line of defending the farming industries.

All of this taught me a great deal – as Robert Burns wrote, 'O would some power the giftie gie us to see ourselves as others see us.' The various perspectives that were expressed (often defensive in tone) enabled me to explore my chosen lifestyle from the viewpoint of others, and this ultimately changed the way that I communicate my feelings and ideals. Like many individuals, I don't like being labelled or categorised, and prefer instead to let my personal beliefs and convictions be reflected in how I live, not simply by what I eat.

So, I am not here to take the moral high ground. This book is all about flavour. When I became vegan at first, despite being a competent cook, I experienced what I can only describe as a sort of paralysis in the kitchen. Suddenly, some of my staple ingredients were no more. It was my research background and experience in the flavour industry, and then as an aromatherapist, essential oil educator, writer, and student of artisan perfumery, that came to my rescue. I began looking at vegan cuisine from the aroma perspective of herbs and spices, and from there it was a natural progression to explore the flavours of all the amazing plant ingredients at our disposal. I realised that neurogastronomy was the key to elevating plant-based cuisine to where it belongs – up there with the very best of vegetarian and omnivorous cuisines! Greg is integral and instrumental in this – his recipes embrace the spirit of neurogastronomy and are inspirational in every sense of the word. Go on – explore, immerse yourself, create, share, enjoy!

To those who might think that a plant-based diet is difficult to follow and missing your favourite animal-derived ingredients, I would say this: focus upon all the plant ingredients that you *enjoy*, rather than what you *choose not* to eat, and

you might come to realise that this way of eating is about abundance rather than restriction, and about kindness and compassion – and that in itself is a very good feeling indeed.

Preparing food for others is an act of love. A form of giving, and directing our attention away from the self, it goes beyond simple 'feeding' and extends into the realm of nurturing minds, bodies and souls. Eating together is important too; we can form rewarding and enduring friendships over plates of food. And when our palette of ingredients comes exclusively from the plant kingdom, we are also being kind to the planet and our fellow sentient beings that live here with us.

The Recipe Collection will inspire you, and encourage you to stretch and develop your palate and culinary repertoire, while the **Exploring Flavour** section can be your own voyage of reflection and discovery.

This book is for everyone who would like to deepen their understanding of cooking with plant ingredients and flavour creation – a vital part of our global culinary future – and so it is also a handbook for a new era of eating 'well', in every sense of the word.

For the animals which share our world, and show us how we can become better humans,

Jennifer

Exploring Flavour

Understanding Taste and Flavour

We are the only species on the planet which prepares meals.

Let us take a moment to reflect upon this statement. Why is eating such an important sensory experience for humans?

If we watch our omnivorous canine companions eating dinner, we see perhaps a quick sniffing session followed by a head in the bowl, swallowing or even 'bolting' food, courtesy of their adapted tongues and their 'open/shut' jaw motion – there is no chewing or savouring of every bite! Leeloo, our first exuberant gold-and-white Tibetan Terrier, ate quite voraciously, whereas our chic and gentle, black-and-white Gertie is much more circumspect and dainty. Then, if we look at our carnivorous feline friends catching and eating their prey (or, in Harry the black panther cat's case, illicitly sampling the Iberian ham), we see their little needle-like, sharp teeth and claws tearing at the flesh; again, anything that is consumed is accomplished with little evidence of chewing – because feline jaws are not adapted to chew. Now consider the cow – the big, gentle herbivore – and observe its jaw motion as it 'chews the cud' at a leisurely pace while taking in its surroundings. I am sure that you will agree that no other species, whatever the facial adaptations, appears to take the same sort of pleasure that we humans take in eating – indeed, some make a profession out of eating well and are known as gourmands!

Apart from discovering fire and cooking food, humans are uniquely adapted to perceive flavour – and this is the key! Flavour is so very much more than 'taste'. Although the foods that we prepare and eat contain flavoursome molecules, flavour itself is created by the relationship between our anatomy, physiology and nervous system, and it is interpreted in the brain. The relatively new science of neurogastronomy shows us how we perceive flavour, and from this we can begin to understand the human palate and its idiosyncrasies, and how local and regional cuisines have emerged and evolved, right across the globe.

NEUROGASTRONOMY

Now, as someone who has a professional interest in the sense of smell, and who is also a perfume lover and happy home cook, the concept of neurogastronomy is stimulating and intriguing. However, when we look at using it to enhance our ways of preparing meals and eating, a whole new culinary world is revealed.

As you may rightly suspect, neurogastronomy is a complex science – as indeed is food science. However, we often think of cooking as an 'art' – a skill that is learned by trial and error and by cultivating our sense of flavour. Most of us learn from the accumulated wisdom of our predecessors, from ancient practices and traditional recipes, from our immediate and extended families, from our social circles, and from the interpretations and innovations of talented contemporary chefs. Here, it is not the science of neurogastronomy that is the focus, but the artistic application of its basic principles, and so the act of preparing meals can become an ever-rewarding, creative endeavour.

Rather than encouraging us to be 'cerebral' about our food – perhaps thinking about its ethical and nutritional attributes, or experimenting with gadgets in the kitchen – neurogastronomy teaches us to honour our palate and ingredients; it can help us transform our time in the kitchen into a form of mindfulness and all of the sensory pleasure and sense of wellbeing that this can offer.

We experience our world through our senses – sight, hearing, smell, taste and touch – and also through our so-called sixth sense, which I will call intuition for want of a better word. In this context, intuition can be thought of as a type of higher reasoning, a heart-centred instinct seasoned with prior knowledge, which has become embedded in our sensory memory. I would suggest that any activity that harnesses all of our senses and channels them, focussing them on a single creative endeavour, not only stimulates our potential for higher cognitive reasoning but also takes us into a therapeutic head-space and heart-space. The only activity that I can think of that does all of this is cooking!

So, this is not just about the physical senses through which we gain a perception of our world. We can use science to gain a partial understanding of our physical, material existence, but we are much, much more than what we see, hear, smell, taste and touch. Cooking allows us the opportunity to create and invent, and move beyond these senses, and if we truly cook from the heart, and without the exploitation of our fellow sentient beings, it is an expression of love.

This is why I believe that respecting and cultivating our palates is so important for wellbeing. My personal experience of healing from stress and anxiety was due, in no small part, to practising natural perfumery and experimenting in the kitchen. This is what led me to explore the crucial links between the senses and wellbeing – and, yes, neurogastronomy.

I am going to explain this as I discovered it, when reading Gordon Shepherd's wonderful exploration of the subject, *Neurogastronomy*, and so, for me, that naturally began with the sense of smell.

Smell

When we talk about our sense of smell, we are normally referring to how we receive and perceive and make sense of the odours around us – and this includes the lovely aromas of spices and herbs, as well as malodours such as putrefaction and burning. Odours have an important biological role, as well as guiding our eating preferences. This type of smelling is more correctly described as orthonasal smelling, because it happens when we breathe in through our noses, or sniff. Odour exists in vapour form – where molecules are light enough to evaporate into the atmosphere and reach the nose. These molecules are detected by the millions of nerve endings known as olfactory hairs which are located in our olfactory organ – the very thin twin membranes located on each side of the bony part of the nasal septum. These olfactory hairs are connected with the neurons of the adjacent 'olfactory bulb', which extends to form the olfactory nerve that sends olfactory signals to the brain. Neurons from the olfactory tract extend into several parts of the brain – the *limbic system*, which is associated with emotional response, memories, motivation and pleasure; the *thalamus*, where sensory integration occurs; the *hypothalamus*, where bodily functions are monitored and maintained; the *amygdala*, which is associated with basic emotions; and the *hippocampus*, which is associated with memory. In addition, the olfactory neurons also project into the *frontal cortex*, the region associated with organising and planning, and this is where recognition of the odour occurs. The area known as the *prefrontal cortex* is also influenced by odours – and this is where executive, logical and social decisions are made. It is hardly surprising, then, that orthonasal smell has such a profound emotional impact on us, while affecting cognitive processes, emotions, and every aspect of our behaviour!

As far as flavour is concerned, our orthonasal sense can be the initial attraction or rejection, because we have learned from experience or cultural conditioning that foods that smell a particular way either will or will not appeal to our palates. Anyone who has attempted to eat a French rural speciality known as *tripoux* will understand the latter reaction! *Tripoux* is a dish made from the rumen/guts of a sheep and is noted for its characteristic odour. A good friend, who was determined to eat it, despite several warnings from the waiter, waited in anticipation as the dish was delivered and the lid of the silver salver lifted with a flourish to reveal *tripoux* in all its glory... and then a faecal odour reached his nose, and this was enough to prevent him taking even one mouthful!

When we lose our sense of orthonasal smell – maybe due to sinus problems or a cold – we might claim instead that we have 'lost our sense of taste'. However, there is much more to understand about the role of smell in flavour, and that is because we have another sensory system implicated – and that is retronasal smell.

Just as breathing in facilitates orthonasal smelling, breathing out facilitates retronasal smelling. This can be considered a separate olfactory system, and it is one of the important ways in which we humans perceive flavour.

We mentioned the dog earlier. Most dogs have long snouts, at least in comparison with ours, and they are better adapted to sniffing than we are, and much better at sensing odours in their environment (especially since their noses are near to the ground). That is why we are often told that our sense of smell is so inferior to that of our canine companions. But dogs do not chew and savour food in the way that we do, and that is because they do not have the same capacity for retronasal smelling. Humans are upright, bipedal creatures, and our facial structures allow stereoscopic vision, but we have a lesser capacity for orthonasal smell than dogs. We also have a short nasopharynx, and our teeth and jaws are adapted for chewing food.

So, when we chew a mouthful of food, using our teeth, jaws and tongue to move it around in our mouth (more about that later), the components stimulating our taste buds (more of that later too), and then exhale, something fascinating happens: the air is forced from our lungs to the very back of the oral cavity, where it picks up all of the odour molecules that have been released in the mouth by chewing, and is then pushed into the back of the nasal chamber and out through the nostrils. This process sends signals to the olfactory system. Here, our senses are literally sending mixed messages – we think that the flavour is coming from our mouth, but it is actually our olfactory system picking up the signals which are interpreted in the brain.

Gordon Shepherd suggests that our nasopharynx is specifically adapted for retronasal smell, and so we have a richer repertoire of flavours than other primates and mammals, and that retronasal smell is perhaps the most important part of flavour perception. But he goes even further, quoting Brillat-Savarin (a gourmand and writer) who said, 'Tell me what you eat and I shall tell you what you are' – and hypothesising that retronasal smell makes us humans what we are. Unlike orthonasal smell, retronasal smell is a sense that cannot exist in isolation. It is inextricably bound up with our sense of taste and of touch.

The 'pinch nose coriander taste test' is a good way to experience the role of smell in flavour. Take a coriander (cilantro) leaf, and pinch your nostrils together – and now place the leaf in your mouth and chew to release the flavour. Get anything? No? You see, flavour is mostly aroma, and taste is less important than smell.

Taste

Much of the time, it would seem that it is our taste buds that are credited with detecting flavour!

We say 'that *tastes* good' rather than comment on flavour *per se*. Most of us have a poor flavour vocabulary anyway; we are not encouraged to learn the words to describe what we are eating.

Our taste buds – clusters of sensory cells – are visible on the tongue. Taste buds are also present on the roof of the mouth and in the throat, the stomach and the lining of the small intestine! In the mouth, small buds, known as papillae, are located on the central area of the tongue, larger ones on the sides towards the back, and large round ones at the back and across the middle portion. These papillae are made up of specialised cells that detect different tastes – namely, salty, sour, sweet, bitter and umami or savoury. Umami is a relatively new Japanese word – derived from from *umai* (delicious) and *mi* (essence, flavour). It was initially investigated by Kikunae Ikeda, who identified that it was imparted by an amino acid called glutamic acid and its salts, known as glutamates. These substances are not particularly tasty on their own, but when they stimulate taste receptors in combination with other taste sensations, the effect is one of flavour enhancement. Glutamic acid and glutamates also act synergistically with other food components such as inosinate and guanylate, compounds found in plant foods such as tomatoes, potatoes, asparagus, lentils and spinach.

Ayurvedic medicine identifies a sixth taste, *Kashai* or astringent (think of the 'rough', dry feel on your tongue after a mouthful of black tea, or eating some pomegranate). The balance of these six tastes in line with our individual constitutions is thought to be central to our optimal health and constitution – in stark contrast to the way that taste is viewed in the West.

So, what is the biological significance of taste? Shepherd suggests that we seek salty foods to maintain our salty body fluids, and that this might reflect a dim and distant sea ancestry; that all mammals like sweetness (think of mother's milk and ripe fruits) because it signifies a high energy value; and that savouriness (meatiness) also indicates a high energy source and is very attractive to us. On the other hand, bitterness often warns of toxic plants and herbs, and sourness can indicate food that is going off.

However, our palates have adapted to enjoy all of these tastes – reflecting a type of learned behaviour. Liking salty, savoury and sweet foods comes naturally to us. The food industry has exploited our innate desire for these tastes, and incorporates sugar and salt and artificial flavourings in many foods to make them more attractive to our palates – often to the detriment of our health. However, we also learn to enjoy the bitterness of dark chocolate and coffee, and the quinine in tonic water, and the sourness of pickled and fermented foods.

Many other factors can condition our tastes and reactions. For example, if a food you have eaten makes you sick – even hours after ingestion – you can lose your taste for it permanently and refuse to consume it on future occasions. This is known as 'bait shyness', or sometimes 'Béarnaise sauce phenomenon', after the psychologist Martin Seligman blamed the Béarnaise sauce on his steak for an episode of violent sickness – even though the actual cause was an enterovirus that was doing the rounds! Bait shyness is also well known to ship stewards, who maintain that seasick passengers often blame the buffet. Shepherd has suggested that bait shyness may be one of the underlying causes of childhood food phobias, and I must agree – for me it is whelks (sea snails)... gathered on a beach on a family holiday near Portmahomack on the northeast coast of Scotland and etched on my memory for ever.

Now, it is well accepted that smells can elicit strong emotional reactions, but so can taste. We can witness this in facial expressions when foods are tasted, ranging from delight to disgust. This can be seen in all phases of life – from infants to the elderly – and it is known as the 'hedonic' quality of food. Like the sense of smell, which is hardwired into our brains, our tongues also vary in our ability to detect tastes. Those who are able to detect tiny amounts of a bitter compound called propylthiouracil are called 'supertasters', and they have a larger number of taste buds than normal. Supertasters are, allegedly, more likely to dislike vegetables but they tend to be leaner, while the rest of us (myself included) tend to enjoy fatty and sweet foods, and alcoholic drinks, and, unsurprisingly, are more likely to be overweight! So, our taste receptor genes are linked to our food preferences and, as a consequence, diet-related health issues.

Texture

Sometimes it is the texture of a food that is closely related to its appeal – or otherwise. Texture – also known as mouth-feel or mouth-sense – incorporates touch, pressure/resistance, temperature and even pain, and is detected by somatosensory nerve fibres in the mouth. Now, pain is a special case, because it is the pain receptors that are responsible for our fondness for chilli and hot spicy foods. Naturally, if something causes discomfort, we instinctively recoil. However, chilli contains an irritant called capsaicin, and we can not only learn to tolerate the burning sensation but also come to enjoy it! It is true that our tolerance can grow, and that the more chilli we use, the more we seek it.

Moving back to mouth-sense, think about how food feels in the mouth when it is introduced and then chewed, to release the flavour molecules. There are many textures to appreciate. Here are the main ones as listed by Gordon Shepherd (with some embellishment)...

Smooth, creamy, thick (viscous), unctuous, velvety
Crunchy, crisp
Springy, chunky, stiff
Soft, yielding, claggy (thick, sticky and gooey)
Slippery, slithery, silky
Rough, gritty, granular
Astringent, mouth puckering

Hot, cold, warm, lukewarm
Pain – burning, aching, prickling
Dry, moist
Light, dense
Ease of fragmentation – sticky, crumbly, chewy

Sometimes, textures are just as important as flavours and tastes in terms of preferences and dislikes. For example, I do not enjoy the texture of badly made risotto, slippery barley risotto is my idea of 'food hell', and I have difficulty even swallowing claggy porridge! This has little to do with taste and everything to do with texture. Texture is all-important in food acceptability. When composing dishes, we also need to look for textural contrasts to bring the food alive and make it exciting. But there is another factor at work: there are some interesting interactions between smell, taste and texture that we can exploit. For example:

The scent of vanilla can make a dish taste sweeter.
Sweetness enhances smoothness and creaminess.
Sourness emphasises thinner textures.
Salt diminishes bitterness.
We are more sensitive to tastes in foods that are presented at body temperature.
Warmer foods taste stronger.
If a dish contains chilli, we will be less able to detect other tastes and smells.
Gel-like textures reduce the capacity for retronasal smell.
Heat increases the capacity for orthonasal smell.

This is where we can start to think about the principles of neurogastronomy in the kitchen! But there are two other senses that play a part before we get the whole concept – sound and vision.

Sound

Now, this might seem a little strange, but sounds can influence flavour and our reactions to foods. When we listen to how food sounds when it is being eaten, we glean a lot of information about it – how hard or soft it is, whether it is ripe or unripe, overcooked or undercooked, crunchy or smooth, and so on. Hearing the sounds of another person eating noisily can, for some of us, be very irritating, and slurping or chewing with the mouth open can be singularly unattractive. These are examples of external sounds, made by others in the environment. But when we bite into a raw carrot, we *expect* to generate an internal crunching sound within our mouth – one that is *congruent* with freshness and crispness – confirming what we expect from a carrot. Or consider a well-executed chip (French fry) – our tongue detects a superficial roughness before we hear the crunch as we break through the surface, experiencing a savoury chewiness while exposing the smooth, unctuous interior which then becomes amalgamated with the exterior as we continue to chew...and the crunching sound fades. Similarly, we hear a characteristic snapping and splashing sound when we bite into a crisp green apple. We can think of many other examples – such as crackly, when the bones of the jaw respond to the vibration of sound – and it is thought that the clearer the sound is, and the lower its frequency, the more we enjoy it!

These congruent sounds enhance our perception of flavour. The use of sound to enhance the experience of eating has been demonstrated in molecular gastronomy. Heston Blumenthal created a dish named The Sound of the Sea, which combines our visual sense (the plate is presented as a tideline, with flotsam and jetsam, beached greenery and foam) with a soundscape of the seaside, and a gentle breeze scented with 'sea odour', to include an enhanced orthonasal element.

And finally, *glou-glou* – the sound of wine as it is being swallowed after swishing around the mouth. According to an anecdote relayed by Shepherd, and attributed to the chef Paul Bocuse, a good wine is said to satisfy all of the senses through its colour, its bouquet, its mouth-feel, its taste and its *glou-glou*!

Appearance

We are all familiar with the saying 'We eat with our eyes' – often that is our very first impression of a dish. We are ending this exploration of neurogastronomy with sight, because it completes our multisensorial picture, and although it is not directly related to the taste of food or the act of smelling, it has an enormous impact on flavour.

Our dominant sense is sight. In neurogastronomy, the most important aspect of sight is colour. Colour can suggest the way something will smell and taste – in other words, it is strongly implicated in our perception of flavour. A simple example: the colour of a wine will immediately give us an indication of what to expect when we take a sip. We can gauge this through the hue and intensity of a red, or the colour of whites, from pale straw to golden.

Have you ever been presented with a wine blindfolded, or, for that matter, a morsel of food? Even those of us who like to think that we have reasonable palates can be fooled if we are denied the sight of what we are eating and drinking!

Again, we can see examples of how the palate can be tricked in the world of molecular gastronomy – perhaps by presenting savoury dishes in the guise of sweets and desserts, and vice versa...when our eyes tell us what to expect only to be confused and contradicted by our palates!

This is why careful, thoughtful and congruent presentation of our dishes is important. It is not about being 'chefy' or clever, but about using our visual sense to enhance the perception of flavour and enjoyment of our food!

Sensory images

Each of the sensory signals received by the brain forms the basis for flavour perception. It is easier for us to understand that vision gives rise to 'spatial' images and that sound frequencies form 'tonotopic' maps, than to accept that smell also stimulates images in the brain. But, in fact, smell does give rise to neural images, and the patterns generated can be detected with functional magnetic resonance imaging (fMRI). With fMRI, we can see parts of the brain 'lighting up' in response to flavours!

These images are the brain's way of interpreting the world around us, but they are constantly modulated by other internal sensory signals, and also by 'external' factors, which include atmosphere and ambience. Even our emotions are implicated, and maybe this is why we are advised not to cook if we are in a bad mood, and that our food tastes better if we are happy! It is certainly why we do not linger in fast-food places, but are more than happy to spend an entire evening around a table in relaxed and convivial company. Or, indeed, why décor and lighting are important in the overall eating experience – we are less likely to relax and enjoy our food in either sterile or dirty surroundings, or when there is harsh, bright, dim or incongruent lighting.

From the womb to old age

Neurogastronomy also explains how our palates evolve as we develop, grow and mature and age. We do know that the flavours of the foods eaten in pregnancy reach the unborn child via amniotic fluid, and that these flavours influence future preferences, starting at the weaning phase. A new-born child is fully equipped for hedonic responses to foods – just look at the facial expressions of babies! Breast milk accurately reflects the mother's preferences, and so these also influence the baby – and this tells us that from a very early stage we are forming flavour images in our brains. In childhood, we are very sensitive to taste, especially sweet, salty and sour foods – a fact not overlooked by the fast-food industry, guaranteeing customers for life. Sadly, our children are being overwhelmed by the amounts of sugar, salt and fat in their diets, and their palates are being destroyed; and along with this we are witnessing many strong food aversions that may be very difficult to change. Indeed, it is believed that the brain flavour system continues to develop through adolescence, when new flavours become attractive while familiar ones continue to overstimulate – and when the concept of 'dieting' as a means of control assumes importance, no wonder obesity and eating disorders develop! However, the role of flavour in all of this is rarely discussed. Flavour perception has a strong emotional and motivational aspect; indeed, it has been shown that we all produce 'emotional flavour images' – also known as 'images of desire' – and food cravings are similar in many ways to the desire for addictive drugs. We are looking for the 'reward'. Whether we are hungry or satiated also has a strong influence on these internal images. We will tend to overeat when there is an abundance of sensory stimuli – think of a Western-style buffet. Some of us have been exposed to long-term overstimulation, and so although our internal flavour images give us pleasure, they are also responsible for eating habits that can be hazardous to our health! Flavour is inextricably interconnected with nutrition. Shepherd makes an important observation here. Traditional cuisines are the key – they contain a balance between quantity and flavour, so that the stomach is stretched just enough to signal satisfaction at the same time as the flavour reward is delivered. In other words, this balance is crucial to optimal flavour system functioning.

At the other end of our lifespan, it all changes, again. Very often, the elderly and those suffering from dementia lose their sense of smell – with subtle yet devastating consequences on both quality of life and appetite, because aroma is such a crucial part of flavour. Neurogastronomy tells us that even if orthonasal and retronasal smell is diminished or lost, we can still sense tastes – sweet, sour, salty and bitter – and heat from chilli, ginger and pepper can still be appreciated. This is why we often see the elderly responding favourably to taste contrasts such as sweet and sour, stimulating combinations such as sweet chilli and robust spices. Texture takes on even more significance, because mouth-feel will relate to flavour memory, and so, for example, the salty crunch of crisps, or cold-sweet-smooth ice cream, is often enjoyed. Contrast is so important! Presentation needs care too; we can help stimulate the appetite by offering an attractively presented selection of small portions which reflect an abundance of taste, flavour and textural contrasts. So, when cooking for the elderly, sensory stimulation is all-important, and neurogastronomy shows us how to achieve this!

Thankfully, over the course of our lives we are able to 'train' our palates, and the process has parallels with the way in which a trainee perfumer learns their art and craft. In essence, we need to learn the flavour vocabulary and use it appropriately, and expose ourselves to foods and flavours and combinations. We can then begin to really understand our own palate and learn about preferences and discuss these in a meaningful way. Of course, we all need to follow recipes – whether we are starting from scratch or experimenting with new cuisines and their herbs, spices and cooking techniques. But, as Alec Lawless (2009), the artisan perfumer (and excellent cook), noted, 'in Ottoman cooking, the cultivation of taste is preferred to following recipes'.

USING YOUR PALATE

It is so important to taste and smell as you are progressing. By this I mean evaluating seasoning, the balance of herbs and spices, and proportions of other ingredients. Only by doing this, as well as consciously appreciating the results of our endeavours, can we learn.

Most of the time we might follow recipes – and a cookbook stand on your workspace is a great idea, especially for those of us who are unable to retain recipes in our heads for any length of time – but at some point we will experiment and invent. This is when experience is needed as well as a sense of adventure. So, never be afraid to make your own judgement calls, based on your own preferences. Educate and stretch your palate. Enjoy experimenting with colours, textures, tastes and flavours to provide contrasts, common threads and coherence in your dishes.

I have always been struck by the parallels between natural perfume construction and classic herb or spice combinations – and indeed entire recipes! In natural perfumery, we form 'accords', combinations of a few aromatics which can either share characteristics or notes – for example, natural pairs such cinnamon and clove will augment spiciness – or contain elements which provide contrast and can enhance one another, such as rose and clove bud, where the spicy facet of rose is awakened by clove, while rose softens and harmonises the strident spice. These accords are then combined to give a fragrance with top, heart and base notes – a fragrance that evolves as it sits on the skin. Fragrance, like flavour, is not one-dimensional. Sometimes, when ingredients or accords do not share any characteristics, or when there is no mutual affinity, we need to think about 'aromatic bridges'. These are ingredients which share some characteristics of both accords and can bring balance and coherence. For example, bergamot has citrus, floral and peppery qualities which can bridge the floral neroli with spicy black pepper; and geranium is a rosy floral with a strong herbal/minty aspect, and small doses can bridge rose and herbal elements. It is the same when combining ingredients, herbs and spices... Or is it?

For many years, it has been thought that foods that share flavour compounds will combine well – a concept called 'food pairing' – and you will find numerous examples throughout this book. The classic book *The Flavour Thesaurus* by Niki Segnit explores this in depth, and in a very engaging manner. Research has shown how foods that pair well together often share flavour molecules. Chefs such as François Benzi and Heston Blumenthal have used this knowledge to push culinary boundaries, creating novel recipes which combine ingredients that do not normally share a plate, such as chocolate and blue cheese, which share a staggering 73 flavour molecules!

However, there is more to recipe creation than food pairing...and, as we shall see, perfume theory has parallels with our current understanding of how flavours work together in successful dishes! In 2011, scientists at Harvard began to explore the flavour links between ingredients from across the globe – and the results were fascinating. They found that in the cuisines of North America and Western Europe, flavour pairing dominates, but in East Asia it is the complete opposite. For example, in Japanese and Korean recipes, ingredients which do not share flavour molecules are often used together – very successfully.

In April 2017, Tiago Simas (of Barcelona University) and his team published their research which culminated in a new concept which they named the 'food-bridging hypothesis'. This goes a long way to explaining the complex interrelationships between ingredients and successful recipes. If two ingredients do not share any flavour molecules, or do not have any affinity with one another, they can become linked via a third ingredient which shares some characteristics of the other two – or indeed by chains of paired molecules. When they analysed Latin American cuisine, they found both food pairing and bridging, and in Southeast Asia it emerged that food bridging is common. Pairing has the effect of intensifying flavours because of the shared flavour profiles of the ingredients. Food bridging smooths and harmonises contrasting flavours. So, here is my perspective on how this all manifests...

East Asian recipes (from Japan, Korea and China) avoid both food pairing and bridging, providing striking flavour contrasts in their cuisines. This can be seen in Japanese *sushi* and *sashimi* with the contrasting *shoyu* or *wasabi*, and in the Korean *kimchi* – fermented, pickle-like vegetables seasoned with spicy pepper. China is too vast to generalise and there are regional variations, but we can find contrasts between salty umami soya sauce and sweetness from sugar, or sweet spices such as star anise and cinnamon, with heat from chilli, warmth from ginger, and sourness from vinegar. Interestingly, in Chinese cuisine, star anise and cinnamon/cassia are important in masking the unpleasant cooking odours that emanate from the fat in meats. See Mushroom Sheng Cai Bao; Singapore Rice Noodles.

Southeast Asian recipes (from Indonesia, Malaysia, the Philippines, Thailand and Vietnam) avoid pairing and use bridging, so although we perceive the contrasts, they are smoother and more integrated. For example, we find combinations of sweet, salty and sour tastes in dishes with themed spice blends – for example, Indonesian *bumbu* spice blends, Thai green curry, spicy *laksas*, and in the salty-sweet-umami soya-based condiments such as *kecap manis* and hot chillis. See Vietnamese Sticky Carrots; Southeast Asia-Inspired Butternut Squash and Spinach Curry; 'Long Pepper' Pineapple Koftas.

Western, Southern and Eastern European and North American cuisines follow food-pairing principles and do not use bridging. These cuisines are noted for ingredients which are all in harmony and amplify each other, so turn up the volume! Contrasts are provided in other ways such as through texture and colour. To get a sense of this, think about all of the big, mouthwatering flavours of Mediterranean cuisines where their vibrancy is augmented by regional herbs and exotic spices, and the robust dishes of Eastern Europe such as hearty soups and stews, paprika and dill, and contrasting salads and pickles. See Mushroom Caldereta; Ratatouille with Black Garlic; Lentil and Italian Herb Ragù; Briam.

In **Latin America**, comprising Caribbean, Central American, South American and Mexican cuisines, we find both pairing and bridging, resulting in dishes with vibrant flavour intensity, spiked with contrasts which provide intrigue and excitement.

Just think of the complex Mexican *mole* sauces and vibrant salsas, and the soups and stews of Caribbean cuisine with their spicy accents, and hot pepper condiments. See Mojo Verde Sauce, and White Beans with Smoked Chilli and Lime Pickle.

It is my perception that the creation of a natural perfume has rather a lot in common with Latin American cuisine! And, in the light of these revelations, we can understand even more about flavour and how different cuisines have evolved, and what is so distinctive about them.

Cultivating our most complex sense and letting it shine is one of the most creative and rewarding things we can do, and it will bring so much pleasure to others too. So I urge you to take the time to learn about the real nature of our ingredients, explore their hidden virtues and think about how neurogastronomy and flavour theory can transform the way we approach cooking, and can help us understand why some recipes, such as the ones Greg developed for this book, are so successful! We need to be knowledgeable and mindful – our time in the kitchen is too special to be anything else.

MINDFULNESS IN THE KITCHEN

Meditation and mindfulness are much discussed topics these days – from teaching children in schools how to meditate, to using mindfulness to improve mental health or help us through illness. I mentioned earlier my own experiences with anxiety and how I discovered that practising natural perfumery and spending time in the kitchen were my ways of returning to balance. Here is how it works.

When we *actively* use our sense of smell and taste – and by this I mean consciously directing our full focus on this in a relaxed and pleasurable context – we are engaging our brains in a very special way. Our limbic system is involved, as is cognitive processing. We will breathe differently

– sniffing and also taking deeper breaths – and this too will help return our physiology to a more balanced state. It is difficult to focus on our fears when we engage with the senses in this particular way – there is no space for them. Then, once we start to prepare our ingredients, and we give them our complete focus and respect, we can appreciate their beauty as we clean and peel and chop and slice, and measure out our treasured herbs and spices, or sense the changing textures of dough as we knead – and we experience gratitude, even for the most humble ingredients. Then, when the cooking process commences, our senses can become fully engaged with the aromas and flavours that are being created, and we can observe the changes in colours and textures, and we can taste and adjust. Creating flavour is alchemy – and what a joy to be part of this process!

So, when you practise mindfulness in the kitchen, for a little while you can experience what it is like to live in the moment. And the more you do this, the more that you will find your own path back to inner peace and balance. 'So what?' you might say. 'I am not anxious or stressed.' That is wonderful, and thoughtful preparation and cooking will simply make you feel very happy and content. And what if you are in a really bad mood, or are angry, upset or just plain tired? Best stay out of the kitchen and it will pass... These states are transient!

Of course, mindfulness extends to eating too – noticing all the elements of flavour that we have been talking about. Then, of course, we discover that making food for others and sharing the enjoyment has exponential 'happy' effects – creativity, selflessness, gratitude, giving and sharing...and being kind to each other, our fellow animals and planet Earth is what life should be about!

I am not saying that cooking should become a new therapy. But I am saying that if we consciously use all of our senses in the kitchen, it can make a difference to our wellbeing – as can any truly creative endeavour.

Ingredients and Flavours

Plant-based cuisine is inherently different from the cuisine of omnivores, because our palette of flavours and textures comes exclusively from non-animal sources. Ponder this: meats are cooked with seasonings and additional flavours from the plant kingdom in the form of herbs and spices, and with a bit of help from oils, to develop the anticipated savoury flavour during the cooking process. Also, the textures vary, but the mouth-feel of animal flesh, whether raw or cooked, is unmistakable. Because of this, many omnivores might believe that flavour could be compromised. Also, where can we find umami – the savoury flavour which abounds in animal-derived foods, especially when roasted or fried? How can we make authentic Italian pasta dishes without dairy ingredients such as parmesan or mozzarella, or Spanish-inspired plates without cured meats such as Iberian ham or chorizo? We can overcome these issues with the help of neurogastronomy...and, of course, by looking at the *cucina povera* of various regions, because many of these cuisines were developed by people who did not have access to or could not afford costly ingredients – see Ribollita and Orecchiette con Pangrattato.

In reality, plants, being non-mobile, produce thousands of different types of molecules as forms of self-defence – because they cannot run away from danger or predators. Often these are highly aromatic and strong-tasting chemicals, such as the irritating capsaicin in chilli, or the tear-inducing factor in onions, or the bitter chemicals in coffee, or cyanide compounds in some beans and fruit seeds, or the astringent tannins – the list is massive. Animals have learned to avoid the toxic chemicals and humans have learned to exploit the flavoursome ones. Plant metabolites can also be highly attractive – for example, sweet, ripe fruits are *meant* to be eaten by animals, so that their seeds can be distributed.

It is generally accepted that a plant-based diet will provide most of the nutrients that we need to stay healthy – indeed, many insist that this way of life poses fewer health risks than the modern omnivorous diet, and it will certainly ensure an excellent supply of dietary antioxidants. Antioxidants can help prevent many degenerative processes, they can reduce inflammatory responses and even help prevent cancer, and they can help prevent osteoporosis and support intestinal bacteria. A plant-based diet will also provide adequate fibre – the insoluble fibre provides bulk ensuring a healthy digestive tract and elimination, while soluble fibre can protect against cholesterol-related heart disease and diabetes.

However, we do need to find a balance in what we consume; like any other way of eating, we need variety to ensure optimum nutrition. There are only a couple of areas where, at least in my opinion, a vegan would be wise to consider supplementing – and that is with vitamin B12 (non-animal-derived versions are made by microorganisms), Omega 3 (ALA) and vitamin D3 (derived from lichen).

Vitamin B12 is crucial for the nervous system – and it is only found in animal products, although small amounts have been detected in some species of mushroom. Many modern supplements combine B12 with other B vitamins, and it is strongly suggested that you supplement if you follow a vegan lifestyle, to avoid deficiency and the damage that this can cause.

For omnivores, the main dietary source of Omega 3 is oily fish. The Omega 3 from oily fish contains two fatty acids, namely EPA (eicosapentaenoic acid) and DHA (docosahexaenoic acid). Omega 3 alpha-linolenic acid (ALA) is found in plant sources such as nuts and seeds, and in some vegetables and fruits. ALA can be used by the body to make EPA and DHA, but an excess of Omega 6 can inhibit this conversion. Omega 3 fatty acids are important in cardiovascular and brain health, and they can be converted into anti-inflammatory compounds in the body, but sometimes it can be difficult to achieve optimal levels in a plant-based diet. Paul Clayton and Colin Rose (2013) suggest supplementing with 1000mg per day and in conjunction with marine polyphenols, which are antioxidant and anti-inflammatory compounds produced by seaweed.

We make vitamin D in response to exposure to the sun. It is found in only a few foods such as oily fish and eggs, and in portobello, maitake, morel, button and shiitake mushrooms. It has been shown that if we expose mushrooms to sunlight, even for a minute or so, their vitamin D content increases. It is believed that most of us are deficient – or at best are only getting sub-optimal levels – especially if we live in sun-deprived parts of the world. According to Dr Michael Holick, a professor at Boston University School of Medicine, deficiency or sub-optimal levels of vitamin D have been linked to auto-immune diseases, heart problems, stroke, over a dozen cancers, Type 1 diabetes in children whose mothers were deficient and arteriosclerosis in those who were deficient in

childhood (cited in Clayton and Rose 2013). There is no universally agreed level of supplementation as yet; however, based on current understanding, adults can safely supplement at up to 2000 IU (62.5mcg) of vitamin D3 per day. Vitamin D3 is cholecalciferol – the form that our bodies make in response to sunlight. Many foods are fortified with vitamin D2 (ergocalciferol), but this is less well utilised in the body.

And what about the quality of our ingredients? This is determined by growing conditions, harvesting practices and storage/distribution, but how does it affect flavour and nutrition? Although it is good practice to purchase seasonal and locally produced ingredients, there is also the organic issue. To me, it seems very sensible that if you eat exclusively a plant-based diet, you should buy organic ingredients wherever possible – to minimise exposure to environmental toxins such as pesticides and herbicides. I contacted Whitmuir the Organic Place to find out more... and what they said was more than enough to convince me!

Whitmuir the Organic Place is located at Lamancha near West Linton in the Scottish Borders. Heather Anderson and farmer and horticulturalist Pete Ritchie explain that in organic cultivation the key is the avoidance of artificial fertilisers, herbicides, pesticides and insecticides so that the plants are not subjected to multiple coatings of chemical sprays. The crops are grown in rotation in order to avoid disease build-up in the soil, and companion planting is used to combat diseases and pests. They weed rather than spray, and the plants are irrigated less – so they grow more slowly and with a fundamentally different root structure, and are denser. Another reason for the slower growth is that they don't use soluble nitrogen fertiliser, which stimulates rapid leafy growth, so that the plants need to take up more water and require more irrigation; it also means that the plants don't need to do as much work at getting their own nutrients out of the soil. The soil under non-organic management also tends to have fewer symbiotic fungi. Pete tells us that chefs who use their vegetables immediately notice the difference in flavour compared with non-organic produce. Indeed, when they started up the organic farm, their children asked if 'we could buy shop carrots instead of our own, because ours taste too carroty'!

A study at Newcastle University in 2014 confirmed that organic food not only has a better flavour than conventionally produced equivalents, but also has a better nutrition profile. Pete adds that, in their view, another reason for organic veg being tastier as well as healthier is that the few organic plant breeders who do exist pay more attention to taste, and organic growers tend to rely more on older varieties (partly because there are fewer new varieties!) because in the past these were bred for taste, not just for supermarket values such as regularity of shape and size (so they can fit in a multipack), shelf life and yield/cost.

The Newcastle University study can be found at www.ncl.ac.uk/press/news/2015/10/organicvsnon-organicfood

www.whitmuirtheorganicplace.co.uk

Until we know more about genetically modified crops, it is prudent to avoid those too. I filter tap water for cooking and drinking, and avoid water if it is bottled in plastic. By making these lifestyle choices, we can cease to support the large corporations who manufacture and market products that might be detrimental to the health of the planet and all those who inhabit it. It's your choice, so make it an informed one, and one that fits with your own values!

So, without further ado, let's start looking at the sensory characteristics of our palette of ingredients, beginning with the core ingredients – vegetables, fruits, seeds, grains, nuts and legumes, then herbs, spices, oils, vinegars and salts, and finally some dairy substitutes.

VEGETABLES

What is the definition of a vegetable? Basically a vegetable is a plant part that is not a fruit or a seed, but it has come to include the tissues that surround some seeds – aubergines, cucumbers, corn kernels and tomatoes are just a few examples of fruits that are regarded as vegetables. We can find a wide variety of tastes, aromas and textures – and these can be modified by cooking processes – so it is no wonder that vegetables take centre stage in plant-based cuisine: they provide us with structure, excitement and limitless potential for the creation of flavour. Once we understand the flavour profiles and characteristics of the main groups, we can begin to explore compatibility and synergy.

Roots and tubers

We are all familiar with roots; tubers are swollen roots. More often called 'root vegetables', these are the often starchy stalwarts of plant-based cuisine, and staple foods for billions. Harold McGee, author of the classic reference book *McGee on Food and Cooking*, tells us that these underground starch stores provide a 'concentrated and long-lived package of nourishment' for both the plants and us as consumers! Starch is formed from the sugars produced by photosynthesis, and is a form of energy storage for the plant. Some are starchier than others – potatoes can be more than one-third starch, but carrots and beets are less so.

POTATOES

One of our staple foods, and a much-loved and versatile ingredient, potatoes are starchy nourishment. We do not eat them raw, because the starch resists out digestive process, but when cooked it absorbs moisture and gives a pleasing texture. Native to the Americas, there are more than 200 species of this tuber, but generally, when cooked, they have either 'mealy' textures which are more starchy (these often have russet or purple skins) or 'waxy' textures (such as new potatoes, and many red- and white-skinned types). Potatoes have an interesting flavour – earthy, slightly sweet, but with a very slight hint of bitterness – and cooking intensifies the earthiness and introduces nuttiness and fruitiness. You might question the bitter aspect. This is given by tiny traces of toxic alkaloids known as solanine and chaconine. These pose no problem in the context of the potato, but they are harmful if consumed in larger amounts. If harvested potatoes are stored in the light, chlorophyll is formed, giving a greenish colouration, and this can indicate higher levels of these alkaloids. So, if your spuds look even slightly green, they should be very deeply peeled, obviously green potatoes must be discarded, and if a potato is notably bitter, do not eat it.

We have a lot of cooking options with potatoes – and they can happily be the hero of a plant-based meal. The mealy types are ideally suited to baking and mashing, and the waxy ones are better in gratins and salads because their texture allows the dish to hold its form. Baked potatoes will develop a more intense savoury-sweetness because the heating produces a browning reaction known as the Maillard reaction, which also creates umami. Mashed potatoes should have a smooth texture, but take care not to overwork or over-process them – they will become glue-like, and this unpleasant texture will be to the detriment of flavour. Similarly, if you are making a potato-based soup, do not over-process or you might find that you have created something that resembles wallpaper paste! Fried potatoes (*pomme frites*) are very popular, and range from the chunky 'chip' to the stick-like French fries and potato chips ('crisps' in the UK).

Although potatoes generally have a lovely flavour, some are notable. A cultivar known as Mayan Gold has a yellow flesh, a rich flavour and a good umami element when cooked – especially when fried. *La Ratte* is often hailed as a good potato for salads because of its nutty-sweet flavour and waxy texture – and I do agree, but sometimes I find that the skins are somewhat tough and papery. For salads, I would suggest Jersey Royals, when in season. Truffle potatoes are purple-hued salad potatoes that really engage the visual element of flavour, hence their name. You could dress these with truffle-infused oil to play with the concept. Or, if you can find them, try the blue-violet variety *La Prunelle...*

Appearing in French markets in early spring, *La Prunelle* is an ancient variety, also known as *Blaue St Galler*, which originated in Switzerland. It has small to medium, evenly shaped tubers with an almost black-purple skin. When peeled, a violet-blue flesh is revealed, but after boiling this fades to a less vivid hue (but the water turns a lovely pale emerald-green!).

I peeled and halved them longitudinally; then they were par-boiled, tossed in olive oil, seasoned with *fleur de sel* and black pepper, and roasted for about 40 minutes in our temperamental caravan oven. What a delight! The texture is very creamy and smooth – and so they would make a stunning purée. But when roasted, the interiors develop an amazing indigo colour – I have not seen anything like this before (at least in nothing that is edible). The flavour is excellent – sweet, definitely 'potato' – but the astonishing thing is the aromatic element. If I were to have tasted these 'blind', I would have insisted that they had been roasted with rosemary!

We ate them along with a simple red oak leaf lettuce salad, and pale green flageolet beans combined with purple scallions and diced red peppers, dressed with golden green olive oil from Provence, red wine vinegar and Burgundy mustard. We had our meal outside our caravan, in the peaceful Dordogne countryside, accompanied by the birdsong which echoes through the valley in early spring. A feast for the palate, the eyes and the ears. Neurogastronomy defined – and gratitude expressed (as my dear friend Courtney likes to say)...

With all types of potato, we can intensify sweetness by introducing a salty-sour element – try capers. Potatoes work well with a wide variety of vegetables, including those which share their sweet-earthy flavour profile, such as beetroot and asparagus, mushrooms (especially *porcini*) and truffles – and just think of all the dishes that have successful pairings with potatoes – onions, leeks, garlic (in the Greek *skordalia*), cabbage and kale (the Irish *colcannon*), and aubergines (the Greek *moussaka*). They are excellent with tomatoes, where we can also find umami, and this combination is perfectly illustrated by Gennaro Contaldo's *Patate Arraganate*, where sliced potatoes are roasted in olive oil with red onions, tomatoes, dried oregano and fresh basil – simple, rustic and fabulous. For Greg's take on this combination, see You Say Potato, I Say Tomato – which demonstrates what we mean by flavour synergy, where the flavour of the dish far exceeds what we might have expected from the simple combination of potatoes and tomatoes.

When talking potatoes, we really must mention gnocchi – the small, light potato dumplings that originated in Italy. Many recipes use egg for binding and to impart a springy texture, so if you are using ready-prepared gnocchi, check the packet. At home, gnocchi can be made with old, mealy potatoes which require less flour, resulting in light, tender dumplings. For Greg's gnocchi recipe, see Homemade Gnocchi.

Needless to say, many spices and herbs are very compatible with potatoes – from the hot chillies and *pimentón*, and the spicy nutmeg and fenugreek, to the aromatic coriander, basil, mint, parsley and rosemary. I really need to mention

saffron at this point too – add a good pinch to the cooking liquor to give a subtle earthiness and glorious colour!

In his book *A Passion for Vegetables*, the chef Paul Gayler gives a sublime recipe for Saffron-braised Potatoes with Paprika, where new potatoes are sautéed with garlic, coriander seeds, hot Spanish *pimentón*, saffron and tomato purée, and then simmered in stock (I use a light vegetable stock). The stock reduces to a thick sauce (courtesy of the *pimentón* and coriander seeds), and the dish is garnished liberally with fresh coriander leaves. This really illustrates how ingredients can work together to produce truly beautiful flavours.

SWEET POTATOES

Sweet potatoes are from South America, and there are many varieties. Those from tropical regions have dry and starchy textures, whereas others are more moist and sweet. Regardless of the variety, cooking intensifies the sweetness, thanks to the action of an enzyme that converts starch to a sugar called maltose. The colour of the skin gives us a clue to the flavour. The paler and reddish-purple types have a nutty element, and the orange ones are pumpkin-like, partly due to their carotenoid pigments. The texture is softer and much less mealy than potatoes – they are less starchy.

Sweet potatoes can be baked whole, or roasted in wedges, or baked in gratins, or steamed until soft and then mashed – and this can form the basis of sweet potato cakes. In his book *Plenty*, Yotam Ottolenghi gives a simple but delicious recipe where they are paired with spring onion for a fresh pungency and chilli for some heat. He suggests a lemon and coriander, sour cream and yogurt-based sauce to accompany them, but I find that a sharp-tasting relish is an equally suitable partner, perhaps because of the acidity and crunch! And, of course, sweet potatoes can form the textural backbone of many curries – including

Thai-style ones, where we might find herbs and spices that work together to enhance their sweetness by contrast – perhaps lemongrass for an oily-citrus element, green chilli and ginger for subtle heat, coriander herb and root for green-aromatic pungency, and lime leaves for a fresh lemony greenness!

In his book *Exploring Taste and Flavour*, which focuses on dishes of the East, chef Tom Kime offers a sweet potato recipe which encompasses all of the 'tastes' – where the sweetness of the potato is emphasised by the saltiness of sea salt and augmented by a little sugar; sourness is contributed by lemon juice; bitterness by lemon zest; and some heat is contributed by green chillies – and, of course, the baking process enhances the caramelisation of sugars and formation of umami. Herbs that complement sweet potatoes include fresh rosemary with its fragrant, piney and resinous notes, and fresh sage which can add a pleasant herbal bitterness – both provide a contrast to and thus enhance the sweet element. Spices that work well are green and red chillies (think of the classic pairing in sweet chilli sauce), and the aromatic nutmeg and cinnamon, while the sharpness of lemons and limes can provide a contrasting sourness (think of the well-established concept of sweet and sour!). See Roasted Sweet Potatoes with Spiced Coconut Yogurt.

CARROTS

Carrots are almost universally enjoyed, and are often popular vegetable accompaniments. However, here we will show how they can play starring roles in dishes of all sorts, rather than being relegated to the sides. Carrots are less starchy than potatoes; they have a lovely aromatic sweetness and are often used in soups and stews. Their history is interesting and we have several different types. The Asian carrot has a reddish-purple exterior due to pigments known as anthocyanins, a yellow interior, and sometimes red roots due to the presence of lycopene (which is also found in tomatoes). The Western types are characterised by the orange pigment called carotene and these are derived from the yellow, sweet Mediterranean carrot, and the more aromatic wild, northern European white carrot with its bitter taste. Our commonly available carotene varieties retain colour during cooking – but the Asian ones bleed their colour into the dish.

Now, we mentioned their aromatic element, which plays a key part in carrot flavour. Volatile components called terpenes give delicate fresh pine-like and woody notes in raw carrots, and when cooked, the broken-down carotene pigment gives an almost iris or violet-like aroma. As an aside, in perfumery, an iris note can be created by blending essential oils of cedarwood and carrot seed – so the iris-violet impression might be a culinary manifestation of this aromatic phenomenon!

When carrots are being prepared for a dish, it is worth knowing that peeling will reduce any bitterness, and that cooking will free up sugars and increase their sweetness. The most flavoursome part of the carrot is the area between the core and the outer layer.

We have worked hard to ensure that our carrot recipes are designed to make the most of the positive attributes of the humble carrot – because, for some, carrots taste too carroty! The recipe for Vietnamese Sticky Carrots really allows the carrot to shine, making the most of its texture and showing how comfortable it is with typically Asian flavours, and Med Deli Ribbons pairs carrots with the Moroccan *chermoula*.

So, what herbs and spices and flavours work well with the carrot? There are some ubiquitous examples, not least carrot and coriander leaf and seeds (usually soup), and orange (often soup and salads) – and the three of them are very happy together too! Carrots are also good with star anise (aromatic-sweet), cardamom (spicy-citrus-penetrating) and cumin (earthy-sweaty); green, fresh parsley is an excellent pairing, as is the potent tarragon for an anisic nuance. Carrots can be caramelised too, emphasising their inherent sweetness. Other ingredients that enhance the carrot flavour are olives (salty), citrus (especially orange), ginger and chilli. In salads, raw carrots can be grated and paired with all manner of nuts and seeds for both flavour and texture – try walnuts or toasted sunflower and pumpkin seeds; sesame is also a good choice. Botanically related vegetables such as celery and fennel combine well with carrot, and fruits such as apple and grapes can add sweetness and a textural contrast. Finally, grated carrots can be used in cakes, where they can add texture and help retain moisture.

PARSNIPS

Parsnips are less popular than carrots. There might be several reasons for this. My mother grew up in Scotland during the Second World War, when much was rationed – especially sugar. So, the ever-abundant parsnips were sometimes used in cakes and jams, and, because of their pale creamy-yellow colour and sweetness, they would sometimes be flavoured with artificial banana essence. Mum does not like bananas much either – but she maintains that this is mainly due to their texture. I don't think that a parsnip ever crossed the threshold of our home. I was in my early twenties when I first met a parsnip, when my flatmate Pauline made a memorable pot of soup.

Parsnips are related to carrots, but they are starchier, and because of this they were an important staple food in Europe before potatoes were introduced from the Americas. They have a more open, almost spongy texture and a thick, fibrous, woody core. Like carrots, parsnips are sweet, and you will find that winter parsnips – when the cold temperatures allow the conversion of starch to sugar – are even sweeter. They also have an earthy element. But none of this is enough to fuel strong dislike. I finally got to the bottom of the matter when browsing

Niki Segnit's book *The Flavour Thesaurus*. When reading about the volatiles that contribute to the parsnip aroma and thus flavour, I had a 'eureka!' moment. The culprits are terpinolene (piney and disinfectant-like), myristicin (the component responsible for the warm spicy aroma of nutmeg) and one member of the group of wildly pungent methoxypyrazines (very intense, cut green pepper, green peas). Now, I 'fixate' on the terpinolene (we all fixate on certain aromas and flavours), and so somewhere in my brain flavour image, raw parsnip is disinfectant. It is unrelated to my mother's aversion. It is nature, not nurture! However, this gem of information does explain the affinity between nutmeg and parsnip, and why it goes rather well with peas.

To make the most of parsnips, roast them in chunks or quarters with plenty of seasoning – they would be overly sweet without salt. As you might expect, nutmeg is an interesting spice to add, as it too is earthy, aromatic and sweet, and maple syrup can turn roasted parsnips into an almost candied accompaniment for robust savoury dishes, or in salads with a bitter element – maybe chicory, rocket or watercress.

SUNCHOKES

Sunchokes – sometimes known as Jerusalem artichokes – are the tubers of a sunflower from North America. They are not particularly starchy, but they are rich in fructose carbohydrates known as fructosans and inulins – which prevent freezing in the winter months. This is a very useful mechanism for the sunchoke; however, it can be somewhat problematic for us. We do not have the necessary digestive enzymes, so when the sunchoke arrives in our intestines, our gut bacteria take over, and in return for breaking down the fructose carbs, they give us gas – and in (how shall I put this delicately?) copious volumes! The only way to overcome this little problem is to cook them for 12–14 hours at a low temperature (90–100°C or 200°F); this turns them sweet, translucent and brown, and breaks down their carbs into fructose – which we can digest. If you feel brave enough to sample these delicious, sweet, almost nutty tubers, you might throw caution to the wind (pun intended) and think of making a soup, or a gratin – perhaps with spinach and a crunchy breadcrumb and hazelnut or brazil nut topping – or eat them raw, thinly sliced, in a salad with radishes and mangetout, and dress with a nut oil (hazelnut is very good), a little Dijon mustard and some white balsamic or sherry vinegar. When peeled, they do discolour very quickly, so it is best to put them into acidulated water to prevent this.

SALSIFY

Salsify is even less used than the sunchoke. I learned to love it in France, when the best season is in the late-autumn and winter months. It looks like a sad specimen of a carrot – long and thin, with a rough brown skin. But inside, the flesh is crisp and almost white. Like sunchokes, you must transfer them into acidulated water as you are peeling, but, unlike sunchokes, you are unlikely to suffer any abdominal discomfort after enjoying them. Salsify is very good sautéed, then simmered in a little vegetable stock until tender, and then eaten cold in a salad with a simple lemon and oil dressing. Paul Gayler suggests combining salsify with sautéed girolles and trompettes in a salad dressed with white truffle oil and lemon juice – what an excellent way to enjoy salsify!

Underground stems and bulbs

BEETS

My adoration began in childhood, where I liked the way that pickled beetroot turned my mashed potatoes pink. I was an imaginative little girl, and I remain driven by aesthetics, so pink mash was very pleasing indeed. This shows how our visual sense is such an important element in the brain flavour image, and indeed how our brain flavour image develops as we grow. Nowadays, I am less obsessed with creating pink potato mash, but I

still love beetroot for its wonderful colours, which range from the jewel-like deep red/purple, to the delicately pink varieties with their Saturn-like rings, to the vibrant, warm golden types. I love it for its aroma – when raw, it is so earthy, and slightly musty – and I would say that it is the food equivalent of my beloved patchouli attar! Its damp earthiness (or 'petrichor', describing the smell of rainfall on the soil) is related to a naturally occurring aroma compound named geosmin. And its texture is good – it doesn't fall apart when cooked, and it keeps its form well; whether you have created wedges, dice, thin carpaccio-like slices or discs, or are celebrating the perfect spheres of baby beets, you just know that your dish will look good. And the flavour – it is robust, sweet and earthy, and so we can pair it with equally robust herbs and spices that could overwhelm more delicately flavoured vegetables.

Beets have been enjoyed since ancient times. Their attractive colour is due to a pigment called betaine, and beets are the most abundant source of this essential nutrient. Betaine is water-soluble and so will bleed the colour into dishes (and your fingers). You may even have noticed that you produce pink urine and reddish-purple faeces after eating beetroot. This is fine – and if you don't, it simply means that the acidity in your stomach and iron in your large intestine have decolourised it! The variegated, pink varieties, where pigmented and non-pigmented tissues occur in alternating layers, look wonderful thinly sliced and eaten raw in salads, simply dressed and arranged over deep-green watercress – it seems criminal to do anything else with such beauty!

Beetroot can be boiled, braised or roasted, or puréed in soups; in fact it can be the hero of a myriad of dishes, and add colour and interest to many more (try adding some seasoned, roasted and puréed beetroot to hummus). Some writers tell us to peel after cooking, but I prefer to trim and peel first. It's a personal thing. OK, your fingers turn deep pink, but it will disappear soon enough. It is cooked when the flesh yields to the tip of a sharp knife – and it will never become soft or mushy.

So, what herbs and spices can be paired with beetroot? For a start, earthy cumin seed could have been made for beetroot, and the more delicate yet persistent coriander seed, with its light citrus-orange element, is also very good. Dill is beautiful – its feathery bright green leaves contrast well with beetroot – but the delicate appearance does not reflect its pronounced sweet-sour-bitter-green flavour. In fact, beetroot and dill is a traditional combination that we can find in Eastern European beetroot soups such as *borscht*. Other good pairings are beetroot and garlic, or horseradish – another match made in heaven, and witnessed in the Ukrainian *tsvikili*, where grated cooked beetroot is combined with a little grated fresh horseradish and seasoned with salt, pepper and vinegar, and sometimes a little sugar. Beetroot likes the salty acidity of capers. It is also compatible with fruits (try apples, pears or oranges) and nuts (especially pecans and walnuts) in salads. Beetroot can take on a hefty dose of acidity and is excellent in pickles and relishes.

Beetroot can be the star of a curry – and for this you could consider the golden variety, with potatoes and spinach (also a source of betaine). Its robust sweetness can also carry classic North African spices and herbs – such as coriander seed, cumin, cinnamon, saffron, preserved lemon, fresh coriander and mint. It is a striking, versatile ingredient indeed!

SWEDE (RUTABAGA)

Swede (rutabaga) is a hybrid, a cross between a turnip and a species of kale or cabbage – the botanical origins are lost in time, but it has been known in Eastern Europe for more than 400 years. The swede is the swollen part of the main stem. Many folks disregard it because they think it is 'woody' and unpleasant, and we might notice hundreds of swedes scattered in fields as food for sheep. I learned to love swedes, or 'neeps' as they

are known in Scotland, at a very early age – it was often served at our table. My father was born in 1921. He told me that when he was a young child, he was very sickly and apparently had difficulty keeping food down. He claimed that mashed swedes saved his life, as it was the only food that agreed with him! Does that not command respect for this humble vegetable?

Often interchangeable with turnip (see below), swede is also known as 'yellow turnip' and 'Swedish turnip'; it is round, with a purple-green skin, and a yellow-orange flesh, but it is sweeter in flavour than turnip and has a higher starch content (about half of that found in a potato), and this means that it is very good for mashing, either on its own or in a root vegetable mash – particularly tasty when paired with carrots. The smaller swedes are the most sweet and tender. A typical Scottish dish is mashed neeps – and this, along with mashed potatoes ('tatties'), often accompanies the haggis on Burns Night – celebrated on 25 January. We can now buy plant-based haggis, so it would be a simple matter to enjoy this traditional meal, followed by a *digestif* in the form of a good single-malt whisky – and I am completely sure that Robert Burns, who was a great humanitarian, would approve. Swede is also good roasted, and it can carry some robust spices, but, most of all, black pepper and also the contrasting freshly ground nutmeg.

TURNIP

Turnip is cultivated as a staple food in many parts of the world. It is a member of the cabbage family; when cut, you can notice the characteristic sulphur-like aroma. There are many varieties – the small mild types can be eaten raw in salads, but the more pungent large types must be cooked. However, be careful not to overcook turnip, as the texture will become waterlogged and mushy, and the cabbage-like aroma intensifies and becomes unpleasant.

Turnip can be peeled, cubed and boiled in salted water and dressed with a little rapeseed oil and black pepper, or roasted with other 'roots', and shallots and garlic.

Cumin can work well with turnip, as can mustard. Turnips can be sliced and combined with potatoes in a gratin – thyme would work well in this combination. Or you might layer sliced turnip with shredded and blanched Savoy cabbage, sliced onions, along with some cumin, mustard and salt and pepper. Baby turnips can be braised too – Paul Gayler suggests a braising liquor of cider vinegar and sugar, which reduces and forms a glaze; the dish is finished with golden raisins and apples which complement the flavours and colours. Baby turnips are sometimes pickled; the process will remove any pungent flavours and aromas, and this makes a lovely accompaniment to many dishes.

RADISHES

Radishes are related to turnips, and hundreds of years of cultivation have resulted in many pretty forms and lovely colours! Most of the ones we can purchase are bright red with a crisp sparkly white interior, but there is also a striking green type, which has a red interior. Radishes have a mild to pungent aroma, and are usually eaten raw, sliced in salads, giving vibrant colour and a juicy-crisp texture. The pungency is due to the formation of a mustard-like component in the skin. So, if you would prefer to reduce the pungency, simply peel off some or all of the skin. Alternatively, try cooking radishes. This destroys the enzyme responsible, and when the pungency diminishes, the sweetness emerges.

CELERIAC

Once obscure, in recent years celeriac has become very popular. Its name suggests a relationship with celery, and this is correct: it is the swollen lower stem of a special type of celery – the *rapaceum* variety. Because of its knobbly appearance, it does need to be peeled deeply before use. In older and larger specimens, you will also find a fluffy part in the centre. This is fibrous and can be removed if desired. Unsurprisingly, the flavour is mild and celery-like, and as it is slightly starchy, it can be cooked like the other root vegetables – boiled, braised or roasted.

Celeriac can make a good soup, with onions, the white portion of leeks and a small amount of potato for body – try serving this with a few drops of white truffle-infused oil. Celeriac makes a good purée (which should be passed through a fine sieve for a super-smooth result) or a more textured sauce which is good with pasta. Celeriac can also be grated and eaten in a slaw-type salad, perhaps with some apple and walnuts, and dressed with oil and lemon, or cider vinegar, and flavoured with some mild mustard or horseradish. See Carrot and Celeriac Pickled Slaw (under 'Long Pepper' Pineapple Koftas).

ONIONS

Onions form the basis of so many dishes – when they are fried gently in oil, sometimes until soft and translucent, sometimes until golden brown and starting to caramelise. One word – umami – really is the key here. However, we have access to many different varieties of onion, and so choosing the right one for your dish is important in terms of the final flavour. Onions are underground bulbs; they store energy in the form of fructose carbohydrates (like the sunchokes) and need long and slow cooking to break down these carbs to produce sweetness. Of course, some species are better known for their leaves – such as leeks, scallions (spring onions) and chives.

Bulb onions (*Allium cepa* varieties) are more often defined by their harvesting time than by variety. Bulb onions are harvested in spring through to early summer, and before they fully mature. They have a high moisture content and are quite sweet and mild. Some may have been grown in sulphur-poor soil, and thus have less potential to produce their pungent volatile components and the tear-inducing defence compounds. Mature onions harvested in the autumn are less moist and more pungent – and these are the familiar brown or yellow 'storage' onions, their colour being related to the development of flavonoid pigments. Indeed, onions (along with apples) are the most important dietary source of a flavonoid known as quercitin. However, we also see specific varieties in the shops – white onions, which are moist and lacking pigment, and red onions, which owe their colour to the water-soluble anthocyanins present on the surface of each leaf 'scale' – slice it and you will see what I mean. Scallions are green onions, known in the UK as 'spring' onions. These come in several shapes and sizes – from the bulbous types to the ones that are almost all green leaf and the bulb is hardly developed at all. These are often used in salads, but in Asian cuisine we also find them in stir-fry dishes, where the short cooking time is well suited to their delicate structure. Finally, we have shallots – these are clustering varieties which have small bulbs, the texture is fine and they are usually mild and sweet. They are attractive too – with a pale purple-pink tinge on the outer layers – and they cook very well. We will discuss garlic and chives under 'Herbs'.

The onion family is characterised by its strong, pungent flavour – contributed by sulphur-containing components, developed as a defence mechanism to deter animals. Sulphur from the soil is incorporated into molecules which are then stored in the cells. When the cells are disrupted – either by a browsing animal or when we cut into the onion – an enzyme is released which splits these molecules and produces irritating compounds, which continue to react with oxygen in the air, becoming even more irritating, and so on – a sort of chain reaction. These are known as lachrymators ('tear producers'), and include hydrogen sulphide, sulphur dioxide, sulphuric acid and thiocarbonyl S-oxides. To slow the enzyme activity down, and reduce the production of lachrymators, you can pre-soak onions in iced water for up to an hour before preparation. Raw bulb onion thus has a very sharp, edgy, pungent flavour that can be modified by the way in

which we treat the onion – chopping, slicing and puréeing will result in subtly different flavour profiles – but if onions are to be used raw in a salad or as a garnish, it is best to rinse them well, to help subdue the harshest of the lachrymators.

Cooking transforms onions. They are unique and virtually indispensable. Of course, it all depends on the cooking method and medium. If we cook in an oil, and at a high temperature (frying, sautéing, roasting, braising), we can produce a myriad of flavour compounds; the sugars present in onions are important in the browning and flavour-forming reactions, and an onion base thus produced will add a sweet and flavoursome dimension to dishes. They caramelise beautifully too. It is no wonder that the bulb onion has become so indispensable in classic cuisines from around the globe.

Mirepoix is the French chefs' term for a 'holy trinity' of diced onion, carrot and celery (in a ratio of 2:2:1) which is gently fried – and this is the base for a myriad of stews, casseroles and stocks across Europe. In Italy, this is called *soffrito*, which means 'underfried', and their mix often includes parsley too. The resulting flavour is hearty and savoury, so much so that it was once called 'false ragù' (from the French *ragoût*, which means 'to revive the taste'), and is noted for the intense flavour that develops from long, slow cooking! In Spain, the trio is known as *sofregit* or *sofrito*, and in Portugal, *refogado*. The Polish *wioszczyzna* means 'Italian stuff' and this version includes leeks, carrots, celery and parsley roots, and sometimes cabbage and celery leaves, and is similar in many ways to the German *Suppengrün* (literally 'soup greens'), which is onion-based with leeks, carrots, celeriac, swede, celery, parsley roots and leaves, and thyme. In Cajun cuisine, green bell pepper replaces carrot, but the principle is the same. In the East, we find onions pounded with chillies and ginger in spice pastes. So, the onion can act as a highly versatile vegetable ingredient and flavouring.

Leeks are not bulb-forming, and so it is their tightly packed leaves (they look like large scallions) that we enjoy. They are a hardy crop and can be harvested throughout the winter. Leeks require careful trimming and washing, because the horticultural practice of building up soil around their bases causes a gradual accumulation of grit.

It is usually the lower white portion that is used; the inner leaves have the most flavour and the tough, more fibrous outer and green leaves are often discarded. The green parts can be used to give body to dishes; however, when cooked, they become gelatinous and some folks find the resulting slippery texture unpleasant. Leeks are rarely used raw; when cooked, they have a milder flavour than onions, and a silky, almost creamy texture – and they can be chargrilled, sautéed, braised, and used in soups, casseroles, gratins… Leeks are versatile, easy to work with, and there are a few classic pairings to explore and experiment with. Leek and potato probably is the most popular: think of leek and potato gratin, leek and potato soup, or the classic *Vichyssoise*.

Stems

Stems, because of their supportive and conductive role, are naturally strong. They are filled with strong vessels for water and nutrient transport, surrounded by cellulose-reinforced supporting fibres. Thus, some stems, such as those of celery, can be tough and fibrous, and so we need to strip away the outer 'strings' before using – to prevent an unpleasant texture in our dish.

ASPARAGUS

Asparagus was loved in ancient Greece and Rome, and its popularity has endured. Asparagus spears develop from underground roots in the spring. Asparagus does not produce typical leaves – instead, you can see little bracts (phylloclades) which are immature photosynthetic branches. Asparagus is relatively expensive; it must be harvested by hand (the stems must be cut individually because, inconveniently, they do not mature simultaneously) and so the process is labour-intensive. It is, in my view, important to enjoy early-season, freshly harvested asparagus – this is more sweet and juicy, and the flavour is at its peak. Once asparagus is harvested, it continues to grow, the sweetness diminishes, and it loses moisture and becomes more fibrous. You might want to lightly peel asparagus that is less than absolutely fresh, and the little bracts along the stem can be removed with a sharp knife. Another trick is to bend the stem – it will break just beyond the drier 'woody' point, which can be discarded or used to make a stock.

Green asparagus is the most common type. It is characterised by sulphur-containing compounds such as dimethyl sulphide and asparagusic acid – the culprit responsible for 'asparagus pee'. Proust declared in his work *In Search of Lost Time* (1913) that after a dinner at which he had eaten asparagus, his chamber pot was transformed into 'a vase of aromatic perfume'. Now this description of fragrant urine is at odds with most folk, who find the odour somewhat objectionable – maybe not surprising, as it is the result of the metabolism of asparagusic acid to methanethiol, which is chemically related to skunk spray! According to McGee, most, but not all, of us produce methanethiol, and most, but not all, of us are able to smell it!

Asparagus, if very fresh and young (the very thin delicate spears are called sprue), can be enjoyed raw. It has a sweet taste and slightly sulphury aroma. More mature spears can be steamed or boiled, and are excellent if blanched then pan-fried or roasted, or even chargrilled; these processes bring out a savoury aspect that is absent in the raw and steamed versions.

The white type is the result of 'blanching', where the spears are covered in soil, they never see light, and they are even cut underground

– the lack of exposure to sunlight means that the green chlorophyll necessary for photosynthesis does not develop. McGee suggests that it has a more 'delicate' aroma when harvested, while Segnit asserts that it is as flavourless as it is colourless!

Asparagus is also very pretty, and can add visual appeal to a dish either as a component or as the main feature. It has a robust enough flavour to stand up to pungent partners such as garlic, mustard and baby leeks (for the aesthetic appeal too); herbs such as parsley, chervil and the anisic tarragon, and sharp-sour ingredients such as balsamic vinegars and capers, if used judiciously, can enhance the sweetness of asparagus.

CELERY

Celery is a member of the carrot family (the *Umbelliferae*) and was first bred and cultivated in 15th-century Italy, and so is embedded in the cuisines that developed in the region. Celery is noted for its crunchy texture when raw and its distinctive fresh aroma, which is due in part to the presence of piney terpenes and components known as phthalides. Celery flavour is salty rather than sweet, and this is why it is often used to bring out the sweetness of other ingredients. It also works well with salty ingredients such as roasted and salted nuts and seeds, and olives. Raw and carefully 'de-stringed', it can be served in sticks (perfect in a plant-based version of a Bloody Mary[1]), or sliced and diced in salads. To preserve the crisp texture, it can be soaked in ice-cold water prior to preparation. Celery is often paired with grated carrots, with which it shares the terpene aroma-flavour and crisp texture, and maybe walnuts, which also contain phthalides – and here we can use our knowledge of chemistry to create flavour synergy! Salads with celery and apple are also widely loved, and it is easy to see why – an example is the Waldorf salad, based on the apple, celery and walnut trio (see All out of 'Waldorf' Salad).

Celery is an indispensable ingredient in many dishes, especially in slow-cooked stews and casseroles, because it is important in the development of a deep, savoury umami taste. Think of the *mirepoix* concept – slowly fried diced celery, onions and carrots is an aromatic, plant-based way to develop a savoury flavour in all manner of sauces, stews and casseroles. Can you imagine a meat-based casserole or stew cooked without plant ingredients, and, of course, herbs, spices and seasonings? It would be characterless and bland. So, if, even for a moment, you wonder if plant-based cuisine might be disadvantaged in the flavour arena, then think again!

We can also use celery seeds as a seasoning, crushed with salt.

FENNEL

Fennel is a relative of celery, and with the 'bulb' or 'Florence' fennel (the variety named *azoricum*), it is the enlarged leaf stalk cluster that we enjoy. Like celery, fennel abounds in Italian cuisine, and, like celery, we need to remove the tough outer leaves which are thick, tough and stringy. The distinctive aspect of bulb fennel is its aniseed-like aroma and mild sweet anisic flavour. This is imparted by a volatile oil – anethole – which is present also in the seeds of the related common fennel – see 'Spices'. Interestingly, pure anethole is 13 times sweeter than refined sugar! Fennel's feathery, jewel-green foliage has a slightly different aroma profile; it contains a terpene called limonene, and this can make an attractive, lemon-scented garnish.

Fennel is versatile. It is very good in salads

---

1 The vodka and tomato juice-based Bloody Mary cocktail also contains lemon, horseradish, black pepper, cayenne and anchovy-containing Worcester sauce (vegan versions of this condiment are available); celery sticks act as a garnish to add visual appeal, texture and flavour.

if thinly sliced, where its unique sweet flavour and crisp texture can stand alone with a simple dressing and seasoning, or combined with thinly sliced raw carrots, pungent radishes or garlic and salty olives. It is often paired with orange too, where the citrus aroma and flavour is also contributed (at least in part) by the same component – limonene.

Fennel is also excellent cooked – braising and oven roasting are probably the best methods – and it is wonderful in soup (see Fennel Vichyssoise). When blanched, well drained, thickly sliced and seasoned, slicked with olive oil and baked until soft and unctuous in a gratin, with a contrasting crunchy lemon-zest-infused breadcrumb topping, it can be the star of a rustic Italian-style dish. Some ingredients are natural partners for fennel – especially red, orange and yellow bell peppers, sweet bulb onions (red ones look good), courgettes and aubergines – and Mediterranean herbs – especially rosemary, oregano and fresh mint – or spices such as coriander, cumin and caraway seeds. We must also mention the tomato and fennel pairing – the basis for a plethora of fabulous dishes.

KOHLRABI

Kohlrabi is also known as the 'cabbage turnip'! It is indeed a cabbage – the *gongylodes* variety to be precise – and it is the swollen main stems rather than the leaves that are eaten. McGee describes its flavour as resembling the stalk of broccoli – mild, crisp and moist, and suited to consuming raw or lightly cooked; he warns us not to use over-mature stems, which have a woody texture. See Carpaccio of Beetroot and Kohlrabi.

Leaves

We have mentioned several members of the cabbage family already. The botanical name for the cabbage genus is *Brassica*, and we have already alluded to the sulphury element present in many relatives. Sulphur and nitrogen-containing compounds called isothiocyanates and glucosinolates constitute the cabbage family defence mechanism – and are responsible for strong odours and tastes, including bitterness. These components can even affect our metabolism – some are mildly toxic whereas others are protective and help us eliminate dietary toxins. Often, the strongest concentration is found in specific parts, such as the central and core parts, which are associated with active growth. Consequently, we find seasonal variations in the production of defence chemicals and thus flavours, because growth is encouraged in the warmth of the summer, and reduced in the cold damp winters – and so summer crops have a stronger flavour, and autumn/winter crops are milder.

We also need to be aware that the way we prepare brassicas affects their flavour. Think about preparing a cabbage to make coleslaw... When we slice the leaves finely, we increase dramatically the production and liberation of the defence chemicals, so it is a good plan to soak the prepared material in cold water to help remove some of the more pungent odours and flavours before incorporating with other ingredients and acidic dressings. Now think about cooking a cabbage... Heat – around the boiling point of water – inactivates the enzymes responsible for the production of the chemical arsenal. If a brassica is put directly into boiling water, there will be less opportunity for the enzymes to create these chemicals – but this might mean that although pungency is reduced, bitterness can remain. Or, if a large amount of water is used, many of the components will be removed from the tissues, and the flavour will be diminished – compare the flavour of a boiled cabbage with that of steamed or stir-fried cabbage and you will see what I mean. I am also sure that many of us of a certain vintage will remember, probably with a shudder, the smell of overcooked cabbage (trisulphides) emanating from school canteens.

CABBAGE

The name comes from *caput*, the Latin word for 'head'. Familiar varieties include the white and green 'heading' types, sometimes called Dutch cabbages, with tightly packed leaves that form elegant spheres, red cabbages with their vibrant anthocyanin pigments, and the more loosely packed and elongated sweetheart, and the round, almost frilly, crinkly-leaved Savoy cabbages. If we are looking for vitamins and antioxidants, we should choose the 'loose' green types, although the heading varieties are sweeter and will keep for longer. Steaming and stir-frying are the best ways to cook cabbage. The exception would be red cabbage, which responds well to braising, and the flavour improves over time, after cooking.

So, what might we pair cabbage with? It is pungent, and so can take on other pungent flavours – especially garlic, onion and mustard, and salty tastes. Or we can think about juniper berries with braised red cabbage, and caraway seeds with braised white or green 'heading' types. Cabbage is an essential part of the much-loved dish known as bubble and squeak – a savoury, fried combination of crushed or mashed potatoes, sliced onion and shredded cabbage (any type will work, but the Savoy ones give a lovely visual effect).

BRUSSELS SPROUTS

Brussels sprouts seem to have acquired a love-or-loathe reputation in popular food lore, but I think that this reputation could be changed. So let's consider how sprouts have divided us into two camps. Closely related to cabbage, sprouts form small 'heads' along a central stalk. But, unlike cabbage, they are bitter – and perhaps they are just too bitter for supertasters (see page 17). The bitterness is conferred by high levels of sulphur- and nitrogen-containing compounds called glucosinolates (which are the precursors of both bitter and non-bitter compounds) and they are affected in different ways by the cooking

process – but the bitterness remains, regardless, and concentrated in the centre of the sprouts. So, we could theorise that no matter what we do, supertasters will still refuse to eat sprouts, but we can try to enlighten the non-supertasters! There are ways of cooking sprouts that celebrate their astringent bitterness – we can shred them and stir-fry with onions, and we can roast them with plenty of salt and seasoning to balance the bitterness, and maybe add some sweet chestnuts – should some seasonal cheer be on the menu.

KALE

The profile of kale has improved dramatically since my father grew it in the 1970s – in those days it was always called 'curly' kale, and he grew it in such profusion that it became hard to think of soup or family meals without it when it was being cropped! Now it is classed as a superfood, and it has websites dedicated to it! Kale contains both lutein and zeaxanthin, which thicken and protect the macular pigment in the eyes, and quercitin, which can protect us from cholesterol oxidation products. Anything which is that good for one's health should be taken seriously and, of course, eaten in industrial quantities. The best way to do this with kale – other than to remove the tough stalks and central stems with sharp scissors, and include it in chunky vegetable and bean soups and stews – is to give it the Brussels sprouts stir-fry treatment. That way, you can consume rather a lot at one sitting, and congratulate yourself on your intake of protective compounds, antioxidants and vitamins. You can also add some seeds to the mix – maybe sesame, sunflower or pumpkin – to add some sterols and flavonoids to the dish! Or, you could try Indian-Inspired Kale and Kasuri Methi Potato Cakes.

CAVOLO NERO

A close relative of kale, sometimes called 'black kale', this is the striking, delightful and flavoursome black cabbage which features in

Italian cuisine. The tough central vein is removed, and the leaves are usually wilted or blanched, then dried and stir-fried, or lightly boiled or steamed. They can carry robust flavours such as garlic and chilli. See Greg's variation, Black Kale Bubble and Squeak, and the traditional, delicious Ribollita.

LETTUCE

Lettuce is a non-bitter leafy green, and is most often consumed as a salad vegetable. The early varieties were very bitter, due to the presence of lactucin, but this has been bred out to give us a whole range of non-bitter varieties of lettuce (*Lactuca sativa*) to choose from – loose leaf types, or the butterhead types with their soft tender leaves, the Batavian types which have crisp dense leaves, Cos and Romaines with their loose heads of sweet, crisp, elongated leaves, and the crisphead types such as the watery, crunchy Iceberg. In general, you will get more antioxidants and vitamins from the types that are not shielded from the sun by the formation of tight heads, and from the red-leafed types with stunning colours from their anthocyanins. Preparation and dressing of salad leaves requires care – if leaves have to be divided, use a very sharp knife to minimise cell damage, and add any oil-based dressing at the very last moment; otherwise, the oil will penetrate the leaf cuticles and cause darkening, discolouration and wilting. Lettuce can be cooked too – you can braise 'Little Gem' lettuces, or include lettuce in dishes such as Petit Pois à la Française, where you will see how they can add flavour and textural contrast.

CHICORY AND ENDIVE

Chicory and endive, both members of the lettuce family (the *Compositae*), have retained their bitter qualities, although this has been controlled by careful breeding. Chicory (*Cichorium intibus*) itself forms an open cluster, while the Belgian type (also called *witloof*) has a tightly packed head of white, crisp leaves, and the *radicchio*

has a round-elongated head of red leaves. The bitter endives (*Cichorium endiva*) all form open clusters and range from the curly endive, to *frisée* with its finely divided 'frizzy' leaves, to *escarole* with its broader leaves. These bitter leaves are best dressed with salty dressings, because salt balances bitterness, and indeed suppresses our perception of bitterness! Some types can be cooked. For example, chicory can be braised very successfully with sweet (and sour) ingredients, and caramelisation really enhances its complex flavour.

SPINACH

Spinach – the leaves of *Spinacia oleracea*, a member of the beet family – is widely used. It has a mild flavour and soft texture, and marked astringency, and it is hailed as a superfood! This is because it contains vitamin A, the phenolic antioxidants lutein and zeaxanthin, and folate (a B vitamin). So, although spinach leaves can be eaten raw and in salad leaf mixes, to consume meaningful amounts we do need to cook it lightly until it wilts – when it reduces dramatically in volume! Spinach makes a welcome addition to a whole host of dishes, from soups to curries – see Southeast Asian-Inspired Butternut Squash and Spinach Curry.

CHARD

Chard is the leaves of beet (*Beta vulgaris*) varieties selected for their leaves and stalks rather than their storage roots. The charm of chard lies in the visual realm – its stalks and leaf veins can be vivid yellows, oranges and crimsons thanks to the presence of betaines – hence the title 'rainbow' chard. Heirloom varieties are available, and these date from the 16th century. It can be used in much the same way as spinach, but if you are going to cook it, the stems should be removed and added first – because they take longer to cook than the leaves. Ideally, it should be served simply so that the lovely colours can be appreciated.

MÂCHE

Mâche, or lamb's lettuce, has tender leaves which have a distinctive floral green-fruity aroma; these are often found in salad mixes and sometimes as the sole salad leaf. The texture is slightly mucilaginous.

ROCKET

Rocket is sometimes called arugula or *roquette*, and is related to cabbage. It is very much associated with the Mediterranean region and is a versatile leafy green – at home in salads, especially the traditional *mesclun* mixes (chervil, rocket, sweet leaves such as red and green oak leaf, baby spinach and endives), or stirred through pasta, and in pesto, purées and soups. It has a distinctive peppery flavour, and you will find that the cultivated varieties are milder and tenderer than 'wild' rocket.

SALAD BURNET

Salad burnet really deserves to be better known! Often classed as a herb, I have included it here because it makes a delightful addition to a mix of salad leaves. It has small leaves arranged in sprays, and these can be added to your salad greens where they do not just look pretty and delicate, but give a lovely subtle cucumber-like flavour. You could add some borage flowers to augment this theme. Salad burnet works well with the equally pretty chervil, but also the peppery rocket and the bitter endive.

WATERCRESS

This wonderful leaf is a species of nasturtium, which belongs to the cabbage family. The vibrant, tender, green leaf clusters have a distinctive but not overpowering peppery flavour – fresh and bittersweet. Like many of the leafy greens we have mentioned, it is a very happy salad vegetable and an interesting, flavoursome ingredient in soups (including potato-based soups) and pesto-type sauces. However, it has acquired

some regular food partners. It makes the perfect base for a roasted beetroot salad, or a fennel and orange salad (or all together) – maybe with walnuts which echo its astringent aspect.

Flowers

Here we will look at the artichoke – the flower bud of a species of thistle, and three members of the cabbage family – broccoli, cauliflower and romanesco. In their case, the flower development has been arrested and we are in fact eating masses of immature flowering tissues!

ARTICHOKE

The large flower buds of a thistle species (belonging to, believe it or not, the lettuce family) and often cursed with the spectre of difficult preparation, artichokes have been considered a delicacy for a very long time – they were loved by the ancient Greeks and Romans. The edible part is the fleshy bases of the bracts (protective leaves) and the base of the flower – known as the heart. The so-called 'choke', which is discarded, consists of the flowerlets – if left to flower, this turns a blue-violet. The flavour of artichokes is due to an array of phenolic compounds, including one named cynarin. These phenolics have been associated with antioxidant and cholesterol-lowering effects; however, despite this, artichokes have not yet been elevated to superfood status. The phenolic compounds react with oxygen, so when the tissues are cut, they cause discolouration. Preparation is not so very difficult; just a tad more effort is needed than with some other vegetables, but it is absolutely worth it! The rough outer bracts should be removed, the top third sliced off, and the stem cut to around 5mm from the base. Some careful knife work can allow you to 'turn' the base to create a pleasing form. The central choke and small inner bracts also need to be removed. This can be done after cooking if you like, using a teaspoon. Cooking – for example, in well-seasoned braising liquor – minimises the browning and any astringency. Their flavour is complex – Segnit mentions that there are elements of asparagus and Calabrese broccoli, and that their texture is dense, yielding and velvety. I would not argue with any of that, and this explains why they are considered a delicacy! It seems a shame to add anything other than simple seasoning, or maybe some freshly squeezed lemon juice, but some classic dishes are worth exploring.

In Italy, *carciofi alla Romana* is a dish of artichokes with chopped mint and garlic stuffed between their leaves, before braising in water, lemon juice and mint. *Artichautes à la Barigoule* is a classic Provençal dish of artichokes braised in a white wine liquor – often with onions, garlic and carrots, sometimes with fennel or celery, and usually flavoured with parsley and lemon. It is truly delicious. The name comes from *barigoules*, or saffron milk caps, which are wild mushrooms – but these are no longer included in the classic recipe!

Artichokes also have a reputation for distorting the flavour of other foods and wines. The cynarin binds with the sweet-receptors on our tongues causing a temporary inhibition. Then when the next mouthful is taken, the food or beverage will taste sweeter than it really is as the receptors kick in again!

BROCCOLI

Broccoli is thought to be the ancestor of cauliflower, appearing in Italy before the 16th century and remaining to the fore in Italian cuisine. The heads of broccoli are the result of additional flower stalks which fuse into 'spears' and form masses of green flower buds. The type we come across most often is the Calabrese type and it has a sweet flavour, with just a trace of bitterness. The purple sprouting type is stronger in flavour and has a more pronounced bitter element – this type is not true broccoli, but is the leafy parts of a variety of turnip – hence its alternative name 'broccoli rabe'. We also find broccolini, with its long tender stalks and small florets; it is a hybrid of broccoli and Chinese broccoli, and has a sweet, green-earthy flavour.

Broccoli can be consumed raw, but cooking will improve it immensely. The key is to use plenty of seasoning. Although it is often boiled or steamed, roasting brings out, as you might expect, a sweetness and depth of flavour. Broccoli is robust enough to carry other pungent and hot flavours such as garlic and chilli.

CAULIFLOWER

Cauliflower is a dense mass of immature flower-stalk branches, known as a curd. It is white to creamy in colour; this is achieved by protection from sunlight – growers tie its leaves over the developing curd to prevent the formation of chlorophyll. Cauliflower can be broken into florets or cooked whole – either by steaming or boiling, and, even better, by roasting or frying. It can also form an excellent purée or be used to make a raw 'couscous' – but remember, the more you disrupt the cells by cutting, the more you will intensify its sulphury element. The flavour is undeniably earthy, and it can carry many other flavours well – especially the equally earthy cumin, the heat of ginger and chillies, and the savoury pungency of garlic – and so cauliflower is wonderful in spicy dishes and curries. For example, the classic *aloo gobi* is a potato and cauliflower curry, and see also Tandoori-Style Cauliflower. Cauliflower can handle sour-salty flavours, it is excellent with capers, and it can take sweetness too, perhaps from raisins and dates. Cauliflower crops up regularly in Middle Eastern cuisine. Roasted cauliflower in a Lebanese-style tahini sauce now seems so much better than the 'cauliflower cheese' that I learned to make at school!

ROMANESCO

Romanesco is an angular variant of cauliflower – rather like a pale green version designed by Gaudi! Now, Gaudi was known for his amazing 'organic' architecture, and in the natural world 'shape' and 'form' are dictated by the Fibonacci sequence,[2] and romanesco exhibits this biological signature so very well! Each floret is a replica of the whole head – reminding us of fractals, the complex never-ending patterns repeated at every scale. And that is, of course, its main attraction! See Romanesco.

Fruits

The fruits that are used as vegetables are an interesting and diverse group. Here we find the *Solanaceae* – the nightshade family – named after its most notorious member, deadly nightshade, with its toxic component 'belladonna' – but also potatoes (remember we discussed the traces of toxic alkaloids?), tobacco (more alkaloids) and the much-loved tomatoes, capsicums (bell peppers, chilli peppers) and aubergines (eggplants). Now, alkaloids are potent defence chemicals, and although they are absent in the tomatoes, bell peppers and aubergines, they may be present in their stems and leaves. Interestingly, tomatin – the alkaloid found in tomato leaves (and in green, unripe tomatoes) – does not actually cause a problem because it binds to the cholesterol in our digestive system which prevents absorption.

This group also includes the cucurbit family – the starchy sweet winter squashes; sweet, delicate-textured courgettes; crisp, watery cucumbers and gherkins; legumes, which are pods that contain several seeds – such as green beans, sugar peas, snow peas, fava beans and soya beans; and also avocados, sweetcorn and olives.

TOMATOES

We owe a huge debt of gratitude to Mexico, where tomatoes were first domesticated! Their name is derived from *tomatl*, which means plump fruit!

They are the second most popular 'vegetable'; the potato claims the first place. This is due to several factors, including their visual appeal – they encompass a vast range of attractive colours and shapes, from dark red to purple to green to yellow to red to tiger-striped, and from cherry-sized to round to plum to fist-sized; they have a unique sweet-sharp-sour taste; and tomatoes are a source of umami – they contain up to 0.3% of the amino acid called glutamic acid. Because of this, tomatoes have been used in cooking to give depth of flavour in a vast range of dishes around the globe. Tomatoes have health benefits too: they contain a lot of vitamin C and a carotenoid named lycopene, which is an antioxidant with anti-cancer and cardioprotective potential (and which is not destroyed by processing!).

To understand tomato flavour, we need to look at its structure, and how cooking affects that. It is easy to examine the anatomy of a raw tomato. Slice crosswise and you will see the thin skin covering the fruit wall. Now, it is the fruit wall that has the highest concentration of the sugars and glutamic acid and its salts, and so this is where the sweet and savoury flavours are concentrated. Then you will see the jelly and juice surrounding the seeds – and this is where we find the citric and malic acids which contribute to sourness. The tough white pithy core doesn't contribute to flavour. So, different varieties have different flavour profiles because of their interior anatomy and the relative proportions of these tissues. Often, before cooking or incorporation into dishes, the skins and jelly-seeds matrix and pith are removed. This practice can improve texture – because the fruit wall is firmer and less watery, and the pith contributes nothing anyway – but acidity can be lost. To rectify this, the skins and jelly-seeds can be cooked down separately,

2   The numerical sequence 0, 1, 1, 2, 3, 5, 8, 13, 21…and so on, was proposed by Fibonacci in 1202 CE, where each number in the sequence is the sum of the two preceding numbers. It was considered an important numerical sequence for many years; recently, it has been shown to play a fundamental role in the growth of plants. When we look at, for example, a sea shell or the seed head of a sunflower, we see the ever-increasing spirals dictated by the sequence.

then strained and added to the fruit wall portion. Cooking also means that the fresh-green aspect is lost, so some chefs add a few tomato leaves at the end of the cooking process to restore this. Sugar and/or vinegar are sometimes added to a cooked tomato sauce – this intensifies sweetness and rebalances acidity.

Raw tomatoes are wonderful salad vegetables – or at least they can be! The vine-ripened ones do tend to have a better balance of sweetness and acidity, and a better aroma – an important contributor to tomato flavour. Furaneol has a sweet-savoury aroma and is responsible for the appetising scent of ripe tomatoes. If tomatoes lack this, don't bother! They may have been harvested while green and artificially ripened or, worse still, chilled. Temperatures below 13°C (55°F) damage the tissues and flavour development. In salads, only use aromatic, ripe, well-flavoured tomatoes, and if they are sublime, all that is needed is a little finely sliced red onion, or perhaps some basil, with a little salt, black pepper and olive oil – and maybe a drop or two of good balsamic vinegar, depending on the acidity of the tomatoes. However, other raw tomato pairings made in heaven are olives and avocados...

Cooked tomatoes often form the sauce in a dish when the backbone or 'hero' is something with a more substantial texture. When tomatoes are in season, they should be the first choice for cooking, as they cook and reduce well, and can be puréed to a fine consistency. Off-season, canned tomatoes are substituted, but – and this cannot be stressed enough – quality is crucial. The best canned tomatoes are from Italy, the entire plum type is preferable to 'chopped tomatoes', and make sure that the brand does not contain added calcium. Calcium is a common additive because it can help with firmness, but it will also interfere with the cooking process, and a smooth texture cannot be achieved. You can roast peeled tinned tomatoes – see Oven-Roasted Tinned Tomatoes. Cooked tomatoes get on very well indeed with

their *Solanaceae* relatives – potatoes, aubergines and peppers. Needless to say, onions and garlic are very good friends, as are chillies, capers, olives – and all of the Mediterranean herbs but especially basil, thyme and oregano.

We also must mention 'sun-dried' tomatoes and oven-dried tomatoes. The former's popularity may well have peaked – sun-drying leads to very intense flavour but a somewhat dry and tough texture, and the ultraviolet light does damage lycopene. Oven-dried tomatoes are easy to make at home – simply halve or quarter tomatoes, drizzle with olive oil and some herbs if you wish, and bake in a slow oven for several hours. This removes water, and concentrates the flavour without damaging the texture or destroying the lycopene. These can be used to make sauces (see Spaghetti with Roasted 'San Marzano' Tomato Sauce) or to add savoury accents to antipasti.

BELL PEPPERS

Bell peppers are sometimes called sweet peppers; they originated in South America but now are associated very much with Mexican and Spanish cuisines. We use varieties of *Capsicum annuum* – these are in effect hollow 'berries', and we have beautiful colours to choose from, from the unripe green peppers to yellows, oranges, purples and reds. Of course, the bell shape is common, but we can also buy elongated varieties. Green peppers have a distinctive aroma when cut, thanks to a pungent nitrogen-containing compound called isobutyl methoxypyrazine – which you might just be able to detect in poor-quality wines made from Cabernet Sauvignon and Sauvignon Blanc. The green types work well in stir-fry dishes and curries – where their clean green-grassy flavour adds freshness, and, of course, the firm moist fruit walls hold their texture. Green peppers contain lutein – the antioxidant noted for its support for the macula of the eyes. Mature yellow and orange peppers are characterised by carotenoids including lutein, but mature red peppers lose the lutein and develop red carotenoids such as capsanthin, capsorubin and beta-carotene. They are also very rich in vitamin C.

Yellow, orange and red peppers are good eaten raw – their fruit walls are crisp and juicy, but they also cook very well. Red peppers in particular have an abundance of cell-wall pectins. This means that when cooked they have a thick and smooth texture. They roast well and can make excellent soups and sauces such as the classic *romesco* sauce, which contains red peppers, tomatoes and ground almonds. As an aside, if you are roasting red and yellow peppers for an antipasti selection, it really does make a difference if you remove the skins after roasting. Simply place the hot peppers, straight from the oven, into a bowl, cover with clingfilm and leave to cool. The skins will slip off easily, and then their beautiful silky texture can be fully appreciated.

Look out for the small red, slightly elongated *piquillo* peppers from Northern Spain – the name means 'little beak', and they are usually roasted over embers to form a sweet, slightly spicy flavour before being skinned, deseeded and packed in jars – see Roasted Piquillo Peppers, where they are stuffed with *skordalia* and complemented with saffron, capers and *mojo verde*!

AUBERGINES

Often called eggplants, aubergines epitomise Mediterranean and Middle Eastern cuisine. Despite this, they actually originated in Africa and Asia and only reached Spain in the Middle Ages. The most common type is oval, shiny and deep purple (anthocyanins), but violet, green, yellow, orange, white and striated varieties can be found, as can spherical and baby versions. Their raw flesh is bitter to taste, cream in colour and very spongy; there are tiny air pockets between the cells. Aubergines are not eaten raw – and the cooking method defines their ultimate consistency. When heated, the air is driven out and the tissue collapses and reduces in bulk. If the flesh is being pan-fried, perhaps in cubes or strips, it will soak up a lot of oil – but this makes for a rich, 'meaty' and creamy texture, and is perfect in dishes such as *Pasta alla Norma*. This dish hails from Catania, an ancient port on the eastern, Ionian coast of Sicily, and was created in honour of the composer Bellini. *Norma* was an adjective used to qualify something that is *ne plus ultra* – in other words, it denotes that this dish is a first course or a single course – and so we do not need to speculate about Norma (although it is fun!).

It is said that if aubergines are deep-fried they will absorb less oil. Aubergines can also be sliced crosswise or lengthwise, or simply halved and baked with olive oil, or strips of skin can be peeled off and rubbed with oil before baking whole. If slices are baked in a Greek *moussaka*-style dish, they will retain their shape. We do need to mention the Arab dish colourfully named *Imam bayaldi* – 'the priest fainted', allegedly because the dish of stuffed halved aubergines baked in lashings of olive oil was so overwhelmingly rich! Aubergines are important in many other regional dishes, and often with peppers and tomatoes – such as the familiar Provençal *ratatouille*; the Sicilian *caponata* (with a sweet and sour element supplied by dried fruit and capers); the Catalan *escalivada* – a dish of roasted or grilled aubergines, red peppers and onions, with olive oil and sherry vinegar – and the Turkish *patlican*, where they are fried in olive oil with green peppers and dressed with a tomato and garlic sauce. See Ratatouille with Black Garlic, and Caponata Revisited.

I have never found it necessary to salt the flesh before cooking. This is said to remove some water and reduce the bitterness, but the process does not seem to make any difference at all – at least not in my experience! However, I often peel before cooking, especially if I am looking for a very creamy, silky texture – perhaps for *baba ganoush*, where the roasted flesh is mashed and flavoured with tahini, garlic and lemon juice. If you roast whole garlic cloves along with the aubergine, and squeeze their softened interiors into the dish, you will get a very mellow flavour indeed!

Courgettes (French) are also known as zucchini (Italian), and are green, yellow-skinned or variegated summer squashes (*Curcubita pepo* cultivars) – and are most often elongated, although round/oval varieties are sometimes available. They are best harvested early. The flesh is pale and slightly spongy in texture. They can be eaten raw – either coarsely grated or sliced into ribbons before dressing – or cooked. Cooking – whether frying, roasting, stewing or baking – does not take long – the texture softens and they develop a delicate sweetness. One of the best ways to enjoy courgettes is to slice diagonally or longitudinally, and roast in a hot oven with some olive oil and seasoning – when just cooked, tender but not on the point of collapse, remove and allow to cool and dress with fresh herbs – marjoram and mint are good – a smudge of crushed raw garlic, a pinch of sugar, maybe some diced red chilli, olive oil and a trace of good red wine vinegar. This allows the courgette to shine in terms of its texture and flavour – delicate, but robust enough to carry herbs, acidity and heat without becoming lost in the process!

Marrows are mature versions of courgettes and they can be very large. They are usually oval to elongated, the skin is tougher and firmer – often green or striped – and the flesh is firm and quite bland. For these reasons, they do lend themselves to stuffing – see Marrow Boat to France.

SQUASHES

Winter squashes have been matured on the plant for much longer than the summer types, and so they tend to be larger, with tougher skins and firm flesh. Their seeds should be discarded, and sometimes the skins are better removed too. They all have sweet, very slightly earthy, but somewhat bland, flavours, and so they can carry a whole range of spices and herbs – making them very versatile ingredients indeed. However, their textures vary. Perhaps the pumpkin is the best known – it has a slightly fibrous texture – and

butternut has a thinner skin, a dense and smooth flesh and is probably the sweetest of the squashes. It has become very popular – but look out for kuri squash (see Roasted Kuri Squash and Coriander Soup), acorn squash and kabocha squash too. Squashes can be roasted, puréed and made into sauces and soups, but a word of warning: they do need generous seasoning. There is a Sicilian proverb – *sali mitticinni nà visazza conzala come vuoi è sempre cucuzza* – which translates as 'add a lot of salt and seasoning because pumpkin it always remains'. Butternut in particular can be sweetly cloying if not well seasoned with salt, and other herbs and spices can offset this too – try the acidity of capers or citrus (orange or lime), the heat of red and green chillies, or pungent herbs such as rosemary, thyme and sage, and spices such as black pepper and nutmeg.

CUCUMBER

Cucumber is one of the freshest salad vegetables in our palette. Its texture is crisp and moist, and the slightly bitter, melon-like, refreshing flavour is instantly recognisable. There are different varieties, but the best ones have smooth skins, small seeds and very tolerable levels of bitterness. Some varieties have been bred for pickling, and these have thinner skins to ease the penetration of brine (for sour pickles) and vinegar. Cucumber has an affinity with dill (think of gherkins and dill pickles), but the coolness of mint complements it well. Some gins are served with cucumber rather than citrus slices – for example, Hendrick's Gin, which includes both cucumber and rose among its flavourings.

GREEN BEANS

Green beans are the pods of a climbing plant (*Phaseolus vulgaris*) originally from the Andes and Central America. They come in several colours – the so-called 'wax' beans are yellow, and there are purple ones too – but by far the most common is the green type. We also see long, round thin pods and flat pods; and the strings that join the two walls of the pod are now only found in heirloom types – modern varieties are stringless. Their flavour is fresh and green with a slight hint of sulphur and mushroom! It is imperative that they are enjoyed fresh, because they do not store well. Even after harvesting, metabolism continues, and their sugars are depleted; to make matters worse, cold storage damages the tissues, resulting in loss of crispness.

FLAGEOLET VERT

Flageolet vert is a French variety of *Phaseolus vulgaris*. The pods are picked before they are fully mature and dried in the shade to retain the pale green colour. The beans within the pods are small, light green and kidney-shaped. They have a fine creamy texture and lovely flavour, and they are excellent in salads.

LIMA BEANS

Lima beans are closely related to green beans, they come from *Phaseolus lunatus* – and, like *flageolet vert*, we eat the immature green seeds within the pods. These are large beans and very nutritious, and have high levels of plant sugars and amino acids. Along with corn, they are an ingredient in *succotash*. This is a traditional Algonquin Indian dish made by boiling broken and/or whole corn kernels and lima beans, sometimes with green and red bell peppers. When *succotash* was introduced to the USA, we start to see the introduction of other ingredients such as onions and tomatoes – and it became a national favourite, because it was easy to make and affordable. We also know lima beans as butter beans, because of their starchy-buttery texture, and they are perhaps more familiar in their dried form (see 'Legumes – beans and pulses'). See Gigantes Plaki and Gigantes Escabeche.

FAVA BEANS

Fava beans, also known as broad beans, are the immature green seeds of *Vica faba*. They feature in many cuisines, and their consumption dates from ancient times. With a sweet and starchy texture, they can be prepared in many ways – from frying to make salted or spiced snacks (*habas*), in soups (*sopa de habas*), in stews (they are good with potatoes), and boiled and served with purées such as the Greek *skordalia* or with pesto. In Italy they are sometimes cooked with artichokes. Fava beans can be puréed and served as part of a *mezze* – for example, the Maltese *bigilla* is made from fava bean purée with olive oil, garlic, parsley and mint, and the Middle Eastern *ful* is flavoured with cumin, and sometimes lemon juice, garlic, parsley and chillies. And, of course, they are the main legume in falafels.

Many writers suggest that they must be double-podded so that the slightly tough skin that surrounds each bean does not spoil the texture of the dish they are destined for. Some of us agree that this is time well spent.

PEAS

Peas are the immature green seeds from the pods of a Mediterranean climbing plant called *Pisum sativum*. We sometimes eat the entire pods (as in sugar snap peas and mangetout), and pea shoots can add freshness to salads. They are small, spherical and have thin skins, with a pleasantly smooth and starchy texture, and their flavour is fresh and green, with a green bell pepper aroma (thanks to the nitrogen-containing isobutyl methoxypyrazines). Like the other green legumes, they are nutritious, containing sugars and amino acids – including glutamic acid – so here we have another plant source of umami. There are several types to choose from, from the tiny, sweet petit pois, to the more mature, larger 'garden peas', to the largest marrowfat peas (from the starchy *medullare* variety) – these are mature peas that are dried out in the field before harvesting. They are the basis of 'mushy peas' where the peas are dried, rehydrated and then mashed, and the snack 'wasabi peas'. Before the advent of frozen foods, peas were a real luxury; now they must be one of the most widely consumed vegetables!

Avocado is probably valued and loved as much for its creamy smooth texture as for its flavour. It is also very pretty, and very moreish, however it is served! Avocados are the fruits of the Central American tree named *Persea americana*. The common name is derived from *ahuacatl*, a word meaning 'testicle' – no doubt inspired by its shape and irregular surface. Avocados contain virtually no starch or sugars, and around 30% of largely monounsaturated oils. This is very unusual in a fruit, and McGee tells us that they might have evolved to attract large animals with big calorie requirements. Avocados only ripen about a week after they have been picked, and the process begins at the stem end and progresses to the base. The ideal temperature range for this is 15–24°C (59–75°F). It is imperative that they are not refrigerated when unripe – they are warm-climate fruits, and cold storage causes considerable damage to their metabolism, and they will never ripen. You can, however, store a *ripe* avocado in the fridge for a few days with no ill effects. So, the ideal storage for an avocado crop is on the tree! Mexican avocados are generally small and have very smooth flesh, and of all the types they are best suited for storage at the cooler end of the ripening range. The lowland, Western Guatemalan avocados have a more fibrous flesh and are the least tolerant of cold – temperatures of less than 12°C (54°F) cause damage; however, the Highland Guatemalan varieties have smooth flesh and smaller seeds. The avocados that we purchase have probably been grown in Southern California, and we can choose from several varieties including the pebbly, dark-skinned Hass, or the smooth green-skinned types such as Fuerte, Pinkerton and Reed with their rich-textured flesh, or some with lowland origins such as Bacon, Zutano, Booth and Lula, which tend to have firmer flesh and up to 50% less fat than the Hass avocados! You can select the variety according to what you are making, rather like you can with potatoes. The high-fat, creamy, soft Hass types are best for making glorious purées, or even a raw chocolate mousse (the avocado supplies the silky texture while cocoa powder gives the intense flavour), but if you want the visual appeal and texture of slices, and would like the flavour to be to the fore, you may be better using the firmer sorts. Avocados turn brown very quickly – but this can be minimised by including something acidic such as lemon or lime juice. How do we describe their flavour? Well, it is certainly delicate, green-grassy-woody, the aroma is slightly spicy-woody, from caryophyllene (in itself this is clove-like) and also fatty acids, and the texture is fatty and smooth, often described as unctuous. Avocados are best eaten raw – sometimes they are cooked or served warm, but we will not go there. For the record, heating generates bitterness and an unattractive 'eggy' quality. Just don't. They were made for dips, salads and salsas. They are wonderful with lime, garlic and chilli, tomato and coriander, and fully ripe mango with fresh chilli. See the delicious Alison's Breakfast Avocado.

As an aside, avocado leaves can be used much like bay leaves, but they have an anisic, tarragon-like aroma and flavour thanks to estragole and anethole. Avocado oil is very bland, but can make a good dressing for a salad – select cold-pressed and unrefined types (they are green and cloudy), store in the fridge and use up quickly!

SWEETCORN

Each little sweet, juicy 'grain' on an ear of corn is a tiny fruit – consisting mostly of a seed, surrounded by its own dedicated food supply of proteins and starch. Fresh corn (*Zea mayes*) must be harvested before the fruits are mature and this is a mere 18–21 days after pollination. After this, the sweetcorn loses its sugars and moisture. The yellow colour is due to zeaxanthin – well regarded for protecting the macula of the eyes – but you can also find other colours including white (which lacks the carotenoids), and red-blue-purple (anthocyanins). Sweetcorn differs from standard corn (the type used to make corn meal) in that it contains more sugars and soluble polysaccharides, and less starch, giving the sweet, almost creamy quality. There are also 'supersweet' varieties; as you might expect, these have even more sugars but less of the soluble polysaccharides, they contain more water, and the texture is less creamy but crisp. However, it is worth knowing that all sweetcorn varieties must be eaten as fresh as possible – even three days' shipping results in a loss of 50% of the sugars! If you can, grow your own!

Sweetcorn is a delight simply served on the cob, but it lends itself to all manner of cooking techniques – it can be roasted, which really brings out the sweetness (see Griddled Sweetcorn Cobs, complemented with lime and chilli), or cooked and puréed, and it is the basis of chowders. Chowders are associated with seafood (especially clams) and usually have a substantial dose of cream too. However, you can make plant-based corn chowder too; make sure that you include potatoes, and you can use oat, soya or even coconut cream to give the desired thick creamy texture. Corn fritters can also be made entirely with plant ingredients – serve with Spiced Tomato and Mint Chutney. Herbs and spices that complement sweetcorn include chives, coriander leaves, black pepper, garlic and chillies.

OLIVES

There are entire books and websites dedicated to olives – such is the variety of their flavours and textures, and their rich history which runs parallel with that of human civilisation. But here we must be brief and restrict ourselves to neurogastronomy! These small fruits of the long-lived, Eastern Mediterranean tree *Olea Europa* have large central seeds surrounded by an oily flesh. Interestingly, their oil content is about 30% – the same as avocados. In their raw state, they are really unpleasant – they are unpalatably bitter thanks to phenolic components, especially oleuropein – but they can be cured,

which reduces this considerably. Curing is best when done the slower traditional way, where the fruits are packed in salt prior to being steeped in brine. The industrial process involves the use of a 1–3% sodium hydroxide solution (alkaline lye) which leaches out the bitter phenolics and breaks down the waxy, impermeable cuticle on the skins, making them more permeable to the brine phase. This is quicker, but involves washing and adding acid to neutralise the lye. The brine phase also involves a lactic acid bacteria and yeast fermentation, which can take up to a year if the olives have not been subjected to the alkali treatment.

Green olives are fermented when they are unripe, and we often see these described as 'Spanish-style' olives, such as the Manzanilla type, and Greek Halkidiki olives. The darker, purple-hued olives such as the Greek Kalamata are less bitter, more fruity and are already ripe when they are fermented. Black, ripe olives such as the Greek type, Italian Gaeta and French Niçoise will have been fermented without chemical leaching and de-bittering, and the result is a more bitter and less tart (sour) flavour, and a fruitier aroma.

Of course, many olives are marinated after curing, with herbs and spices that complement and augment their flavours. We find green olives stuffed with almonds, lemon rind, slivers of garlic or red pepper, or cracked and marinated in crushed coriander seeds and lemon rind, or oregano and garlic, or indigenous dried herbs and spices. Olive tasting is a lot of fun... Our favourites are the large, succulent Spanish green Gordal Reina olives, which have just a hint of chilli.

Usually enjoyed with an aperitif or two, olives also form the basis of an intense, coarse French spread known as *tapenade*. It can be made with green or black olives, capers, thyme and sometimes garlic – anchovies are an essential part of the traditional recipe, but can be omitted for a plant-based version.

Samphire and seaweeds

There are a few salt-tolerant coastal plants and seaweeds that can add interest (and iodine!) to plant kingdom cuisine – samphire, and members of the green, red and brown groups of algae (not plants, but we will include them here because this is where they fit).

The edible seaweeds all have a salty, briny-savoury flavour attributed to the presence of minerals and glutamic acid. McGee explains that it was the glutamic acid in seaweed that provided the breakthrough in understanding umami. Their aroma evokes the seashore – thanks mainly to a chemical called dimethyl sulphide. Samphire and seaweed should be cooked briefly – if seaweed is overcooked, it can become unpleasantly fishy. Often the larger types such as kelp and kombu are cooked in broth, just briefly, to release the flavour that has crystallised on the surfaces and within, and they are then removed, leaving behind their distinctive umami signature! If, like me, you find the texture of some seaweeds unpalatable, but you appreciate their particular version of umami, you can use seaweed salt, or even dried flakes, in all manner of recipes!

SAMPHIRE

Samphire is also known as sea beans (glasswort and pickklebeans), and is the fleshy stems and branchlets of *Salicornia*, which belongs to the beet family. It grows in coastal regions and is salt-tolerant – look for the marsh variety which is emerald green, crisp and succulent. Samphire is often used as an accompaniment to fish and seafood because of its crisp texture and pleasantly briny flavour which is evocative of the sea. However, that is a very limited role for such a unique vegetable! It is quite salty and so works well in dishes that are comfortable with this. It can be eaten raw, but is best boiled in water for a few moments to ameliorate the saltiness. It looks fantastic with asparagus and a simple oil and lemon dressing, and is quite at home in linguine,

spaghetti and gnocchi dishes. You could also use it in a Japanese-style stir-fry, maybe with some mirin which will temper the briny aspect with its sweetness.

GREEN ALGAE

Unusual, but you might like to try the delicate sea lettuce (*Ulva lactuca*) in green salads or soups, if you can find it! Try it with a mirin dressing...

RED ALGAE

More common in tropical and subtropical waters, the red algae store starches and sugars, which is why some are exploited for their gelling and thickening properties. This group includes the delicate nori (*Porphyra* species) which is used as a sushi wrapper; agar agar (*Gracilaria* species) for its gelling properties; carrageenan (*Chondrus crispus*) for its thickening properties (you might see it listed on the ingredients of some plant milks); and dulce or sea parsley (*Palmaria palmata*) which is eaten with potatoes and in soups in Ireland.

BROWN ALGAE

Brown algae are more substantial. They often have a jelly-like texture which is an acquired taste (and one that I have not been inclined to cultivate since my early days experimenting with macrobiotics). Examples include kelp and kombu (*Laminaria* species) which flavours Japanese *dashi* (soup), and they are sometimes fried. Wakame (*Undaria* species) is also common, and it is an ingredient in Japanese *miso* soup.

MUSHROOMS AND FUNGI

Mushrooms are not from the plant kingdom; they are the fruiting bodies of fungi. Here, when we are talking about mushrooms, we are referring to the edible gilled varieties. The white mushroom – *Agaricus bisporus* – is fairly typical; it has a stalk and a cap with gills on the underside. This is where the tiny spores are produced. However, some types look very different – such as the crinkled morels or the frilly chanterelles.

Mushrooms are popular in plant-based cuisine because they are said to be 'meaty' in texture. Now, this is perhaps a bit unfair – they are not necessarily dense and chewy – and it does imply that they could be a substitute for something that is missing in our repertoire! But they do, undeniably, have a pleasing, substantial texture and distinctive rich savoury flavour, and can easily be the hero of a dish. Unless you are an expert, it is better to buy cultivated mushrooms, or purchase wild mushrooms from reliable sources – foraging might be fun, but there are some poisonous species out there too. We have a wide variety to choose from; apart from the standard white *Agaricus bisporus*, we have its variants including chestnut, crimini and portobello. We also have cultivated Japanese shiitake and oyster mushrooms. Some mushrooms are difficult to cultivate, and so we can only buy wild-harvested porcini (*Boletus edulis*), which are known as *cèpes* in France, chanterelles (also called girolles), trompettes, and, of course, truffles (not mushrooms, but fungi nonetheless).

Mushrooms are 80–90% water, the cap is covered in a cuticle that allows the passage of gases and moisture, and their cell walls are reinforced by chitin – the same as insects and crustaceans. They are rich in protein and vitamin B12, and even contain vitamin D – and so are valuable foods for vegans.

Mushroom flavour is fascinating. The mushroom aroma is due to the presence of an alcohol named octanol and a ketone called 1-octen-3-one, which are released in response to tissue damage. Some mushrooms such as shiitake produce sulphur compounds with meaty aromas. Chanterelles have a fruity, apricot-like aroma. Now, as we know, aroma is an important component of flavour. Mushroom octanol is produced mainly in the gills – and not all mushrooms have prominent or even exposed gills. That is why we have a more intense flavour in, for example, the mature, wide, flattened portobellos, with their dark prominent gills, than in the immature closed white button mushrooms. The savoury taste comes courtesy of amino acids, including glutamic acid.

Fresh mushrooms should be consumed as soon as possible after harvesting, because metabolism continues along with increased cell-wall formation; storage is therefore important – we need to keep them cool and free from moisture. They must be well dried and cooked immediately after cleaning. Of course, some mushrooms such as porcini are often dried – and this intensifies the flavour considerably. These need to be cleaned and rehydrated before use.

Cooking methods are important too. We can generate an intense flavour if we use dry heat over a long period. This is because heat collapses the air pockets and moisture evaporates, so that the flavour compounds are concentrated and the texture becomes firm. But, more importantly, this process develops umami, via the Maillard reaction between sugars and amino acids. See Mushroom Caldereta.

Mushrooms are often used to give flavour and character to dishes – the suffix *forestière* denotes this. However, if the mushroom is to be the main feature of a dish, and we are looking to enhance our mushrooms with other flavourings, it is worth taking a few moments to establish the character of the type we are using. Here is a quick guide to some mushrooms and flavours.

BUTTON AND CHESTNUT MUSHROOMS

These are the most common and typify the mushroom fresh-earthy flavour and firm texture. The brown chestnuts are said to be more flavoursome, but the two varieties can be used interchangeably. They can be fried, sautéed or roasted, and a wide range of herbs complement their flavour, from the fresh-green anisic tarragon, or dill, or the green-grassy aromatic parsley, or the more intense, woody thyme or the pungent sage. Mushrooms are very good cooked with shallots and garlic; we can make *duxelles* – a savoury combination of finely chopped, fried shallots and mushrooms – which can be used as a stuffing for vegetables such as butternut squash, or layered in lasagne, or used as a topping for bruschetta with a liberal dose of parsley. Walnuts and mushrooms are a common pairing in French cuisine; indeed, walnut oil is often the choice for sautéing mushrooms. Try adding chopped toasted walnuts to *duxelles*.

CÈPES OR PORCINI

If you are lucky enough to obtain fresh *cèpes*, you are in for a treat. Slice and gently fry in olive oil with some finely sliced garlic and some sea salt. Parsley can be stirred through at the last minute.

CHANTERELLES OR GIROLLES

Apricot colour, apricot aroma – these are wonderful if you are looking for a fruity accent!

CRIMINI

The crimini is a mature button mushroom, younger than the portobello, and often called 'baby bello' or 'baby portobello'. It has more flavour than the white button mushroom, but this is not as fully developed as the mature portobello.

MORELS

Shaped like a date, with a honeycombed surface, and packing a strong flavour punch, you can play with their smoky element by pairing with carvacrol-rich herbs such as oregano and thyme.

OYSTER

Characterised by thin tissues, this pretty, pale-gilled mushroom is often torn or cooked whole rather than sliced. They are excellent in stir-fries, or simply sautéed with seasoning and garlic and served over a bed of mixed green leaves, or *mesclun*.

PORTOBELLO

Aromatic, rich and savoury, the flavour can be intensified by roasting with just a little oil and seasoning. Try removing the stalks and stuffing the gill surface with a mixture of ciabatta breadcrumbs, garlic, parsley, lemon rind, sea salt and olive oil before baking.

SHIITAKE

Grown on the logs of hardwood trees (often oak), these firm, almost tough mushrooms have unusual cell-wall carbohydrates, which are believed to have anti-cancer properties. They also are said to be immune system stimulants. Shiitake produce an unusual aroma molecule called lenthione. They are well suited to East Asian cuisine and flavours – stir-fried, or steamed, or simmered in aromatic broths with *shoyu*, *tamari* or *teriyaki*. Their texture is slightly slippery, and their flavour is intense. See Mushroom Ceviche.

TROMPETTES

Trompette de mort has a sinister ring to it...so you might just want to call them trompettes or the sunnier-sounding 'horn of plenty' instead! These are dark and horn-shaped with wavy edges and a curved stalk. The nickname 'poor man's truffle' gives us a clue about their flavour – which is strong and earthy. If finely sliced, the dark colour and flavour could almost pass for truffle – at least to the uninitiated! The best way to use them is to slice or pull into strands, sauté in olive oil with some seasoning, garlic and parsley or tarragon, and pile on to bruschetta or toasted sourdough, maybe with some capers – rather like *tapenade*.

TRUFFLES

We debated where to include the truffle. It is here because it is a fungus; however, it is not used like a vegetable, but as flavouring. Truffles are the fruiting bodies of the *Tuber* genus – dense, knobbly masses of thickened tissue which can be as small as a walnut or larger than a fist. Hidden underground, growing in symbiosis with oak, hazel or linden trees, they emit a musky and persistent aroma which is hugely attractive to truffle flies and some animals – including pigs and dogs. It came as a bit of a shock to us to discover that they are not approved by the Vegan Society, because dogs or pigs are trained to find them. Now, I suppose that, strictly speaking, this is animal exploitation, but it does not appear to involve any cruelty, so we are more than happy to include them in this book. There are two types of truffle, and both are much sought after, but they are always in limited supply, and so are very expensive.

The black winter truffle (*Tuber melanosporum*) comes from the Périgord region of France. Subtle, earthy, musty and foresty, and with some interesting aromatic compounds, black truffles also contain androsterone. This is an androgen (a male hormone) and possibly a pheromone (a biological messenger chemical) which is present in the saliva of male pigs, and is also found in the armpits, sebaceous glands and urine in human males. Pig androsterone induces mating behaviour in sows, but it has also been shown to impact on human behaviour. It has a musky odour that many people cannot detect – and the ones that can describe it as unpleasant! Usually, black truffle is cooked gently to bring out the best in its flavour.

White truffles (*Tuber magnatum*) are found in the north of Italy. You might expect them to be more subtle than the black ones, but you would be so wrong. They are more pungent and have a distinctive savoury garlic aspect, possibly related to some unusual sulphur compounds. White truffle is best used raw – shaved finely and scattered over the dish just before serving. This is a real sensory treat – they are attractive, the aroma is appetising and the flavour is exquisite.

FRUITS

Fruits are sweet, attractive, colourful, and destined to be eaten – at least from the biological perspective. They are versatile ingredients and can be included in both sweet and savoury dishes. Some of us prefer to eat raw fruit between meals rather than as a dessert course because of the demon indigestion, but this is personal preference, of course. There is one benefit of ending your meal with fresh fruit, however, and that is as a breath freshener. Some fruit enzymes (the ones that cause discolouration when we prepare fruits) can react with the smelly sulphur-containing components of garlic and onions, and render these odourless, helping to counteract bad breath. The best fruits for this are the stone fruits, grapes and blueberries.

Fruits have an interesting taste profile, characterised by a balance between sweet and sour. The sweetness is due to the presence of fruit sugars which are usually in the region of 10–15% by weight in ripe fruit; unripe fruits store sugar as starch and are less sweet to taste. As the fruit ripens, the sour component contributed by fruit acids – such as citric, malic, tartaric and oxalic acids – falls, and this has the effect of intensifying the sweetness.

Aroma is also important. Often just a few volatiles will impart the characteristic aroma of a particular fruit, while many hundreds are in the background, adding layers of complexity. Fruity aromas are formed when alcohols and acids react to form constituents known as esters (these have names that end in '–ate'). For example, ethyl acetate is characteristic of apples, hexyl acetate of pears, ethyl butyrate of pineapple and isoamyl acetate of bananas. Finally, think about the wide variety of fruit textures – which completes the flavour profile. We have juicy, tart citrus fruits and soft, smooth bananas, crunchy apples, gritty pears and so on. Once we have established the flavour/aroma profile, we can make links with compatible ingredients when composing a dish.

The pomes

The pome fruits belong to the rose family. The word 'pome' comes from the Latin word meaning 'fruit'. Apples are classed in the genus *Malus*, and we have several thousand named varieties to choose from! Here is a quick guide...

DESSERT APPLES

Dessert or eating apples have a good balance between sour and sweet when raw, their pH is typically 3.4 and the sugar content is around 15%. About 25% of an apple is air, which occupies the spaces between the cells. This is important in the texture. When an apple ages or becomes over-ripe, the texture becomes mealy because the cell walls lose integrity and the moisture is lost. So, dessert apples are best enjoyed fresh, solo or in salads. We have the crisp green sort with their refreshing, tart flavour (Granny Smith), the yellow, soft-watery and honeyed type (Golden Delicious), pink types which are crisp and tart-sweet (Pink Lady), russet, crisp, aromatic and floral varieties (Cox's Orange and Ribston Pippins), russet and red types with firm texture, crunch and sweetness (Royal Gala, Braeburn and Jazz), and deep red, soft-textured and sweet-winey varieties (McIntosh Red). The flavour (and texture) of apples goes very well with beetroot, carrots, celery and nuts, especially hazelnuts, pecans and walnuts (see Gnocchetti Sardi and Apple Pesto Salad).

COOKING APPLES

Cooking apples are very tart and sour when raw, with a pH of 3 and sugar around 12%. However, their texture holds up when cooked. Most eating apples – with the exceptions of Granny Smith and Golden Delicious which are 'dual-purpose' varieties – disintegrate when cooked – some even turn to froth! When an apple is baked whole, the air spaces fill with steam and the apple expands – this is why we need to make a slit in the skin to avoid an explosion. Cooking apples are used in pies and crumbles – often with blackberries – and they make excellent rosy-floral-scented purées and sauces. Varieties include Bramley's Seedling and *Calville blanc d'hiver*.

CRAB APPLES

Crab apples are the fruits of wild species rather than domestic ones. They are bitter and virtually inedible when raw, but can be used to make a wonderful jelly, maybe in conjunction with rosehips, or delicately scented with clove – for me, memories of childhood. Crab apple jelly can contribute a lovely sweet accent to many savoury dishes. All apples are rich in cell-wall pectins and this is why they make such good jellies.

CIDER APPLES

Cider apples need a mention here. The fruits of *Malus sylvestris* are used only for cider making. They are acidic – which is an important factor in the fermentation process – and they are rich in tannins – astringent constituents which bind to cell-wall fragments and help these precipitate out, aiding clarity. Cider apples contain an indigestible sugar alcohol called sorbitol – present at around 0.5%. A large volume of cider can therefore cause a fair degree of bloating – similar to the aftermath of eating sunchokes. You have been warned! Cider can also be used as an ingredient – see Pears Poached in Craft Cider.

Pears are also popular dessert fruits and ingredients. They belong to the genus *Pyrus* and do not have the acidity or the keeping qualities of apples. They must be picked when mature but still hard; ripening is achieved off the tree. If they are picked when ripe, the texture suffers very rapidly, becoming mushy. Pears will also suffer if they are wrapped in plastic. They are juicy and crisp, with a grittiness which is due to cellulose-rich 'stone cells'; however, modern European varieties have a softer texture and fewer stone cells.

SUMMER PEARS
Summer pears include Bartlett (or Williams), which is sometimes used for canning and pear brandy. It is the typical pear in every way – from its shape to the definitive pear flavour. Most are green and become softer and more yellow as they ripen, but red cultivars are available too.

AUTUMN PEARS
Autumn pears include the Doyenne du Comice and Bosc varieties; they are good for eating, being highly aromatic and with buttery-soft textures.

WINTER PEARS
Winter pears include the sweet dessert pear Winter Nellis and the green or russet D'Anjou, which has very good keeping qualities and is suitable for eating, baking and puréeing; it is juicy, subtly sweet and with a slight lemon-lime character.

Pears are widely used in desserts – they are often poached in spice-infused liquors, and are particularly good with star anise, cardamom or cinnamon. *Saffa* is a sweet dish from Morocco, where dried pears are combined with toasted flaked almonds and sweetened couscous, orange flower water and cinnamon. Pears can add a lovely flavour dimension to savoury dishes too.

Like apples, they are a delight in a roasted beetroot and toasted hazelnut salad, or with raw grated carrots and walnuts on a bed of bitter leaves. Or try a salad of thinly sliced pear with caramelised fennel and rocket leaves, and All out of 'Waldorf' Salad.

Citrus fruits
The citrus fruits that we enjoy today are all descended from ancestral varieties – namely the citron, the mandarin and the pommelo. Some are eaten for their own sake, some are used to give sour accents to sweet and savoury dishes, and citrus peel can add character, aroma and bitter accents.

Citrus colours vary; unripe fruits are usually green, ripening to vivid shades of orange and yellow. Often commercial fruits are treated with wax to slow moisture loss – so try to purchase organic, fresh, ripe and unwaxed fruits when possible, especially if you are planning to use the rind. The typical citrus flavour is due in part to sour citric acid, sweet sugars, bitter phenolic compounds, and glutamate (umami!) – which makes citrus a very useful ingredient indeed. The aroma is also very distinctive and unmistakable, largely due to the lemony limonene; some such as orange, mandarin and grapefruit have a floral element (linalool) which is backed up with some sulphur-containing compounds that give a musky note (especially in grapefruit) and nitrogen-containing aromatics (in mandarin peel). Quite unique! So let us see how we can incorporate citrus in our dishes, to add character and flavour.

We can use the carefully prepared flesh in many dishes – just ensure that the bitter pith (albedo) is removed along with the peel, and that any seeds are discarded. A good way to prepare citrus fruit for the flesh is to immerse the fruit in simmering water for a few moments – this loosens the rind. The peel is very useful too. It has an intense and typical citrus aroma because the volatile oil glands are abundant in the peel. The peel can be removed and grated, but sometimes the presence of the pith can impart bitterness. Because the aromatic oils are insoluble in water, and the bitter elements in the pith are soluble in water, some chefs place the peel in hot water to leach out the bitterness without affecting the aromatic oils.

ORANGES
Oranges are the offspring of the pommelo and the mandarin, and come in many varieties, from the fresh, juicy Navel and common types (*Citrus sinensis*), and the Italian blood oranges with

their anthocyanin-coloured flesh (the best for dietary antioxidants) and which have a delightful raspberry element, to the sour or bitter Seville oranges (*Citrus aurantium*) destined for orange flower water production or marmalade. Orange with raw or caramelised fennel is a classic and delicious combination, and blood orange and thinly sliced roasted beetroot, sprinkled with the lemony-herbal dill, is a delight. Orange flesh and grated carrot on a bed of watercress, with some walnuts and capers, makes a simple and refreshing salad. Some soups work very well with orange – the juice and grated rind can be added to carrot and pumpkin soups, perhaps with aromatic-citrus coriander seeds, and then garnished with coriander leaves, which have the orangey aromatic decanal; or in beetroot soup along with ginger, which will add warmth and underpin the citrus element, and again a liberal application of coriander leaf is perfect.

Orange flower water, made from the blossoms of the bitter orange, is used in many Middle Eastern dishes, especially Iranian ones. Despite sounding gentle, floral and mildly aromatic, it is actually powerfully scented, so only a very few drops are needed!

GRAPEFRUIT

Grapefruit is the Caribbean child of the sweet orange and the pommelo. It is pretty – we have yellow, pink and red (ruby) varieties. The pink and red colours are given by lycopene, and the ruby ones are slightly sweeter. Grapefruits have a complex aroma and flavour, and are mouth-puckeringly bitter, thanks to a phenolic compound called naringin, but the riper the fruit, the less naringin it will contain. This is probably the only health 'warning' in this book: grapefruit phenolics can interfere with some drugs, causing them to persist for longer in the system – so if you are on medication, heed the warnings on the packaging! However, on the plus side, the same phenolics are being developed to act as activity-enhancing ingredients in some drugs! There is

another bitter culprit lurking in grapefruit: when it is cut and the cells are disrupted, enzymes act on an innocent compound and convert it into the intensely bitter limonin. So if you want to enjoy grapefruit, it should be fully ripe and it *must* be freshly prepared and consumed before the dreaded limonin makes its presence felt!

LEMONS

Lemons are hybrids of hybrids, and we have many varieties at our disposal. They are acidic and tart, and have an incredible, mouthwatering aroma. The zest is indispensable in the kitchen, it can add brightness and freshness to so many dishes, and it is an important part of *gremolata*. The juice is good in salad dressings – especially for Middle Eastern dishes – and it is important in Lebanese tahini sauce. Lemon works so well with many herbs – from the anisic basil to the citrusy herbs such as coriander leaf and dill, and, of course, parsley and thyme. Lemon and ginger is also an excellent combination, and it is very happy with coriander seed and black pepper. Preserved lemons are important in Middle Eastern and North African cuisine. These are made by salting sliced lemons and allowing a fermentation to take place over a few weeks; the bacteria and yeasts transform the sharp flavour into something much more mellow. Preserved lemons, if used judiciously, can add an incredible depth and complexity to tagine-style vegetable dishes.

LIMES

Limes are the most acidic citrus species, and they are also fragrant – with floral, pine-like and spicy elements within the citrus framework. There are two types on the market. The 'true' lime is known as Key lime, or Mexican lime – the botanical name is *Citrus aurantifolia* – and it is widespread in tropical regions. In the traditional Ayurvedic medicine of India, lime is something of a cure-all, and modern research is indicating that the volatile oil from the peel has cancer-fighting activity. We might also find the Persian or Tahiti lime (*Citrus latifolia*), and this is possibly a cross between the true lime and the pommelo – so, as we might expect, it is larger and seedless. This is more tolerant of the cold, and it is the more common variety in stores in Europe and the USA.

Despite these differences, the uses are the same. Lime juice can be used in many ways – in salad dressings, in salsas with chilli and coriander leaf, in curries – and it is a natural partner for the smooth, unctuous avocado. Lime has an affinity with basil – you can make a speedy green soup with watercress, spinach, rocket, spring onions (scallions) and peas, with a handful of basil added at the last moment. Simply halve a lime (or two) and let it simmer as the soup is cooking – remember to remove it if you are blending the soup. Or add a squeeze of the juice along with some black pepper before serving. Lime pickle is a classic accompaniment for a curry, adding a sour and spicy accent, while dried limes contribute an earthy, aromatic sour-lime flavour to Iranian vegetable stews. Yasmin Khan explains the best way to use them – the hard outer surface should be pierced several times before adding whole to soups or stews. They rehydrate during the cooking process; just before serving, they can be squeezed against the sides of the pot to release the juices into the dish.

Stone fruits

Stone fruits belong to the rose family and belong to the *Prunus* genus. Often, they are enjoyed fresh, they can be poached in liquors to make delightful desserts, and when dried they can be incorporated as sweet accents in savoury dishes.

APRICOTS

Apricots come in many varieties – the familiar orange, but also white and red, the colour being due to lycopene. They have peach-like notes due to aromatic chemicals called lactones, but also floral-citrus characteristics. When fresh and ripe, the flesh is structured but yielding, but they are delicate and do not travel well, and so they are often sun-dried. Dried apricots are sweet-sour, and feature in some classic Middle Eastern dishes, including tagines and vegetable stews.

PLUMS

Again, there are numerous varieties of plums. I must confess to a particular fondness for Victoria plums – succulent, heady, sweet, almondy, floral, spicy and even peachy. When I was born, my grandfather planted a plum tree in his garden. Many years later, and having survived a hurricane and bracket fungus infection, it still bears the loveliest fruit that I have ever tasted! However, there are many other examples, such as the European 'yellow-egg' and 'imperatrice', greengages, and many purple-blue varieties – which are usually destined for drying into prunes. Asian plums are normally eaten fresh. Damsons and sloe are English types – rather astringent when fresh, and better appreciated in damson or sloe gin!

Prunes are deep, rich and caramelic. They have a somewhat negative connotation in many households – offered up as a laxative rather than something to be actually enjoyed! They do contain a lot of the indigestible sugar, sorbitol, and a lot of fibre, so this probably helps transit through the gut, but inevitably with some accompanying gas! They are also fantastic antioxidants due to the presence of phenolic compounds. Maybe we should revise our opinion of them. Prunes are sometimes included in Middle Eastern tagine-style vegetable dishes, but we do find them more often with meats – probably due to their good preservative and moisture-retaining actions.

PEACHES AND NECTARINES

Peaches and nectarines are varieties of the same species – *Prunus persica*. Peaches have a softly fuzzy skin, and nectarines are smooth and more aromatic. There are several types – white- and yellow-fleshed, 'clingstoned' and 'freestoned'. The aroma and flavour comes from lactones – compounds which also have a coconut-like aspect.

For this reason, they can accompany coconut milk ice cream very well indeed! Just beware of fruits that have been chilled below 8°C (46°F) – this causes pectin breakdown, which has a negative impact on their texture.

Shiny black-red-purple (anthocyanins), sweet and succulent, or red and yellow with a sweet-tart flavour, sweet cherries are the fruits of *Prunus avium*. They must be picked when perfectly ripe, and enjoyed fresh – and there is really nothing I can add, except to mention that their distinctive flavour is given by benzaldehyde (almondy), linalool (floral) and eugenol (clove). Heating intensifies the flavours, especially if the stones are left in (that is where the benzaldehyde lurks – see 'Almonds').

I love to eat cherries just as they are. However, you could create a plant-based version of the classic Escoffier dessert Cherries Jubilee by gently cooking pitted cherries in a brandy or kirsch syrup; flambé before serving over a coconut-vanilla ice cream.

Sour cherries (*Prunis cerasus*) are very popular in Iran – they are more tart and less sweet. They are the types that you might find in dried form, and they are great for adding an aromatic sour accent to dishes.

Tropical fruits

Tropical fruits still evoke a sense of luxury, even though they are now commonly available. I am a bit of a fruit purist, enjoying it as nature intended, especially where tropical fruits are concerned. Their flavours are intense and complex, and so evocative of the tropics.

BANANAS

Bananas are the most popular fruit. They are actually seedless berries from *Musa sapientus* – a large herb! They are born in clusters, picked when still green and unripe, and they are starchy – with sugars being formed and acidity rising as they ripen. A very ripe specimen will contain 30% sugar. They are quite unique, with their smooth texture and distinctive aroma and flavour. Banana aromatics include esters such as amyl acetate (pear drops). The big down side is that they rapidly over-ripen, turning brown-black. We normally see the large, elongated, curved types, but there is a whole world of bananas to discover – look for the Asian and Latin American varieties which are shorter and straighter and with distinctively different flavours!

MANGOES

Mangoes are the fruits of the Asian tree *Mangifera indica*. They are intensely aromatic and juicy. The texture is variable – there are many, many different varieties, which range from fibrous to smooth. I prefer to eat the less fibrous types, but these are not always easily identified! Mangoes have a deep orange (beta-carotene), succulent flesh, and an astonishing flavour profile – you will find fruitiness (esters), coconut-peach (lactones) and caramel, depending on how ripe the fruit is. Chilli or cayenne pepper can really emphasise the sweetness and a little sea salt will pull it together. Look out for Alphonso mangoes, which are said to be the finest; see Mango and Coconut Frozen Yogurt. Green, unripe mangoes are not sweet; they are tart and are sometimes pickled or dried and powdered to make *amchur* – a souring agent in curries.

LYCHEES

I have a fascination for these perfumed Asian fruits. The outer skin is dry and loose, covering a pale milky-white flesh that surrounds its small seed. The sweet flesh is so fragrant and complex – it is very floral, due to linalool and rosy geraniol, and also rose oxide. The flesh is delicate, and it turns brown if chilled excessively or if it loses moisture. If you have eaten cooked lychees, you will maybe have been aware of a lovely pink tint, due to the development of anthocyanins. Delicate yes, but well worth the aromatic experience!

PASSION FRUIT

Another perfumed treasure! The fruit of a tropical vine, it has a wrinkled, sometimes brittle outer skin, and inside we find hundreds of small round seeds, each with its own jelly-like covering. The child in me thinks of frog spawn, and my texture police scream 'no!', but I cannot help but be entranced by the aroma and flavour. It is intense, slightly acidic-tart, fruity-floral (esters and lactones), violets are there (ionones) and musk (sulphur compounds) – strange, intriguing, heady, euphoric and beautiful.

PINEAPPLES

Like strange mutant pinecones, these are the fruits of a bromeliad, and we could say that they epitomise tropical fruits – exotic and exuberant! They are constructed of individual baby fruits that are fused together and arranged in a spiral. They are picked before they are fully ripe, because they do not travel well, but sadly they do not actually improve over time. Best to enjoy them, fully ripened, in the tropics! Like many other tropical fruits, the flavour can only be described as intense. A ripe pineapple is sweet, but with a good balance of sourness. The scent is exotic and fruity, with pungency from sulphur-containing compounds, and interesting vanilla and spice elements. Different parts of the fruit have distinct flavours – the base consists of older and sweeter fruitlets, and the outer layers are more tart. The texture is fibrous, but that can be forgiven! Pineapple enzymes can cause problems in conventional desserts, because bromelain (a member of the protease group) breaks down gelatine and milk proteins – and conventional cooks need to cook pineapple before incorporating it into gelatine-based or dairy desserts. We might question why some plants produce these protein-digesting enzymes. It is possible that it is a limiting factor, so that if an animal eats too much, its digestion will suffer; or it might be that moderate consumption aids in the expulsion of intestinal parasites. These enzymes can dissolve live tapeworms!

Cane berries

Cane berries belong to the genus *Rubus*, and their fruits were the inspiration for Velcro, because the tiny fruitlets are held together by a network of small surface hairs! There are many varieties and hybrids, such as the loganberry, which is a cross between the blackberry and raspberry.

BLACKBERRIES

There are many varieties, from the gentle, sweet European ones to the spicy American varieties. Wild blackberries ripen in the autumn, and so are often associated with comforting desserts – with their tart, spicy, woody sweetness.

RASPBERRIES

Raspberries are jewel-like and pretty, and with a distinctive sweet and sour flavour; they must be one of the best-loved soft fruits. The flavour is partly given by raspberry ketone – now sadly better known for its alleged weight-loss effects. I first encountered it when studying perfumery, and it really does smell of mouthwatering raspberries! However, raspberry flavour also has a beautiful violet aspect, given by another set of aroma compounds called ionones. I love eating freshly picked raspberries, but they are also wonderful when paired with peaches or blackberries.

Berries

It is difficult to think about blueberries and cranberries without thinking superfoods. Both hail from North America, although the *Vaccinium* genus is widespread, thriving from the Tropics to the Arctic.

BLUEBERRIES

Blueberries are the fruits of a bush belonging to the *Vaccinium* genus – small and spherical, a deep purple-blue and with a white bloom, and filled with lots of tiny seeds. The flavour is concentrated in the skin – fruity and just a little bit spicy. They are noted for their array of phenolic antioxidants and anthocyanins. The European bilberry is closely related – from *Vaccinium myrtillus*.

Cranberries are the fruits of the vine *Vaccinium macrocarpon*. Cranberries are small, spherical and red in colour. Fresh cranberries are harvested using the 'dry method' – they are picked mechanically when ripe – usually in autumn and winter. Cranberries destined for juice are harvested by the 'wet method'. Here, the wetland where they are grown is flooded with 45cm of water the night before harvesting, and the berries are then loosened mechanically, and they float to the surface for collection.

Fresh cranberries are acidic rather than sweet, and they are very well endowed with phenolics which act as both antioxidants and antimicrobials. One of their pigments, a flavonoid, prevents bacteria from adhering to body tissues – hence their use in managing urinary tract infections. Raw cranberries are unpleasantly sour and astringent – thanks to an abundance of terpenes, cinnamates and phenolics, to name just a few. The European type has a more herbaceous flavour than the more common North American sort. Cranberries are also notable for their pectin content – hence the omnipresent cranberry jelly which makes an appearance in many Western households at Christmas!

CURRANTS AND GOOSEBERRIES

Currants and gooseberries are the fruits of species in the genus *Ribes*. We have both red and black currants. The blackcurrant, *Ribes nigrum*, is a native of the British Isles, but is widely distributed. It is cultivated for its berries which are used in jams, jellies and as flavours for desserts and alcoholic drinks. Apart from its small purple-black, spherical berries, it is notable for the strong aroma of its leaves and flower buds. In Siberia, the juice of the berries is a folk remedy for sore, inflamed throats. Goats enjoy the leaves, and bears like the berries, it is said...

Blackcurrants have a high acidity, and an incredible spicy-fruity-catty aroma! The catty element is given by traces of a sulphur compound (4-methoxy-2-methylbutan-2-thiol) that you can also discern in Sauvignon Blanc wines. They are rich in anthocyanins and vitamin C, but are rarely consumed freshly picked, sadly.

Gooseberries, deliciously sweet and tart, slightly hairy with a tough skin and jelly-like interior, have a similar fate, and they are usually destined for purées, sauces and tarts. But I have fond memories of picking both blackcurrants and gooseberries and eating them on the spot!

GRAPES

Grapes are the fruits of woody vines of the *Vitis* genus, and there are thousands of varieties. Most of the world's harvest goes for wine making, and the rest for eating fresh or as raisins. Grapes for eating as fruit are the sweeter varieties, and we have a huge choice – seedless and seeded; thick- and thin-skinned; blacks, reds, purples, greens; green and citrus aromas, floral aromas and even musky aromas. Grapes can be preserved by sun-drying to make fruity-caramel-scented raisins, and again the variety is enormous – we have brown-gold raisins, yellow-gold raisins, 'sultanas', and black raisins or 'currants' from the Corinth grape.

KIWI

Kiwi fruits were originally named by growers in New Zealand, but they are the berries of the Chinese vine, *Actinidia deliciosa*! They are unusual berries – with a thin, hairy skin, and a striking green translucent flesh embedded with tiny black seeds around the core. When they are harvested, they are starchy, but during storage this is converted to sugars – and a ripe kiwi has a soft, tart-sweet flesh and an aromatic, fruity-green aroma. It reminds me of gooseberries. Like the pineapple, kiwis contain a protease enzyme – in this case actinidin – but the challenge is the same, and they do not cook well. Kiwis also contain crystals of calcium oxalate, which can be irritating to the tissues – and puréeing or processing can intensify these effects. Kiwis are best enjoyed raw, when their unique flavour and beauty can be appreciated.

STRAWBERRIES

There are more than 20 species of *Fragaria*, but most of our strawberries come from a relatively recent European cross of two American species. Bright red and undeniably pretty, rich in vitamin C and red anthocyanins, strawberries bear their tiny seeds, unusually, on their surface rather than in the interior. A ripe strawberry contains air in tiny pockets – a consequence of cell enlargement and separation – and this is why if a strawberry is frozen, the structure weakens, the pressure is released and the shape is lost. They must be picked when ripe and consumed within a day or two – but that is not arduous, is it?

Strawberry flavour is sweet and intense; some have pineapple nuances (ethyl butyrate) and a fruity-caramel element. Woodland or wild strawberries are more aromatic, more grape-like and spicy. Strawberries can be enhanced by the cucumber-tinged borage, fragrant elderflowers will add a heady, honeyed flavour, and spearmint is also a good pairing.

Melons and watermelons

In ancient times, melons were associated with abundance and fertility because of their rapid growth and size. Nowadays we have many types to choose from.

MELONS

Here we have the 'summer' varieties including the highly aromatic cantaloupes, such as the orange-fleshed, rich and caramelic charentais (this is intense, heady and verging on savoury – OK, it is my absolute favourite); and muskmelons such as the sweet and aromatic galia, with its delicate, green-cucumber aspect. Then there are the 'winter' ones – which are less aromatic, and have a crisper texture and a milder, less sweet flavour – but unlike the summer types, they keep well! The winter types include the yellow honeydew and the canary. All melons must be ripened on the vine – if you spot a small piece of stem, this is an indication that the melon was harvested before it was fully ripe. We often sniff a melon to check for ripeness. This is possibly misleading, because it is only the aroma that intensifies during storage! All melons are best enjoyed fresh and raw – and be sure to wash them before slicing, because bacteria from the fields are often present on the outer skins. Melons are happy with orange and also strawberries – and this is the basis of a beautiful summer fruit salad, maybe with some freshly picked spearmint!

WATERMELONS

Watermelons are the fruits of an African vine called *Citrullus lanatis* and they were known to the ancient Egyptians. Watermelons are very large and heavy; inside, the vivid ruby-red flesh (which is a rich source of lycopene) is crisp and watery, and sweet, scattered with black seeds. Like their relatives, they are always eaten fresh and raw. Mark Twain claimed that watermelons were the 'chief of this world's luxuries'. I have to agree. Chilled watermelon is such a joy, but you can also use it in salsas, with some fresh green chilli, coriander leaves, finely sliced red onions and a squeeze of lime! Tomatoes and capers would not be out of place either.

Dates, figs and pomegranates

This trio of fruits share one thing in common: they originated in hot, dry climates – the Middle East, Africa and arid and semi-arid areas of the Mediterranean. To this day, they feature in the cuisines of these regions.

DATES

Dates are the fruits of the desert palm – *Phoenix dactylifera*. The name comes from the Greek *daktulos* which translates as 'finger', reflecting their elongated form surrounding long torpedo-like seeds. Typically sweet, and an interesting merger of succulent and dry, there are thousands of varieties. Ripe fresh dates are soft and delicate, while tree-dried dates are deeper brown rather than golden, wrinkled, chewy and very sweet. Dates make a simple yet delicious end to a meal. They are the nearest we can get to a healthy sweet – full of fibre and antioxidants including polyphenols. Buy the best you can afford – Medjool dates are wonderful – large, plump, succulent and with a caramel flavour! I'm not surprised that they were once called 'the fruit of kings'. Don't go for the dried-out ones crammed into a box with a plastic fork!

FIGS

Figs are another fruit beloved of the ancients; indeed, they were one of the first cultivated fruits. They are not, strictly speaking, fruits – but rather infructescences (i.e. more flower than fruit) of the tree *Ficus carica*. Figs are squat and round, and the body is actually a fleshy flower base which has folded in upon itself. Within what we think of as seeds are small, dry fruits which develop from florets. Here's what happens... Figs have a symbiotic relationship with the fig wasp. These little (2mm) wasps are free living and have a very short life cycle – they locate the fruit they want to pollinate and enter via a tiny hole in the crown of the fig opposite the stem. The female wasp pollinates the florets, lays her eggs and then dies. As the fig develops, enzymes will digest the wasp. Now, in recent years figs have had very bad press because of this natural ecological relationship with their pollinating wasps – and it has been claimed (rather sensationally) that if you eat figs, you are eating dead wasps, and therefore figs are not suitable for vegetarians and are disgusting anyway! It is up to you...

Not all figs require pollination, but it is believed that those that are pollinated will have a different and better flavour. There are many varieties, green-skinned and purple-skinned, and the interiors range from pink to ruby-red. Ripe figs are very moist and succulent, with a sweet, fruity, almost spicy aroma-flavour (phenolics) and a floral element (linalool), and the outer skin contains tannin which gives an astringent aspect. You might also see a white milky sap at the stem end – this is a type of latex which contains the enzyme ficin, a protease. The sap is sticky and can be irritating. So if you are not disturbed by the ecological aspects of the fig, you can enjoy this unique fruit and benefit from its considerable calcium and antioxidant content along with fibre and potassium.

If you are buying fresh ripe figs, remember that they are 80% water and are delicate and perishable. Dried figs are commonly available – and yes, you should choose the best you can afford, preferably organic. Flavour pairing? For me, it has to be rosewater.

POMEGRANATES

Pomegranates are the fruits of the tree *Punica granatum*. They are loved across the Mediterranean and West Asia, and especially in Iran (where the best are grown). Rich in history and symbolism, pomegranates occupy a unique place in regional cuisines. We all know the Greek myth about Persephone (the daughter of Demeter or her Roman counterpart Ceres) who was abducted by Hades and taken to his Underworld Kingdom. She refused all food and drink, which would have bound her there for eternity; however, she was tempted to eat some pomegranate seeds, and as a consequence was destined to spend the winter months with Hades, before returning to her mother in the spring, heralding the new season of regeneration and growth. This is a powerful myth, and it undoubtedly influenced the creation of pomegranate-shaped goblets in Troy.

In Persia, the pomegranate symbolised fertility, and to this day it is thought that pomegranate juice can support fertility and conception, and possibly prevent brain damage in babies. It is certainly rich in vitamins – notably folic acid.

I always think that knowing a little folk history can enhance our respect and enjoyment of foods! Pomegranates do not appear interesting, with their dull, yellow-blushed-with-pink rinds... until you look inside. They are neatly packed with layers of small, translucent, jewel-like, pink-red fruitlets, bursting with a sweet-tart, slightly astringent, faintly perfumed juice. Inside each fruitlet there is a seed. Now, this does have a textural implication – contributing a definite crunch. Maybe this is why the juice is more popular. The beautiful colour is due to anthocyanins and other phenolics – pomegranates and their juice are an excellent source of antioxidants. Pomegranate juice can be cooked and reduced to make pomegranate molasses – this is sweet and tart and intense, and is an indispensable ingredient in Persian cuisine. The juice is also used to make grenadine – a sweet syrup used in desserts and as a cordial for dilution.

A vegetable masquerading as a fruit

We end this section on fruits with a vegetable. Now, many fruits are treated as vegetables, but rhubarb is a vegetable that is treated like a fruit.

RHUBARB

The bright red stalks of a large perennial herb that rejoices in the name *Rheum rhubarbarum* are wonderfully and spectacularly sour! In Iran and Afghanistan, rhubarb is indeed used as a vegetable in stews, along with spinach, and in Poland it is cooked with potatoes. However, it would seem that the rest of the world has followed the 18th-century English cooks who treated rhubarb as a fruit in sweet pies and tarts. McGee tells us that there was a rhubarb boom between the First and Second World Wars, and this might account

for the proliferation of rhubarb patches in many suburban gardens. I remember our lovely Kerry Blue Terrier, Tara, lurking under the large leaves, hiding in a sulky silence when he didn't want to come back into the house. I also remember chewing on the vivid stalks, stringy and sour, and dipping the ends into caster sugar when it all got too much to bear!

Rhubarb is rich in anthocyanins, which accounts for the lovely colour, and organic acids including oxalic acid (see also 'Sorrel'), which contribute to the acidity. The leaves, incidentally, are toxic because of their higher levels of oxalic acid and other compounds. Rhubarb can lose its colour, which is undeniably part of its appeal, when cooked, so to retain this, minimise the cooking liquid and time. For Greg's take on a perennial favourite, see Rhubarb and Indonesian Long Pepper Crumble.

GRAINS, NUTS, SEEDS AND LEGUMES

It would be fair to say that grains, nuts, seeds and legumes are fundamental foods in a plant-based diet (or any other type of diet for that matter!). This is for a very simple reason: this group of foods – if unrefined – contains virtually all of our essential nutrients – proteins, carbohydrates, vitamins, minerals, trace elements and fibre.

Grains and their products

What we know as 'grains' are the seeds of certain grasses; they are often referred to as cereals. The word 'cereal' is derived from Ceres, the ancient Roman goddess of agriculture, whose name in turn was derived from an earlier verb meaning 'to feed or satiate'. That in itself speaks volumes about the value of this food group. Some of the grains – especially wheat – are being somewhat demonised because of their gluten content and the apparently rising incidence of intolerance, not to mention the current popularity of 'low-carbohydrate' ways of eating, but wheat and wheat products remain staple foods for millions.

It is best to purchase organically grown grains and products – mass cultivation usually means a lot of crop spraying...and the pesticide and herbicide residues will end up in our breads, and all of the other grain-based products that we enjoy on a daily basis. Here we will outline the merits and delights of the grains and their products.

BARLEY

Barley is always considered to be nourishing and fortifying, especially in my native Scotland. However, it is worth noting that the Romans thought this too – the gladiators were known as *hordearii*, or 'barley eaters' – from *Hordeum*, the Latin name for the genus. The entire kernels – usually in the form of hulled kernels, or 'pearled barley' – can be used in stews, soups and risotto-type dishes, and for those like me who have a problem with the slippery texture, barley can be consumed in the form of processed flakes, or made into barley flour for baking breads – it does contain some gluten, and so is fine for this purpose. Oh, and barley was the original polenta grain!

Robert Burns wrote:
Inspiring bold John Barleycorn,
What dangers thou canst make us scorn.

Here, Burns was praising barley, because it is an alternative to hops for providing malt for whisky. Barley is bland – but malt has flavour! To make malt, barley grains are allowed to germinate until the shoots are a third of the length of the seed, and at this point the starch in the endosperm has been converted to sugars. The malted barley is then kiln-dried – and destined for Scottish whisky, or Irish whiskey, or unhopped beer, or malt vinegar, or ground into flour for bread making.

It is only in the Orkney Islands that 'bere barley' – an early spring variety dating back to the 8th century – is still grown for human consumption. Bere meal is used in making traditional bannocks, mainly for the tourist trade.

MAIZE

Maize is closely associated with Mexico, where it was domesticated thousands of years ago; it is also known as corn. It was a dietary staple of the Incas, Mayas and Aztecs, and was brought to Europe by Columbus. Nowadays, it is the third largest grain crop. We can see parallels with attitudes to oats (see below) – in the USA it is often fed to livestock, but in Europe it is enjoyed in many forms by humans! There are the following types: the protein-rich popcorn and flint corn; waxy, starchy dent corn for animal feed; flour corns for dry-milled grits, meal and cornflour; and sweetcorn. There are many varieties including yellow carotene types, and blue, red and purple anthocyanin types.

Wet-milled maize forms a dough-like *masa* and this is used to make sheet-like tortillas and *tamales* – small cakes that enclose a filling. Tortilla chips are deep-fried tortillas and corn chips are deep-fried strips of *masa*.

We cannot talk about maize without mentioning polenta! This is cornmeal 'porridge' and originated in northern Italy. Traditionally, it is made by long, slow, stove-top cooking with regular and frequent stirring to prevent sticking. This may be labour-intensive, but it does develop the corn flavour because of the intense heat at the base of the pan, and the drying out at the surface. Cooled polenta becomes firm – and this can then be cut into shapes and fried, grilled or baked.

MILLET

Millet is the name given to several grain species, all characterised by being very small and spherical. The millets are native to Africa and Eastern Asia, where they were considered sacred. It can thrive in dry climates and poor soils, and has been cultivated since prehistoric times. Millet is unique: it is the only true grain that can supply us with all of the essential elements, in the correct balance, to sustain life – in the absence of other foods. Thanks to Pythagoras, it gained a reputation for enhancing health and strength, and as a consequence it was favoured by Attila the Hun – enough said! It is versatile, finding a place in breakfast cereals, and it can even be used to make porridge.

OATS

Oats originated in Southwest Asia, and eventually reached Europe and even northern regions because the crop can withstand cold and wet climates. Samuel Johnson – author of a dictionary published in 1775 – defined oats as a grain which in England is regarded as fit only for horse fodder, but that in Scotland it 'supports the people'. This was written just 68 years after the Act of the Union in 1707, which joined the parliaments of Scotland and England...and perhaps was a reflection of the prevailing English perception of the Scots!

However, oats are rich in beta-glucans – carbohydrates which act like a sponge, absorbing and holding water – and so oats make good porridge, and they improve the texture and moisture levels in baked goods. They also have numerous health benefits – they can lower blood cholesterol and they are good dietary antioxidants. The grains are processed to remove the outer husk, and can be made into fine, medium and coarse oatmeal and oat flour, or the grains can be rolled under pressure – these can be used in quick-cooking porridges and in breakfast cereal mixes. Oats do not contain gluten and so need to be combined with wheat flour for making breads (see My 'Isle of Skye' Porridge Bread, which is wonderful with Alison's Breakfast Avocado). Oats really come into their own in the Scottish staples, oatcakes and skirlie – a delicious combination of fried onions and medium or coarse oatmeal, which has to be well seasoned! It is usually a side dish, but it can make a good stuffing. Traditional recipes involve beef dripping or lard – but you can easily make it with plant butter and rapeseed oil.

QUINOA

Quinoa is not a true cereal, as it is not the seeds of a grass, but those of *Chenopodium quinoa*, a plant native to the Andes – the Incas knew it as 'the mother grain'. Quinoa has superfood status; with its full complement of amino acids, fibre and minerals, it has now superseded millet in this respect. The grains are tiny and spherical, and they must be washed and soaked and rinsed to remove their coating of bitter saponins. When cooked, they quadruple in size and take on a translucent, 'curled' appearance; they have a mild, nutty flavour. Several colours are available – Red Quinoa Bowl features the pretty red variety.

RICE

The staple food in Asia, and cultivated in India since 3000 BCE, rice has been hailed as the sustainer of the human race! There are more than 25 *Oryza* species and around 100,000 varieties (mostly of *Oryza sativa*), and it is available as whole grains (brown or polished), flakes, flour, noodles, and even beverages such as milks and rice wines, such as the Japanese *saké*. *Mirin* is a sweet, low-alcohol Japanese rice wine that is an ingredient of *teriyaki* marinade, and it can be used rather like a condiment in Japanese cuisine, to balance saltiness.

The principal types of rice are long grain (when cooked, these are springy in texture and easy to keep distinct and separate from one another), medium grain (tender and with a stickier texture), short grain (also tender and with a tendency to form clumps), sticky (waxy, glutinous and a tendency to disintegrate), aromatic (long- and medium-grain types, such as *basmati* – the Urdu word for 'fragrant') and pigmented (reds and blacks because of anthocyanins). Of course, it is important to select the correct type for your dish.

'Typical' white rice has many words to describe its flavour – McGee mentions green, mushroomy, cucumber-like, popcorn, floral, hay-like – whereas brown rice has these attributes and the additional elements of vanilla and maple syrup! Basmati rice has popcorn nuances due to an aromatic component called acetylpyrroline. This is lost during cooking – but pre-soaking the grains will help to minimise the loss and preserve flavour.

There are many, many methods of cooking rice! A word on safety, however: a spore-forming bacterium known as *Bacillus cereus* is often present in raw rice. Spores are resistant structures and can survive high temperatures, and so if cooked rice is left at room temperature, they will germinate, and the bacteria will produce enterotoxins which cause serious problems with the gastrointestinal system. So, rice must either be served immediately after cooking, or refrigerated and properly reheated before consumption. Rice salads *must* contain acidic dressings, which can help prevent spore germination and enterotoxin formation.

Rice is often served as an accompaniment to curries and stews, but it can also form the backbone of dishes such as the Italian *risotto*, the Indian *biryani* (see 'Sunday Best' Biryani), and the Spanish *paella*. *Pilaf* originated in Persia, but then rice cooked in flavoured broths is a widespread phenomenon! *Pulao* is a rice-based pilaf, and often includes pulses.

What about wild rice? It is not true rice, but a distant relative – it is the long grains of a water grass called *Zizania palustris*. Wild rice has a dark coat – the bran layer – and a chewy texture, and a green, earthy, tea-like flavour.

RYE

I have a soft spot for rye, which has more to do with my glory days than flavour. When I was studying microbiology, and embarking on a career path in mycology, I became fascinated with folk medicine and diseases of the Dark and Middle Ages! I was enthralled to learn that the ergot fungus (*Claviceps purpurea*) thrives on rye growing in cold wet climates, and was the culprit behind the dreaded outbreaks of St Anthony's fire. This was a gruesome disease characterised by mental derangement, constricted blood vessels and progressive gangrene – in advanced stages, the blackened limbs would become detached from the body. The ergot fungus produces several alkaloids – and later investigations revealed that some are stimulants of the uterus, and others are hallucinogens. In 1943, Albert Hofmann investigated a component of ergot alkaloids – lysergic acid – resulting in the social prominence of the hallucinogen 'lysergic acid diethylamide' (LSD). My interest in ethnomedicine, hallucinogens and entheogens has endured, and thankfully has remained on the academic rather than experiential level!

Rye is hardy and thrives in Northern Europe – and it was the principal grain for bread making until fairly recently. Rye is unusual; its main type of carbohydrate belongs to the arabinoxylan group, which can absorb a lot of water – eight times its weight! This means that rye breads do not dry out and have a much longer shelf life than wheat-flour breads and products. Rye breads are common in Germany and Scandinavia – but many combine rye flour with wheat flour for its gluten. Pumpernickel is a type of sourdough wholegrain rye bread, and the mushroomy, potato-like and green elements of rye merge with the malty, sweet, fried and vinegar-like elements given by the sourdough fermentation. We are probably familiar with rye 'crispbreads', the sort embraced by dieters. The arabinoxylans in these low-calorie, thin, crisp 'breads' swell in the stomach so that we feel 'full', and they are only partly digested – so the 'dieter's friend' label is partly justified! Rye also contains substantial amounts of a flavonoid called rutin, which is valued for its support of the capillaries, especially when weakened by diseases such as diabetes, and for other circulatory problems such as haemorrhoids and chilblains.

We mentioned Scottish whisky, so we should also mention bourbon – a rye whisky from America – and rye gin from Holland, and rye beer from Russia!

One of those ingredients where a paragraph or even a chapter will not suffice, the importance of wheat cannot be underestimated, and it is a fascinating grain to study! The original wheat was wild *einkorn*, and a chance hybridisation with a wild goatgrass resulted in two of the ancient varieties – emmer or farro, and durum (semolina). Over time, these too hybridised with goatgrass, resulting in our modern bread wheats, and these include spelt and club!

It is the gluten content of wheat that determines the type of dishes it is best suited to. Glutens are proteins, and when wheat flour is mixed with water, they bond together in long chains and form an elastic dough. Plasticity and elasticity obviously are important for pasta making, and in bread making, the carbon dioxide produced by the action of yeasts can be accommodated in this mass – and so we can have raised breads.

There are many products made from wheat – and perhaps the most important is bread. It can form the basis of the most simple yet delicious dishes – see Pane e Olio e Sal e Pomodoro. Bread can take many forms – from the unleavened flat breads (such as Indian *parathas* and *chapatis* and Middle Eastern *pittas*) and leavened flatbreads (Italian *focaccia* and Indian *naan*) to sourdoughs, *ciabattas* and many, many more! Bread is a wonderful ingredient too – from its inclusion in the Tuscan *panzanella* (a salad based on stale white rustic bread – see Isabella Panzanella) and Middle Eastern *fattoush* (a salad with toasted pitta), or for making croutons to give textural interest and flavour accents, or fried breadcrumbs with pasta (see Orecchiette con Pangrattato). Bread, if accompanying a dish, is best enjoyed fresh. To keep it in good condition, never refrigerate – wrap it in a clean tea towel and store at cool room temperature. If you feel it is becoming dry, it can be refreshed by sprinkling it with water and heating it. Alternatively, you can sprinkle thin slices with olive oil and bake until crisp to make *crostini,* or sprinkle with oil and toast on a hot griddle pan for *bruschetta.* However, some dishes such as *panzanella* must be made with stale bread, which can absorb flavoured dressings much better than fresh.

There are many more wheat-based products to enjoy. We have Eastern noodles (Chinese *mian* and Japanese *udon*), Italian pasta and Middle Eastern couscous.

Whole wheat grains are called 'wheat berries' and these are popular salad ingredients. Freekeh is toasted and cracked young, sweet, green wheat (see Freekeh and Fresh Herb Salad). Bulgur wheat is partially pre-cooked grains of durum wheat which are then dried and become glassy and hard; then they are cracked and the bran and germ is removed. This is an ancient preparation and is the grain basis of *tabbouleh. Maftoul* – which means 'hand rolled' – is a traditional Palestinian couscous made from boiled, sun-dried and cracked wheat which is formed into matchhead-sized spheres, and it is delicious – see Maftoul House Salad.

We also need to mention products made from wheat gluten. In 11th-century China, wheat gluten became known as the 'muscle of flour' – *mien chin* – because when it was cooked it became meat-like in texture. In Japan, it was called *seitan.* In Buddhist monasteries, this was exploited by the vegetarian cooks who developed meat-like dishes with it – and we now know that fermented gluten contains glutamic acid – umami!

Buckwheat is related to both rhubarb and sorrel – both of which are characterised by sour oxalic acid! However, buckwheat does not contain this. It is a hardy plant of the *Polygonum* family – and thrives in the colder regions of the Northern Hemisphere. Buckwheat is a staple food in China,

Korea and Nepal. The grain is unusual, being triangular in shape. The hull is often removed to make buckwheat groats, rich in starch with some protein, but also some oil, so the shelf life is limited. I first came across buckwheat through a Buddhist macrobiotic house guest, when its distinctive aroma drifted through the rooms on occasions. I often thought that, strangely, its nutty taste was better than the aroma, which had a slightly fishy aspect. He sometimes cooked the Russian dish *kasha* – a sort of porridge – and the small pancakes called *blini*. In Brittany, crêpes may be made with buckwheat flour. In the Himalayas, the flour is used to make flatbreads called *chillare*, and also savoury and sweet fritters. In Italy, it is mixed with wheat flour to make flat noodles called *pizzocheri*, and we also have the Japanese soba noodles.

Nuts

In general terms, and indeed botanically, a nut is an edible seed surrounded by a hard shell. Most (but not all) nuts have a high oil content and a high energy value. They are also valued for their protein content and comprehensive array of vitamins and minerals. They can be enjoyed in their own right, or eaten in snack dishes, or crushed and ground for incorporation into a wide range of recipes. Puréed and ground nuts – along with seeds and spices such as turmeric, coriander, cumin, pimentón and dried red chillies – are very useful for thickening sauces as well as adding flavour – just think of Mediterranean *romesco* and *picada* (almonds), and Indonesian *satay* (peanuts and coconut milk) and Indian *korma* (almonds, cashews). Many nuts are the basis of plant 'milks' and 'creams', and 'butters' – notably peanut, cashew, almond and hazelnut.

ALMONDS

From the tree named *Prunus amygdala*, almonds are the largest tree-nut crop. There are two varieties – bitter (*amara*) and sweet (*dulce*). Sweet almonds have a delicate nutty character and have

been eaten for millennia – and not just for their flavour! The Romans called them 'Greek nuts' – and copied the Greek custom of eating a handful before embarking on a feast, in the belief that this would prevent intoxication.

Bitter almonds are extracted to produce an essence that is used for flavouring; however, it must be processed to remove toxic cyanide. Bitter almond extract has a pronounced marzipan-like aroma and flavour due to a component known as benzaldehyde, which is not prominent in sweet almonds. Marzipan is essentially a cooked and crystallised paste of sugar and ground almonds – it hails from the Middle East and Mediterranean and is valued in confectionery because it can be shaped, sculpted and coloured!

Possibly one of the most significant nuts in world cuisine, sweet almonds can be used whole, flaked and ground – ground almonds act as a thickening, protein-adding and flavour-enhancing ingredient. Almonds feature in many classic recipes – *romesco*, *picada* and *ajo blanco* (Spain), *pesto alla Siciliana* (Italy), and many classic curries, especially the *korma* types.

Almond and rose is a classic flavour pairing, redolent of the Middle East – *faludhaj* is traditional marzipan which features rosewater. Rose and almond syrups are key ingredients in cocktails such as Mai Tai and Moresque! And, of course, we must also mention amaretto – the almond-flavoured liqueur of Italy.

Almond can work well with fruits, especially apples and pears, peaches and apricots, and, of course, cherries, and with many vegetables – try toasted flaked almonds as a garnish over Middle Eastern dishes (especially when they contain rice or cauliflower) and over curries which have been thickened with ground almonds.

BRAZIL NUTS

Brazil nuts are the largest of all, and are borne by an enormous Amazon rainforest tree. They are contained in massive pods which can weigh up to 2.5kg (5.5lb) – and so, for safety reasons, they are gathered after they have fallen, rather than being harvested from the trees. The kernels are white and firm-textured and have a wonderful sweet flavour. It is worth knowing that they are very rich in minerals including phosphorus, potassium and calcium, and they are a valuable source of the trace element selenium. Selenium is a renowned anti-cancer agent and a potent antioxidant. They are high in thiamine too. Brazils are often eaten as a dessert nut, or grated and incorporated into stuffing mixes.

CASHEWS

These kidney-shaped nuts, borne by a tree related to the mango and pistachio, are possibly the most unusual of all. They are attached to fruit-like structures called 'cashew apples', and they have two shells – a thin outer one that changes from green to pink as the quasi-fruit matures, and a very hard inner shell. Between the layers lies an irritating oil which causes blisters. So if you ever wondered why we never see cashews in their shells, now you know. The oil is a vesicant (it causes burning and blistering, and poses a hazard to the workers who are tasked with shelling the nuts – so look for 'fair trade' brands), but it does have ethnomedicinal uses as an insecticide, a waterproofing agent and a treatment for warts and ringworm. Cashew nuts are sweet, they can take on spices very happily, and they are nutritious – being high in minerals, fibre, protein and unsaturated fat – so they make an excellent snack, or they can feature in dishes such as Kachin Cashew Nut and Green Bean Curry.

CHESTNUTS

The fruits of trees of the *Castanea* genus are different; they have a higher starch content and lower oil content than most other nuts. They have been used for millennia – their moist, mealy flesh can be dried and ground into flour and used for breads, cakes and pastas. Indeed, in Europe, they were a major source of carbohydrate before the introduction of potatoes and corn; in Corsica,

the chestnut tree was called the 'bread tree'. If you gather your own, let them dry at room temperature for a few days to allow some of the starch to convert to sugar; otherwise, store in the fridge after purchasing. Chestnuts must be thoroughly cooked before consumption. This is best done by making little slits in the skin and roasting in a hot oven (or over an open fire if you are feeling traditional), and then peeling once they are cool enough to handle. Of course, you can buy them already cooked and vacuum-packed if you are pushed for time, or when they are not in season. Chestnuts have a pleasant mealy texture and sweet taste, and so they will need careful seasoning in savoury dishes, but their sweetness comes to the fore in desserts. There are many classic pairings, such as the traditional festive dishes of chestnuts and Brussels sprouts, or red cabbage. Their texture and flavour works well with celery and fennel, white and Savoy cabbage, mushrooms and butternut squash – and in many autumnal and winter dishes.

In our local village in France – Villefranche-du-Périgord – the baker sometimes offers chestnut bread – earthy and moist, with good keeping qualities, and sometimes local walnuts are added – absolutely delicious. Here, we can sometimes purchase vacuum-packed chestnut flour, but we discovered the hard way that it has a short shelf life. A traditional Tuscan unleavened cake, *castagnaccio*, is made with the flour, olive oil and salt. This can also be found flavoured with rosemary and sometimes with pine nuts, walnuts and perhaps dried fruit.

The sweetness of chestnuts has been exploited to make confections – especially in France – where you can find *marron glacés* (whole nuts infused in vanilla and syrup) and sweet spreads in jars.

COCONUTS

Like chestnuts, these are not 'typical' nuts in that the mature flesh is moist, with about 35% fat, 10% carbohydrate and just 5% protein. They are the largest of all our nuts – borne all year round on a tall palm called *Cocos nucifera*. This is a native of tropical Asia, but is widespread because the trees grow by the sea, and their hardy, water-resistant fruits have been swept far and wide by ocean currents to find new homes. The main commercial producers are the Philippines, India and Indonesia. The Portuguese word *coco* means 'goblin', and this is how the nut got its name – the stem end of the nut has markings that resemble a monkey-like face.

The coconut consists of a dry, fibrous and thick husk lined by a woody shell. Within this we find the fleshy 'meat' and the liquid portion. At the age of four months, the nut begins to fill with liquid, and by five months it reaches its full size and begins to develop a jelly which, in time, will form the meat. Between five and seven months, it will yield a sweet liquor called coconut water, and also the delicate jelly-like flesh – very nutritious and known as 'spoon coconut'. When mature – at around a year old – the liquid diminishes and the flesh becomes firm and white. Coconut flavour is unique and instantly recognisable – mild, rich, creamy, nutty and sweet – making it a much-loved and versatile ingredient. The aroma is given by a group of constituents called lactones, in particular octalactone – we have already encountered these when discussing peaches.

When exploring the coconut, we need to address two aspects – the 'meat' and the 'milk'. The meat can be enjoyed fresh as a snack, or removed and toasted to develop the flavour. Toasted coconut flakes are chewy in texture. It is the milk that is more important in Asian and tropical cuisine, however. To make coconut milk, the meat (fresh or dried) is pulverised to form a thick paste – an emulsion of oil droplets and water with disrupted cells and their debris. Water is then added, the milk is mixed and strained, and left to stand, when it will separate into a fatty cream and a thin milk. Coconut milk is widely available (in cans and cartons), as is the cream, and coconut milk powder.

Coconut milk adds body, creaminess and mild sweetness as well as flavour to a myriad of Asian dishes including curries. It is very much at home with spices – especially cardamom and cinnamon with their aromatic-sweet facet, and Thai herbs such as lemongrass, coriander leaves and lime leaves. Its sweetness is exploited in many desserts where it works well with tropical fruits such as bananas, pineapples and mangoes, and also peaches (lactones in common) and cherries, and vanilla intensifies its sweetness.

HAZELNUTS

Hazelnuts are borne by a small bushy tree of the genus *Corylus*, a native of Europe and Asia Minor. The Greeks called it *korys* – which means a helmet – because of its hood-shaped husk. The Romans brought hazelnut trees to Avellino, indicating the roots of its botanical name – *Corylus avellana*. Our name hazelnut is derived from the Saxon word for a head-dress – *haesil*. We have three types of hazelnut. The filbert ('full beard') has an elongated husk, the cobnut (from the Welsh *cobyn* meaning 'tuft') is shorter and rounder and prolific, and the Barcelona is very similar and hails from Taragona, a small port south of Barcelona.

Hazelnuts are highly nutritious and are perfect in a plant-based diet – being superior to animal-derived foods such as milk or eggs in many ways, from protein content (50% more), vitamins E, C and thiamine, to calcium (twice that of milk), potassium, magnesium and phosphorus. But here it is the flavour that we must consider! Hazelnuts are sweet and nutty, and if toasted or roasted (a good way to remove the skins if desired is to simply rub them off on a rough cloth), the flavour and aroma is intensified. The aroma is given by a heptenone compound called filbertone, and although this is present in the raw nuts, it increases 600–800-fold after roasting or frying. Hazelnuts are wonderful in savoury dishes – I love them in apple or pear and celery salads, and carrot salads with a hazelnut oil dressing. In Spain, hazelnuts are an alternative to almonds in *picada* and *romesco* sauces, and in Egypt they feature in *dukkah*.

Hazelnuts can be made into a delicious butter. In Scotland, hazelnut milk sweetened with honey was given to children and to aid convalescence. Hazelnuts are the basis of Frangelico, a speciality liqueur from Piedmont in Italy, where they are paired with vanilla and cocoa – demonstrating their versatility in both the savoury and the sweet dimensions.

MACADAMIA NUTS

From the Australian *Macadamia* species of tropical evergreen trees, macadamias were enjoyed for thousands of years by the native peoples before being 'discovered' and named after the Scottish chemist John Macadam in 1858. They are now produced in Australia and Hawaii – and are always encountered shelled, often salted, and packed to prevent rancidity. This is because their shells are exceptionally hard, and because of their high monounsaturated fat content (65% oleic acid) they are prone to oxidation once removed from their protective shells. They are expensive, pale gold, spherical and pretty, and have a pleasingly crisp rather than hard texture, and a mild nutty flavour – excellent with an aperitif! See All out of 'Waldorf' Salad.

PEANUTS

Just like macadamias, peanuts have been enjoyed for millennia too – originally by Native Americans. Botanically speaking, they are pulses that grow on a vine, but they are included here as nuts, because that is how they are used! After the flowers have been pollinated, they head for the ground and bury themselves in the soil; the seeds are then formed and protected within coarse pods. When they reached North America, they were not considered to be nutritious and were used as pig fodder; but later their value was recognised and cultivation is now widespread and global.

In the West, they are chiefly regarded as a snack food; however, peanuts are in fact very nutritious – they contain 30% high-quality protein (with a full complement of the essential amino acids) and around 50% fat (most of which is unsaturated and includes oleic and linoleic), and they are a rich source of essential minerals. Removing the skins, roasting and salting intensifies the flavour but diminishes the mineral content; however, they remain valuable for preventing the build-up of LDL cholesterol and providing dietary fibre.

The flavour of peanuts is dramatically altered by roasting – they go from raw, green and bean-like (green hexenal and pea-like pyrazines) to crunchy, savoury-sweet and nutty (more pyrazines) – and if salted, their sweetness is emphasised. Peanut butter is flavoursome, with a cloying thick texture, but again judicious salting makes this very acceptable. Commercial varieties can contain up to 6% added sugar.

In Thai and Chinese noodle dishes, peanuts are used whole and puréed. When puréed, they will add flavour and richness and body to sauces and stews. They are found in Indonesian dipping sauces and with coconut milk in *satay* dishes; in Mexico, *mole de cacahuate* is a hot sauce made with dried chillies and ground peanuts. In West Africa, they are common ingredients in stews, soups and cakes. Peanuts can happily straddle the salty/sweet divide! Roasted, they are excellent in carrot salads with punchy citrus dressings; puréed, they are sublime in an aromatic garlic and chilli dressing for the Indonesian salad *gado gado* (a potpourri of raw and cooked vegetables); and simply roasted and crushed, they shine in the Indian condiment *khamang kakadi* (with cucumber, green chilli and grated coconut). So, don't restrict yourselves – peanuts may be ubiquitous, but world cuisine would be much, much poorer without them!

PECANS

Originating in the Mississippi river valley, pecans are members of the hickory genus – they are the fatty seeds of *Carya illinoiensis*. Like all of our nuts and seeds, they were enjoyed by indigenous peoples of the Americas for thousands of years and now they are much valued and sought after – although they do remain inextricably linked with their geographical source because the main areas of production are Georgia, Texas and New Mexico. This is thanks to Antoine, a slave from Louisiana, who perfected the art of grafting to improve the stock. Pecans are almost always mentioned in the same breath as their European relative, the walnut, most writers going as far as to say that they are interchangeable. Like the walnut, pecans have a very high oil and unsaturated fatty acid content – which goes hand in hand with a fragile texture and tendency to oxidise and become rancid. However, pecans are easier to shell, there is more nut in the shell, they are more elongated, smoother and flatter in profile, they have a delightful mild, nutty and sweet flavour (the coconut-scented octalactone is present), and they lack the astringency and bitterness associated with walnuts. Roasting will intensify their lovely flavour, but beware, they will not keep well, so enjoy when freshly roasted. If you have raw pecans, they can be frozen and stored for several years. Apart from the American classic – pecan pie – there are few recipes that showcase them! Going along with the theme of matching local ingredients to traditional recipes, it would seem fitting that pecans could be used to thicken and even feature whole in Creole-style vegetable and bean stews. And I would only use them in place of walnuts if astringency and bitterness was not a consideration!

PINE NUTS

Pine nuts are borne on the scales of mature pine cones. The most important species for pine nuts are the Italian stone pine, the Korean or Chinese pine and the American pinyon (*piñon*). The cones are sun-dried, then threshed, and the pine kernels are mechanically hulled. They have a high oil content (45% in European types but up to 78% in the Asian ones), a soft texture and a unique flavour – aromatic and resinous. Although pine nuts feature in both savoury and sweet dishes across the globe, we are probably most familiar with them in raw purées such as pesto. They are also good additions to dishes where a gentle crunch and resinous accent is welcome – perhaps toasted and sprinkled over pasta dishes and gratins, or in spinach or rocket salads. Flavourwise, they have an affinity with the resinous rosemary, and the green, aromatic and anisic basil.

PISTACHIOS

McGee tells us that pistachios have been found in ancient settlements in the Middle East – dated as early as 7000 BCE – so they have been enjoyed for a very long time indeed! Today they are produced in Iran, Turkey and California. Pistachios are the seeds of *Pistacia vera* (a relative of the mango, cashew and mastic) and they are quite unusual in many ways. They have an outer hull which turns a purple-crimson as they mature, and the cream-coloured inner shell is cracked open by the kernel as it expands. In nature, the pigments of the hull stain the shell, and, within, the kernels have a vivid green hue from chlorophyll – especially if harvested early. If the nuts are hulled before drying, the shell remains light in colour, but you might see some delicate purple-red hints on the green kernel. So, pistachios are not only sweet and nutty, with a delicate astringency, but they are also visually stunning! The lovely green colour can survive brief roasting – but otherwise they must be cooked at low temperatures to avoid losing the chlorophyll pigment. Often found in traditional meat dishes, including cured sausages such as the Italian *mortadella*, they also make a popular ice cream. Like many nuts, they are equally at home in savoury and sweet dishes, giving flavour, colour and thickening actions if ground. In plant-based cuisine, the opportunities are boundless – roasted and used whole in salads (see Freekeh and Fresh Herb Salad), or puréed in pesto, in coconut milk ice creams, and in baked goods (especially sponges).

Like almonds, walnuts have a long history of use and are fundamental to many traditional recipes. They are the lobed wrinkled kernels of species of trees in the genus *Juglans*, of Southwest and East Asia, and the Americas. Most commercially available walnuts are from the Persian walnut tree named *Juglans regia*, which over the years became widespread, and embraced in cuisines across the world. The main producers are the USA, France and Italy. Walnuts have a very high oil content (typically 64%) and so they have a delicate texture and a tendency to go rancid rather quickly (best to keep them cool and in the dark); if you can, buy them in their shells and use them as soon as they are removed – this is the only way to guarantee freshness. They are rich in Omega 3 alpha-linolenic acid (ALA), and so make a valuable contribution to our diet, but let's be honest: we really eat them for their rich distinctive flavour and their slightly bitter and astringent quality! They have a wonderful aroma too – which is carried in the oil – so a light toasting enhances their flavour profile.

It is unsurprising, then, that just like almonds, crushed and ground walnuts feature in many classic regional dishes, providing rich and flavoursome sauces, thanks to their high oil content, ease of grinding and robust flavour. For example, in Georgia, *satsivi* is made from walnuts with garlic, and spices may include cinnamon, cloves, coriander seeds, paprika and cayenne pepper. In Mexico, *nogado* is a dish made with stuffed green chillies in a walnut sauce, and festooned with pomegranate seeds; Niki Segnit informs us that this reflects the colours of the national flag, and that it has pronounced aphrodisiacal qualities (but I will not spoil this anecdote for you – check it out for yourself...). Meanwhile, in Iran, *fesenjan* sauce features walnuts and pomegranate juice; it is used to dress all manner of dishes and is often served with rice. We also can make the sublime Middle Eastern dip called *muhammara* with its delicious combination of roasted red peppers, ground walnuts, lemon juice, pomegranate molasses and spices including red chilli, paprika and cumin. In Russia, Georgia and Turkey, we often find recipes for aubergines stuffed with walnuts and garlic – and again frequently garnished with pomegranate seeds. These will balance out the bitterness because they are sweet, with a slight astringency. Walnuts also lend themselves to raw sauces. In Eastern Europe, Bulgaria and Turkey, there is *tarator* – walnuts with garlic, tahini, olive oil, lemon juice and breadcrumbs. Meanwhile, in the Languedoc region of France, we come across a raw sauce called *aillade* – made simply with crushed walnuts, garlic, olive oil and seasoning.

Walnuts are versatile and make many happy food pairings; however, they have a real affinity with a few special ingredients. They will work well with ingredients that temper the bitterness (hence sweet spices and pomegranate) or ingredients that provide a counterpoint, such as cayenne. Walnuts and fresh green parsley have a real affinity too – hence the creation of walnut and parsley pesto. Like all cold sauces and dips, I prefer to make this by hand in a mortar and pestle, with walnut oil and just a trace of garlic, seasoning and some finely chopped red chilli – this is excellent with broad beans, green beans or roasted beetroot (whatever is in season), and served with a liberal garnish of chopped parsley.

Looking back, I realise that walnuts have been mentioned rather a lot... So without repeating myself unduly, but for the record – they are also very good with celery (pthalides), fennel (sweet), carrots (sweet and woody), beetroot (sweet and earthy), butternut squash (sweet), apples (sweet-tart), mushrooms and parsley (woody, earthy and green), aubergines (savoury and creamy), and bitter greens such as watercress, endive and *frissé*.

It was once thought that the lobed and crenelated walnuts were good for the brain.

According to the 'Doctrine of Signatures' proposed by the alchemist and philosopher Paracelsus, the physical appearance and indeed habitat of a plant signified how it might affect our bodies and minds, and so a system of plant remedies gradually evolved into what we now know as Western herbal medicine. Maybe Paracelsus was not so far off the mark – Omega 3 supports the brain and nervous system!

Seeds

Seeds are an important part of our diet, providing energy and fibre, and in some cases, such as flax, hemp and chia, they are good sources of Omega 3. These tiny seeds can be added to breads and baked goods for flavour and texture. Here we will look at pumpkin, sesame and sunflower seeds, which, as well as contributing flavour, have numerous health benefits – we can use them to add valuable vitamins and minerals to our daily diet.

PUMPKIN SEEDS

Ironically, the seeds are the most nutritious part of the pumpkin! They are borne by fruits of the *Curcubita pepo* vine, and are dark olive-green in colour because of chlorophyll and the yellow-orange carotenoid lutein. They contain around 50% oil (linoleic and oleic), 35% protein and no starch whatsoever, with a good range of vitamins including E and A, riboflavin and thiamine, and minerals such as phosphorous, magnesium, iron and zinc. Most commercial varieties have a thin skin – which is by far preferable to the sorts with a tough seed coat, for both pleasure of eating and ease of grinding or pulverising. As with most seeds, toasting or roasting enhances the flavour of pumpkin seeds, which are nutty and mild. Because they hail from the New World, it is not surprising that we find them in Mexican cuisine. *Pepitos* is a snack of deep-fried and salted pumpkin seeds, while the ground seeds are used to thicken sauces – *mole* is made with pectin-rich dried chillies and pumpkin seeds.

SESAME SEEDS

In the dim and distant past, sesame (*Sesamum indicum*) originated in Central Africa, and nowadays it is grown in the Sudan, India, China and Mexico. Mythology has conferred considerable power on this tiny seed: the Assyrian gods drank sesame wine to give them the strength to create the world, and in Hindu mythology it symbolises immortality. And then we have the magical command 'Open sesame!' in the tale of Ali Baba and the Forty Thieves; the origins of this are obscure, but I would hazard that it is related to ancient magical uses of sesame oil!

The seeds are often golden in hue, but we find tan, violet and black types too. Sesame is rarely consumed without light toasting, which brings out its distinctive delicate nutty flavour and develops crispness. It contains the sulphur-containing aromatic compound furfurylthiol, which is also found in roasted coffee beans. Sesame seeds contain about 50% polyunsaturated oil, 22% protein and lecithin, with vitamins choline, inositol, C and E, and magnesium, calcium and phosphorus.

The Armenian Turks – who, incidentally, were noted for their longevity and vigour – are credited with the creation of tahini – a thick paste of finely ground sesame seeds. Tahini is an ingredient in hummus (with puréed chickpeas), *baba ganoush* (with roasted mashed aubergine, garlic and lemon juice), *tarator* (with walnuts, garlic and lemon juice), and *tahir* (with soya sauce and horseradish). Sesame seeds are also used in many confections such as the Eastern Mediterranean *halva* (tooth-achingly sweet), and baked goods including breads.

SUNFLOWER SEEDS

In older times, the Sun-worshipping inhabitants of Peru revered the lovely sunflower (*Helianthus annuus*), decorating their temples with beautifully crafted golden representations, and their priestesses wore sunflower head-dresses and carried floral garlands. When the sunflower reached Europe around 1510 CE, it was regarded as a purely decorative plant. It was much later that crops were grown for oil production. The types that we eat are larger than the oil varieties. They have a pretty striped hull but the seed itself is pale and somewhat nondescript. However, toasted, they take on colour and flavour, and they can provide interest, flavour and texture in breads and baked goods. Agreed, they are maybe not the most exciting from the neurogastronomical perspective – maybe appealing more to parrots – but they are good for you, being a source of antioxidants, anti-inflammatory sterols and vitamin E!

Legumes – beans and pulses

Legumes are the fruits and seeds of members of the *Fabiaceae* family. This family is notable because its members have nitrogen-fixing bacteria in root nodules – and growing leguminous crops is very good for the soil. A legume fruit is a dry fruit, usually called a pod.

Beans are highly versatile ingredients. They provide structure, bulk and texture; their flavour is subtle and so they combine well with many grains and vegetables, and a plethora of herbs and spices. Beans make a valuable contribution to our diets, and it is often recommended that we consume at least one portion every day. They provide protein, fibre, carbohydrates, minerals and resistant starch. Resistant starch is not digested in the small intestine, but it is broken down in the large intestine by bacterial action – so it acts rather like fibre and supports the gut microflora. However, it is due to this resistant starch that beans and pulses have a reputation for causing flatulence, because the action of large intestine bacteria also forms gas. This is a small price to pay for the considerable health benefits of consuming legumes – and it can be reduced by pre-soaking and long cooking. Soaking hydrates the bean coat, and then they should be cooked in just enough water for them to absorb and cook in – gentle cooking as opposed to hard boiling will minimise

damage and disruption. Hard water will slow softening of the beans, as will acid liquids, but alkaline liquids will hasten softening. Salt will slow softening, but will not prevent it. It is a little known trick, but if you soak the beans in salted water they will cook more quickly! So, how long should we soak? If we blanch them first in boiling water, medium-sized beans will only require 2–3 hours; otherwise, 10–12 hours.

Bicarbonate of soda at 0.5% can reduce the cooking time by 75%, but can result in a slippery texture. Salt at 1% speeds up cooking time considerably, but it will reduce the expansion and gelation of the starch granules, so the texture of the cooked beans will be mealy rather than creamy. Pressure cookers are wonderful for bean cooking – if pre-soaked in salted water, beans can cook in 10–15 minutes.

Canned beans are fine when you are pressed for time – as we all are on occasion. However, if we have the foresight and time for menu planning, we can cook beans and freeze them in advance...

ADZUKI (AZUKI) BEANS

Hailing from Asia, where they have been cultivated for thousands of years, these are small, oval and a pretty deep maroon colour with a sweet flavour. In Korea and Japan, they are often sprouted, and often made into a sweet paste, but in the West we use them in savoury dishes. Their small size has the added bonus of quick cooking!

BLACK-EYED BEANS

Originating in Africa, these were well known in Greek and Roman times. They are a relative of the mung bean – and what makes them attractive is an eye-like marking of anthocyanins!

BUTTER BEANS

Butter beans are also known as lima beans. They were first used in Peru and are named after its capital city, Lima. These large beans reached Africa because of the slave trade, becoming an important legume there too. They are one of our largest legumes, each pod bearing 2–4 flat, cream-coloured, kidney-shaped seeds. When cooked, dried butter beans have a soft, mealy, buttery texture – hence the name – and the flavour is sweet and reminiscent of potatoes. Butter beans are filling and satisfying; they are equally at home in salads, in vegetable stews and soups. They are protein- and fibre-rich, and contain a raft of essential vitamins and minerals.

CHICKPEAS (GARBANZO)

Chickpeas (garbanzo) are an ancient culinary legume – it is believed that they have been cultivated for more than 9000 years. Hailing originally from the dry regions of Southwest Asia, we cannot underestimate the importance of chickpeas. There are three types. The *desi* types of India, Iran, Ethiopia and Mexico are related to their wild ancestor and are small, dark in colour and have a thick seed coat. In India, these are known as Bengal gram or *kala chana*. The *kabuli* type is from the Middle East and Mediterranean, and it is cream in colour, larger and with a much thinner coat. It has been suggested that the name reflects its Afghani origins. Finally, green immature chickpeas are common in Maharashtra in India – these are called *harbhara*. They are roasted over coals and the skin is removed – and these are called *hula*.

Although hardly 'oily', they do contain up to 5%, which is more than double that of most other pulses – and this factor undoubtedly contributes to their pleasing texture, whether used whole or puréed. Chickpeas are fundamental to a myriad of regional dishes. In the Middle East we find hummus – a thick paste flavoured with garlic and lemon – and often tahini is included (*hummus bi tahini*), as are other flavourings such as paprika. Here they are also roasted, salted, spiced and eaten as a snack – *leblebi*. In India, they are probably the most dominant legume, frequently used in curries, and when hulled and split they

form the basis of *chana dal*. However, they are also ground into chickpea flour (gram flour) for making *pakora* and *poppadum*. We see echoes of this in Italy, where they are used whole in pasta dishes and soups, while in Sicily the flour is used to make fritters called *panelle* – a popular street food. In Tuscany, chickpea flour – *farina di ceci* – is used to make oven-baked pancakes. In other parts of the Mediterranean, we come across flat breads made with cooked chickpea flour, such as *socca*. Chickpea dishes are very popular in Portugal and Spain, where they are called *garbanzo*, and are found in many traditional stews, soups and, of course, tapas. In Egypt, we find a wonderful, 'naturally vegan' dish called *kushari*, which is an early example of fusion cuisine, developed in the 19th century, using ingredients from India and Italy. It includes rice, macaroni and lentils in a tomato and vinegar sauce, and it is liberally garnished with chickpeas and crispy fried onions. Sometimes flavours such as cumin are included, as are optional hot sauces and garlic juice.

COMMON BEANS

These are from the *Phaseolus* genus, and include the small oval, quick-cooking haricot (navy); the dark red kidney beans, named after their shape and requiring thorough cooking to remove the toxin phytohemagglutinin, but nonetheless very popular in world cuisines, from Mexican *chili* dishes to North Indian dishes; the speckled pinto beans often found mashed in burritos; the tan-streaked-with-red borlotti that features in Italian cuisine; the large, cream kidney-shaped cannellini with its nutty earthy flavour, tender texture and thin skin which is ideal for purées; and the dense, slightly grainy, great northern bean, popular in the USA.

Their common ancestor came from Southwest Mexico – but nowadays we have hundreds of varieties, with a huge variation in size, colour, texture and flavour. McGee suggests that the larger types developed in the Andes, establishing in the Northeast of America, Europe and Africa, whereas the smaller ones from Central America became established in the American Southwest.

LENTILS

Along with chickpeas, these have been in cultivation for some 9000 years. There are many varieties. The smaller types include the French green *lentille de Puy*, which is a beautiful, mottled, green-blue lentil with a smooth texture; the Turkish *petite crimson*, which has a bright red interior and is ideal for Middle Eastern and Asian dishes and purées; the tiny protein-rich (up to 24%) *black beluga*; and the nutty-flavoured Spanish *pardina*, which holds its shape well when cooked and is ideal for Mediterranean dishes. The larger types come in many colours – the thin seed coats may be brown, black, green or red, but most have yellowish or reddish-orange interiors. Lentils are nutritious and cook quickly – a bonus in the world of legumes. We find them in many traditional dishes. In India, we have *masoor dal*, made with red split lentils, and in the Middle East we find *mujaddara*, a dish of green lentils and rice, flavoured with cumin, coriander or mint, and garnished with caramelised onions. In Lebanon, this is puréed and called *mudardara*. In Egypt, there is *koshari*, lentils with rice and macaroni.

SOYA BEANS

Soya beans are very high in protein and oil, and low in starch, but are better known for the salty soya condiments of Japan, China and Indonesia, and for their textured vegetable protein products, than as a culinary ingredient in their own right.

Fresh, green, immature beans are known as *edmame* (Japan) or *mao dou* (China), and these can be boiled for a short time and are a good source of protein, and very palatable. On the other hand, mature dried soya beans, when soaked and cooked, have a very distinctive beany taste (like grass, oil paint, cardboard) thanks to their high oil content

and prolific enzyme action, and I confess that I do not like the flavour much. They are also noted for their pronounced ability to cause flatulence thanks to indigestible oligosaccharides and fibre.

Tofu (or bean curd) is made from curdled and coagulated soya milk. In the 1980s, when I was working with soya products, we used to make soya milk and tofu from scratch, every week, using the traditional *nigari* – a mixture of magnesium and calcium salts; it is the residue when salt is crystallised from seawater. I had great times with the research team, but my dislike of tofu has endured – it's that beany aftertaste!

However, if soya beans are fermented or otherwise processed, their products are flavoursome, not beany at all, and abundant in umami. I spent several years working in the research and development of fermented soya products, and to this day can take a sip of *shoyu* and estimate the maturity and salt content! The palate does not forget. Here we will mention the Japanese *shoyu* and *tamari* and *miso*, and also the hydrolysed soya sauces which are really very different.

Shoyu is a Japanese fermented soya sauce. It is made from a mixture of equal parts of cooked soya beans and roasted, crushed wheat, which undergoes a double-stage fermentation. The first is a short mould fermentation (with *Aspergillus* species) resulting in the growth of white mycelium throughout the mass and an enzymatic breakdown of the beans and wheat, and this is called *koji*. It is important that the fermentation is stopped at the right time, before spores form and it becomes stinky and ammonia-like! This is done by transferring the *koji* into a brine (around 18% salt), where salt-tolerant yeasts and lactic acid bacteria continue the fermentation – *moromi*. This too can be a bit smelly in the initial stages, as the microbes continue to break down the beans and wheat, but eventually, after a lengthy fermentation, some amazing flavour compounds, including glutamic acid, are formed, thanks to microbial action and the Maillard reaction. The *moromi* stage is lengthy, but at the end it is filtered and pasteurised and clarified to yield *shoyu*, the deep brown, salty condiment with an astounding depth of flavour – savoury and sweet and slightly fruity – umami defined.

The beancake residue is often used to make bean sauce – in China, this is called *yuen-shi chiang*. *Hoisin chiang* uses the residue with some more additional wheat flour, sugar, vinegar and chilli. *Shiro* is white soya sauce – made with a much higher ratio of wheat to soya beans. *Tamari* is made by a similar process – and modern versions are made without wheat. It is darker than *shoyu* and has a richer, deeper, less fruity flavour. *Saishikomi* is a double-fermented *tamari*, the second fermentation using more *tamari* rather than brine – rather like the *solera* process!

Miso is made from cooked grains such as rice or barley, which undergo an initial *koji* fermentation before being mixed with ground, cooked soya beans, salt (up to 15%) and a 'seed' *miso* culture of salt-tolerant lactic acid bacteria and yeasts. Traditionally, the second fermentation phase lasts for upwards of a year; the result is a thick, brown, coarse paste, with a deep, savoury, fruity and complex flavour. *Miso* is usually used as a base for soup (with a *dashi* broth and often little cubes of tofu), or as a seasoning in stews.

In Indonesia, we witness variations on this theme. We find *kecap* – a double-stage fermentation which is followed by lengthy boiling before filtering. The suffix *asin* denotes an extra-salty version. *Kecap manis* is another popular variation, where galangal, makrut lime, fennel seeds, coriander seeds and garlic are added before boiling.

Non-fermented soya sauces are made by chemically hydrolysing defatted soya bean meal – which is the residue of soya oil extraction. This is done by the addition of hydrochloric acid, which breaks the meal down into amino acids and sugars. The hydrolysate is neutralised with alkaline sodium carbonate and then filtered, clarified and coloured (caramels) and sweetened (corn syrup), and the salt adjusted – often up to 22%. Would you want to use this? No, I thought not. Just read the label, so that you know you are using the genuine fermented article!

YELLOW SPLIT PEAS

Yellow split peas have been a staple food for thousands of years. They are dried, hulled and split field peas (*Pisum sativum*). They are nutritious, protein- and fibre-rich, and it will come as no surprise to learn that they are used in many traditional dishes across the globe. In the Middle Ages in Europe, yellow split peas were a staple food – as the children's rhyme testifies: 'Pease porridge hot, pease porridge cold, pease porridge in the pot nine days old.' My father had a spell of eating 'pease brose', as we called it, for breakfast – and sadly my enduring memory is of the smell as it was cooking, and so, to my shame, I refused to taste it. It is strange, because there is a delicious Greek purée made from yellow split peas, called *fava* – and it was a forerunner or relative of hummus, which I like very much. In traditional Persian cuisine, *khoresh* is a stew of vegetables and yellow split peas often flavoured with saffron, and it is served with rice. The yellow split pea *dals* of Northern India are known as *matar ki daal*, and I was intrigued to learn that similar *dals* are made in Guyana, Trinidad and Fiji.

So, from the pease brose of my childhood, my palate and I have come a long way. It demonstrates that once we start to learn about food and flavour and understand our own palates, we can completely overcome preconceptions and prejudices.

HERBS

Herbs can define the geographical or cultural origins of a dish, and they add an aromatic signature and intrigue. Herbs – strictly speaking, the leaves and stalks of aromatic plants – are usually best used freshly picked, when you can really appreciate the volatile oils that impart their characteristic aromas and flavours. In truth, the harvesting is a fantastic sensory experience in itself.

Fresh herbs can be stored for a few days. You can place their stems in a small glass of water in the fridge (for parsley and coriander) or in a cool place for basil (which does not like refrigeration). The more robust herbs such as mint, thyme, rosemary, sage, marjoram and oregano will be happy in a glass of water in a cool place too, or they can be placed in loosely sealed plastic bags and stored in the fridge.

Preparation is important. Careful chopping with a sharp knife or scissors will minimise discolouration and bruising. When working with fresh herbs, a mortar and pestle is preferable to a food processor which introduces a lot of air, and this is detrimental to both flavour and texture. In many cases, fresh herbs are significantly better than their dried counterparts – notably basil, coriander leaf, rocket and chives – all of which are tender and have a high water content, compared with, for example, thyme, marjoram, oregano, mint, sage, bay and rosemary – which can be perfectly acceptable when dried.

Drying herbs preserves them, and they can be stored for some time without losing flavour. Dried herbs are robust and encapsulate concentrated flavours, and are very useful for flavouring many dishes. Some can make excellent tisanes. It is perfectly feasible to dry your own crop of herbs, but in our view it is better to purchase small quantities from reputable suppliers. Let your eyes and nose be your guides! Keep your dried herbs in a cool dark cupboard, tightly sealed and protected from humidity – they can last for 18 months if stored properly.

As an aside, herbs also have therapeutic uses and have played a major role in healing traditions across the globe. They have also been used for their scents. They played vital roles in early perfumery – from the early 'lavender water' – and they continue to play a role in contemporary fragrances. Essential oils distilled from herbs are central to the practice of aromatherapy, especially those belonging to the *Lamiaceae* (mint) and *Umbelliferae* (carrot) botanical families. So, as in aromatherapy, with cooking – it is the *aroma* that contributes significantly to their effects, whether therapeutic or flavoursome (and maybe even a bit of both).

In this section, we will explore the sensory characteristics and culinary uses of a wide range of herbs. We have excluded those that are used mainly in therapeutic and cosmetic preparations, such as angelica, lavender and lemon balm, and others such as stevia (a member of the daisy family) which, when dried, can replace sugar, and those that are very difficult to source, such as anise leaves.

BASIL

Botanically, it is known as *Ocimum basilicum*, and there are many varieties to choose from. 'Sweet' basil is versatile, much loved, features strongly in Mediterranean cuisine and has an affinity with tomatoes. But we all knew that! Some of us might also have heard that its leaves should be torn rather than cut. It is easy to grow, and pots can thrive on a kitchen window sill or, even better, outside in warm climates. Crush a basil leaf between your fingers and sniff – you will notice fresh, pungent, aniseed or clove-like notes. Now taste it, and the peppery aspect comes through. Basil was well known in ancient Greece and Rome, and it became well established in Liguria and Provence, giving rise to the classic pesto and pistou.

Basil is an assertive herb; it can really dominate! So either go for it and use liberally in pesto (use the Ligurian, sweet types) or be more sparing if combining with other herbs such as parsley or mint. As we have mentioned, there are many culinary varieties to choose from, each with its own sensory qualities. You might come across Green Ruffles or Purple Ruffles, or lemon- or lime-scented basil, and red-leafed basil. However, for some regional dishes, it is worth looking out for Greek or Cretan basil (this is a different species – *Ocimum triloba*), and the purple-stemmed Thai basil (*Ocimum basilicum* var. *thyrsiflora*) with its pronounced anise-liquorice note. Basil is certainly best when fresh, but the dried version does have appealing anise and mint-like qualities.

Yes, we did mention an affinity with tomatoes and tomato-based dishes, but other herb pairings made in heaven include basil and garlic, basil and mint, and basil and oregano.

In pesto, basil acts as a thickening agent, creating a stable emulsion with the oil. For a plant-based basil pesto, simply omit the traditional parmesan component, and experiment with pine nuts (toasted and otherwise), walnuts, pistachio nuts and combinations thereof.

Oh, and if you enjoy gin and tonic, try floating a basil leaf along with some lime slices – excellent with Rangpur Lime gin, and perfect on a warm summer evening.

BAY

The botanical name is *Lauris nobilis* – a beautiful evergreen tree of the laurel family. Bay leaves are much used in many cuisines – especially Mediterranean and Middle Eastern. It is easy to grow, although it has a reputation as a slow starter, and it is possible to have a year-round supply of bay leaves – they are good fresh or dried. Next time you have the opportunity, pick a mature bay leaf and crush it, and observe the aroma – pungent, warm, sweet and aromatic, and maybe with a touch of camphor-eucalyptus-pine. When harvesting, select older, mature ones (don't pick the leaves from the tips of the stems), dark green in colour – and if purchasing dried leaves, avoid yellowed and dull ones. Incidentally,

growing your own has an added benefit – the appearance of sweetly scented flowers in late spring! These are attractive to bees. However, do not be tempted to consume its berries, which are toxic.

Elizabeth David (1999) wrote that 'a freshly picked bay leaf gives out a strange scent, bitter and aromatic, with something of both vanilla and nutmeg'. I get the nutmeg part, but I do struggle with the vanilla aspect. Bay can dominate, so use it carefully. It has several natural partners – such as cardamom and rosemary, which share its camphory nuance given by a constituent in its volatile oil – the eucalyptus-scented 1,8-cineole. Bay also appears in the classic herb combination *bouquet garni* (bay, thyme and parsley) and in *bharat*, a Lebanese spice mix (bay, ginger, cinnamon sticks, nutmeg, cloves, allspice, black peppercorns, white peppercorns, cardamom). The warmth of bay can be enhanced by black pepper, and bay can add depth to basil, rosemary, sage, thyme, oregano and marjoram.

Bay can also be used with other flavourings to create depth of flavour. For example, when preparing a plant-based béchamel-type sauce, you can infuse the milk element with a bay leaf, some whole black peppercorns, half of an onion and some freshly grated nutmeg.

We could also give a mention to Indian bay leaves – known as *tejpat*. These are the leaves of the evergreen cinnamon tree (the same laurel family as bay); the young leaves are red, turning a glossy green with white veins. These have a clove-like aroma and flavour.

BORAGE

The botanical name is *Borago officinalis*, and I debated whether to include it because it is rarely used in cooking. However, it can actually add a lot of flavour and visual appeal! Make sure that you pick very young leaves, because the older ones are a bit hairy (not good in the world of neurogastronomy). They have a fresh aroma and flavour – almost like cucumber. The leaves can be fried in a tempura-style batter, or incorporated in soups. Elizabeth Hemphill gives a recipe for Borage and Potato Soup, and claims that the flavour resembles sunchoke soup.

Borage also produces flowers that are edible, and these can add a visual impact to a dish. See 'Edible Flowers'.

CHERVIL

Chervil – or *Anthriscus cerefolium* – is valued as much for its visual appeal as its fragrance and flavour. The herb is delicately pretty, with its lace-like appearance, and the scent and flavour is fresh and mild – you might detect traces of a tarragon-scented compound called estragole. Chervil cannot withstand prolonged heat, and so finds its place in salad leaf mixes where its subtle delicacy is appreciated both for flavour and visual appeal – although it can be added at the very last moment to warm dishes.

Chervil is part of the classic French herb combination known as *fines herbes*, where it is paired with tarragon (now we know why!) and chives.

CHIVES

Rejoicing in the botanical name *Allium schoenoprasum*, chives are the most delicate members of the *Alliums* – both visually, with their fine, emerald-green, grass-like leaves and pretty globes of little purple flowers, and in terms of their mild, fresh, onion-like flavour. Garlic chives are also available; these have flatter, blade-like leaves and a mild, garlic-like flavour. Chives are easy to grow. There are only three rules – maintain them in small clumps to avoid die-back in the centre, remove flowering stalks when they appear by pinching at the base (because the flavour changes once flowering is underway), and harvest by picking rather than cutting the leaves, about 5cm from the base.

Like chervil, chives cannot withstand heat or lengthy cooking, so, to maximise their flavour, they can be finely chopped and used as a liberal garnish for warm dishes, or included in salads. Chives are especially good in potato salads and 'clapshot' – a warm mash of potatoes and swede (50:50). Chives are an important element in *fines herbes*, along with chervil, tarragon and often parsley. Elizabeth Hemphill describes a Jane Grigson dish of a Summer Carrot and Chive Salad – a combination of grated carrots, chives, olive oil, sea salt and fresh lemon juice, with a pinch of sugar – simple and easy to prepare, and epitomising leisurely summer *al fresco* lunches.

CORIANDER LEAF

Coriander leaf is *Coriander sativum* of the carrot family, and is often called cilantro. Native to the Middle East, it is the most widely consumed fresh herb in the world. Coriander is attractive but short-lived. Its leaves are tender and notched, and look rather like flat-leaved parsley (the same botanical family). When crushed, you will notice coriander's distinctive, strong aroma – slightly soapy and slightly citrusy. The citrus element is given by decanal, which is found in orange peel. The flavour is also strong and very distinctive. Like many delicate herbs, it quickly loses its aroma and flavour when heated and so it is best chopped and added to warm dishes at the very end of cooking or used liberally as a flavoursome and attractive garnish.

Coriander root, however, can be chopped and used earlier in the cooking process; it has a different flavour – decanal is absent and the aroma-flavour is more woody-green.

Coriander leaf is very important in Asian and Middle Eastern cuisine, and also in many Mexican and Cajun dishes of South America. So, what does coriander do to dishes to deserve such popularity? Segnit encapsulates what coriander is all about – she asserts that it 'calms saltiness, deodorises fishiness, cuts fattiness and lends a cooling note to hot, spicy food'. Perhaps this also explains its affinity with the fatty avocado, its cooling effect on the heat of chilli and its ability to complement the earthiness of cumin with its own earthy, woody qualities. Coriander leaf can also complement citrus flavours – especially lime but also lemon and orange (decanal again). It works well with tomatoes, especially in the context of salsa, and potatoes, because coriander's earthy, green qualities complement the sweet nuttiness of potatoes.

CURRY LEAVES

Curry leaves are from *Murraya koenigii*, a tree belonging to the citrus family. Native to South India and Malaysia, curry leaves, as the name suggests, are widely used for making curries and other Southeast Asian dishes. Try to obtain fresh leaves – these have considerably more flavour than the dried version, and they can be frozen. Typically, the leaves are fried to give flavour to the oil before incorporating into the dish, and the crispy fried leaves are used as a garnish. The leaves do not, however, have a curry flavour – instead, they are subtle, woody and fresh. McGee mentions that they contain alkaloids called carbazoles, which have good antioxidant and anti-inflammatory actions – another example of how flavour can also be good medicine!

DILL

From *Anethum graveolens*, the pretty, jewel-green, feathery leaves have been used to add character to food for millennia – from ancient Egypt and India, to Northern Europe. McGee suggests that this is because of its affinity with caraway – a typically northern flavouring. Dill has an aromatic, refreshing, green aroma and flavour, and you might detect a faint anise-like element. It tends to be used liberally – and in Asia and Greece, it is sometimes treated more like a vegetable than a flavouring, often in rice-based dishes.

Dill brings freshness and is often used in conjunction with sharp-tasting vinegars, lemon juice and capers – typically in pickles. However, it also works well in potato salads and with beetroot. In Northern and Eastern European cuisine, dill features in *borscht* and other beetroot soups.

FENUGREEK LEAVES OR METHI

Fenugreek leaves or methi – *Trigonella foenum-gracecum* – is an ancient herb. Its botanical name comes from the Latin *foenum-graecum* which means 'Greek hay' – and it does have a hay-like appearance; indeed, in ancient times it was used as a fodder mixed with hay that had passed its best, to make it more palatable. Fenugreek has become integral to Asian cuisine, from India as a curry flavouring and a vegetable (*methi*), in tandoori marinades and in potato and spinach salads, to Iran, where it is combined with fresh herbs and served in salads with flatbread. The fresh leaves are aromatic and have a bitter element (they combine very well with the astringency of spinach), but more often the dried leaves are used in cooking. These retain a stunning emerald colour, and aromatic scent and flavour.

GALANGAL

Galangal is often called Thai ginger, and this gives a clue as to what it is all about! It is the underground stem (rhizome) of an Asian species of ginger – *Alpinia galangal* – although *Alpinia officinarum*, so-called lesser galangal, is also used. Galangal comes into its own when paired with lemongrass, in Southeast Asian cuisine and notably Thai recipes. It is pungent, with penetrating eucalyptus-like and clove elements.

GARLIC

The culinary importance of garlic (*Allium sativum*) cannot be underestimated. Native to Central Asia, it is fundamental in cuisines across the globe. With its unique aroma and flavour, it is a very happy partner to many herbs, spices and vegetables. Of course, there are many varieties to choose from – the smaller Asian bulbs with tight heads of closely packed cloves, the large Californian varieties, the pretty pink bulbs from Lautrec in France known as *ail rose*, and the single-clove types from China. The different varieties do have different flavour profiles – look for variations in pungency, heat, sweetness and earthiness. Garlic's pungency is related to the level of sulphur compounds. Cold growing conditions will produce more intense flavours – and interestingly it is important not to refrigerate garlic, because this will decrease its flavour. And what about the notorious 'garlic breath'? This is due to methanethiol (a sulphur-containing compound which is related to skunk spray) persisting in the mouth, and to methyl allyl sulphide which is generated as garlic is digested – peaking up to 6–18 hours later. The mouth odour can lessened by eating a salad, or with a mouthwash if you are desperate. As for the methyl allyl sulphide, time is the only remedy...

Raw garlic is pungent and hot, but when roasted or braised it becomes milder and sweeter. Even the way it is prepared has an influence on its flavour profile and characteristics. As with other members of the onion family, the more you disrupt the cells, the more you stimulate the production of the sulphur defence compounds. That is why a food processor, or crushing or mincing, gives a stronger pungency than chopping or using entire cloves.

So, what exactly does garlic do for food? Just think of the difference it can make if you rub a cut clove around a salad bowl before dressing a green salad, and the savoury, umami element it imparts to cooked dishes! Indeed, some dishes are even characterised by garlic, such as the Spanish *ajo blanco* – a raw garlic and almond cold soup.

There are very many 'classic' garlic combinations – too many to mention really! Here are just a few. Garlic and basil, garlic and tomatoes, garlic and bread, garlic and olives, garlic and chilli, garlic and aubergines, garlic and ginger, garlic and mint, garlic and mushrooms, garlic and onions (although some cultures such as Chinese Buddhist, Hindu Brahmins and Jains forbid this duo for various reasons including the belief that it excites the passions), garlic and parsley (and lemon, for *gremolata*), garlic and rosemary, garlic and thyme, garlic and walnut, and garlic and pine nuts...

You may come across giant or elephant garlic – *Allium ampeloprasum* var. *gigantica*. This is a type of leek and it has a much milder flavour. Wild garlic (*Allium ursinum*) appears in the spring – and you might notice its presence in the air before you see its lily of the valley-like leaves and starry white flowers. The leaves can be used in salads, or added to savoury dishes at the very end of the cooking process.

Black garlic is another thing altogether. Allegedly, it has been used in Asian/Korean cooking for four millennia – and in the West it is now hailed as a superfood because it is rich in antioxidants! It is made by slow-cooking entire bulbs over several weeks, resulting in blackened, viscous-jelly-like cloves with an intense, savoury-sweet-tart flavour – due, of course, to the Maillard reaction between sugars and amino acids. For this reason, black garlic is absolutely wonderful for imparting umami! See Ratatouille with Black Garlic.

HORSERADISH

Like garlic and onions, the large, fleshy white roots have a pungent aroma which is due to sulphur defence compounds, but horseradish is a member of the cabbage family – the *Cruciferae* – which also includes mustard and cress. Horseradish roots look hairy and a bit wizened; when peeled, the outer parts can be grated and used sparingly to add heat, zest and freshness to dressings. Heating destroys horseradish's pungency and flavour, so it is always associated with cold condiments and relishes – for example, in Germany, grated horseradish is combined with ginger to produce *Moutarde des Allemands*.

Horseradish is very good with beetroot and is an important element of the Ukranian *tsvikili*. It also works well with grated raw celeriac, in potato salads and with celery and apple.

As an aside, *wasabi* is a pungent green paste, made from varieties of *Wasabia japonica*, a relative of horseradish. Proceed with caution – when the stems are freshly grated, more than 20 enzymes kick into action and these generate pungent, green and onion-like defensive volatiles, including an array of isothiocyanates. A few years ago, on holiday in the Maldives, we enjoyed an extensive buffet every night, which reflected the regional specialities of the surrounding countries. I mistook a bowl of wasabi for my absolute favourite avocado dip, and spread a very generous spoonful on some bread. Wasabi's impact on the senses cannot be underestimated. The volatiles enter the airways, so as well as dealing with a saliva-inducing, mouth-burning and tear-inducing episode, I was also spluttering, coughing and gasping for both water and air (and acutely embarrassed!). Now, if I had read McGee, I would have known how to deal with this – by breathing in through the nose and out through the mouth.

JUNIPER BERRIES

We have included juniper berries here under herbs rather than spices because they are best used fresh and preferably foraged! Their aroma and flavour is best described as piney, and this diminishes dramatically with drying and storage. The common *Juniperus communis* is the best known, but other species also produce edible berries. The berries are very slow to mature. The young green ones are unpleasantly piney, but after two or three years these mature to a black-purple hue and have a fresher aroma and flavour – less piney and disinfectant-like and more woody-green-citrusy. Juniper berries feature in Northern European cuisine, and are often associated with cabbage dishes. And, of course, juniper is the most important botanical ingredient in gin. Recipes do

vary, but juniper berry is usually accompanied by angelica, and can include lemon peel, cinnamon bark, cassia bark, liquorice root, cardamom seed, orris root, fennel seed, aniseed, caraway seed and sweet and bitter orange peels. Now, we probably do not want our savoury creations to resemble gin *per se*, but we can take a cue from gin and pair juniper with aromatics from this flavour palette! Next time you are braising red cabbage, and are able to obtain some fresh berries, why not add some lemon and orange peel, fennel seeds and caraway seeds, or a stick of cinnamon, a few cardamom pods and star anise? Interestingly, juniper can also work well with dark chocolate – as I discovered when given artisan chocolate bearing proudly the description 'Gin and Tonic'!

LEMONGRASS

The aromatic grass *Cymbopogon citratus* is related to citronella, and is important in Southeast Asian cuisine. When purchasing, look for stems that have not dried out – they should be firm and white; when preparing, they should be bruised and then sliced across the fibres – and sliced finely, to avoid these spoiling the texture of your dish. The distinctive lemony scent and flavour is due to the presence of an aldehyde derived from the terpenes, known as citral. The edible portion consists of the lower stalk and inner leaves – the tough outer leaves should be discarded, or used to flavour broths or tisanes. The scent is certainly sweet-lemony and green-grassy, and the aroma when it is pounded with other spices to make pastes is wonderful – its presence imparts a vibrancy and freshness that characterises many of the traditional dishes of the region. Thai green curries are characterised by sour, sweet, salty and hot tastes, and in traditional versions the saltiness is given by fermented fish sauce or shrimp pastes – which have an inherent umami element. For a plant version, light soya sauce (*shoyu*) or *miso* can be substituted very successfully. Natural flavour partners to lemongrass in these aromatic pastes are alliums – garlic, shallots, scallions – and green chillies, galangal, lime leaves, lime juice, coriander leaves and roots, while coriander leaves and Thai basil make perfect garnishes for the finished dishes. Lemongrass also works very well with ginger, red chillies and black or long pepper.

LIME LEAVES

Lime leaves (makrut lime, kaffir lime) are the leaves of a very thorny citrus tree (*Citrus hystrix*); the common prefix 'kaffir' has racially offensive, derogatory connotations. It is derived from the Arabic word *kafir* (which came to mean an infidel, or someone who hides the truth), and was used by the early Portuguese explorers who became involved in the slave trade along the east coast of Africa. The leaves are very distinctive – aromatic, dark green and glossy; they are constricted in the middle and so resemble 'double' leaves, comprising a leaf blade and a flattened leaf-like petiole, which is the stalk that joins the leaf to the stem. Its small dark green fruits are similar in appearance to key limes but are slightly pear-shaped, and have an irregular, rough, 'bumpy' surface; they are very sour. In Malaysia, makrut lime is often planted in domestic gardens along with some of the other Asian herbs and spices such as lemongrass, ginger, galangal and pandan. Makrut lime leaves are a very important ingredient in Thai, Cambodian, Indonesian, Laotian, Malaysian and Philippine cuisines, adding their distinctive fragrance and flavour to many dishes. For example, *Tom Yum* Thai soup is flavoured with fresh lemongrass, makrut lime leaves and galangal. The majority of the many variants of Thai curry paste, such as red curry, Massaman curry and green curry, contain makrut lime leaves in combination with other herbs and spices, and often coconut milk.

The leaves have an intense citrus aroma and flavour – and their flavour is fresh but less sweet and more persistent than that of lemongrass. The aromatic responsible for the citrus aspect is another aldehyde – citronellal, which incidentally is related to the rose alcohol named citronellol.

The leaves are best when fresh, but they can be used frozen, and a dried version is available too. See Carrot and Lime Leaf Kebabs, which also features lemongrass – again demonstrating how well carrots carry Asian flavours! Segnit suggests that you can substitute lemon balm if the leaves are unavailable – however, this does have a different flavour profile. Its aroma is, like lime leaf, dominated by citronellal, but it contains higher levels of the rose alcohols citronellol and geraniol, and also some citral. This lemony-rosy-sweet aspect is why lemon balm is found more often in fruit salads and desserts.

LOVAGE

Lovage – *Levisticum officinale* – is a herb belonging to the carrot family; it originated in the west of Asia, and when it reached ancient Greece and Rome it became known as Ligurian celery. So, yes, it has a celery-like scent and flavour but also a herbal-parsley element and a peppery-floral aspect. It is a large herb, resembling angelica, and has large, serrated, lobed leaves. When preparing these, chop them finely as the texture can be slightly coarse. Lovage is excellent in hearty soups and vegetable stews where it imparts a robust savoury-celery flavour; it goes particularly well with potatoes and with carrots, with which, of course, it has a botanical connection. Try the chopped leaves in a salad of carrot, apple or pears cut into thin ribbons, and served on a bed of crisp chicory...

MARJORAM

Origanum majorana is a much-loved Mediterranean herb which is closely related to oregano. Often called sweet marjoram, it has small tender leaves which have a mild, warm herbal aroma and flavour that can be used to give interest to salads and marinades. It also produces clusters of pretty white flowers, and it is often these that are harvested for drying – the flowering herb contains more volatile oils and thus is perfect for drying. Dried marjoram has a lovely warm, subtle herbal quality, and because it is not dominant it combines well with other herbs – sometimes appearing in *herbes de Provence* and *bouquet garni* mixes. Try roasting potatoes with garlic and sprigs of fresh marjoram – a nice change from the more traditional rosemary, and equally pleasing. Fresh marjoram also combines well with mint.

MINT

Now, there are numerous varieties of culinary mint (they interbreed readily), so it is not possible to give a detailed description of them all. Here we will focus on spearmint and mention peppermint. *Mentha spicata* is spearmint; its scent is characterised by a ketone called *l*-carvone. Now the *l*- prefix is important, because another form of this compound – *d*-carvone, its molecular mirror image – smells of caraway and is found in dill! However, nothing related to flavour is that straightforward. Spearmint also has traces of pyridines, which are nitrogen-containing molecules that add depth to its penetrating sweet flavour. Fresh spearmint is widely and copiously used in India, Southeast Asia and Eastern Mediterranean regions. It is an essential flavouring in *tabbouleh*, where it is combined with parsley, garlic and lemon, and the fresh or dried leaves are used to make a popular tisane. In the West, we often find it with potatoes and cooked vegetables such as peas, in mint sauce, and in summer beverages and fruit salads. It is very good with fruits such as watermelon and strawberries... Look out for 'English' spearmint with its smooth bright green leaves and 'Moroccan' spearmint (the common type) which has oval dark green crenelated leaves. Despite the names and appearances, they can be used interchangeably, although you might find that the English type has a stronger and cleaner flavour.

Peppermint is a different matter altogether. It is a hybrid – *Mentha × piperita* – a cross between watermint and spearmint. Despite its relationship to spearmint, it does not contain *l*-carvone or pyridines, but does contain a lot of menthol – a terpene alcohol with a cooling, almost numbing quality. McGee explains that menthol binds to temperature receptors in the mouth, causing these nerve cells to send signals to the brain that they are cooler than they really are, by 4–7°C. Words that go well with cooling are clearing, penetrating and piercing – and there you have a description of menthol! When peppermint is heated, menthol degrades, and that is why it is always used raw. However, most peppermint grown is destined for use in the flavour and pharmaceutical industries, for herb teas and for the menthol itself – rather than for culinary use.

OREGANO

Origanum vulgare or common oregano has many varieties, and is much more assertive than its very close relative, sweet marjoram. Also a perennial herb from the Mediterranean, it is more robust in form and habit, aroma and flavour. The leaves are larger and rounder, and have a piercing herbal aroma, and, like marjoram, it is the flowering tops that are harvested for drying. Oregano is widely used in Mediterranean cuisine. The different growing conditions across the area affect the aroma and flavour of the herb – and it is a nice idea to try to use locally produced herbs for regional recipes. For example, oregano from Greece is more pungent than other oreganos, because it contains more of a phenolic compound named carvacrol. Carvacrol itself has a powerful herbal, spicy aroma with a tar-like aspect. Think of old-fashioned carbolic acid soap, or coal tar soap – if you are old enough to remember these – and you've got it! Italian-, Turkish- and Spanish-grown oreganos contain less carvacrol and more thymol – another phenol but with a less pungent and more thyme-like aroma. Needless to say, oregano pairs well with all of the typical flavours of the Mediterranean – onion, garlic and tomato-based dishes, pastas and pizzas, and in combination with other herbs, but notably its sister marjoram, the penetrating but milder thyme, and mint.

You might also come across Mexican oregano. Now this is not, as you might expect, oregano that hails from Mexico, but a completely different plant belonging to the genus *Lippia* – it is a type of verbena! However, its high carvacrol and/ or thymol content does mean that there are similarities with Mediterranean-grown oregano, but Mexican oreganos are (usually) stronger in aroma and flavour as they contain higher levels of volatile oil. There is even a carvacrol-containing Cuban oregano – from a member of the mint family! Mexican oregano features in White Beans with Smoked Chilli and Lime Pickle.

PARSLEY

Those of us who grew up in Britain in the 1960s and 1970s will remember the curly sort (*Petroselinum crispum*) – that rarely eaten and unpleasantly tough garnish which, in my head, has come to represent the cuisine of the era. If you need to know more, just give yourself a literary-culinary treat and read Nigel Slater's *Toast*! Now, I know I am being very prejudiced about curly parsley, but if you are looking for flavour rather than a frilly garnish, go to the Italian or Continental type – flat-leaf parsley (*Petroselinum crispum neapolitanum*). This is the one with deeply divided and serrated leaves, and the one that is central to Mediterranean and Middle Eastern cuisines – in *tabbouleh*, in traditional tagine recipes, and in some *chermoula* blends – but its flavour is so very versatile that it is not limited to this genre! McGee tells us that the name comes from the Greek and means 'rock celery' and that its distinctive flavour – green, fresh and woody – is due in part to menthatriene, but when it is chopped this fades, and it becomes more green and faintly fruity. Parsley is compatible with many other herbs and flavours – including bay and thyme in a *bouquet garni*, with garlic and mint (*tabbouleh* again) or lemon (*gremolata*) – and is excellent in a *salsa verde*, with garlic, red pepper flakes and fresh oregano in the Argentinian

chimichurri, and in walnut pesto. It can deal with the acidity of lemon, the sourness of capers and the heat of chillies, and many vegetables can be enhanced by its presence – especially root vegetables, and most especially potatoes and carrots. In my ideal world, I would have the time and space for a herb garden (OK, if I am being really honest, a mediaeval physic garden), but even when time and space are limiting factors, I always grow parsley!

ROSEMARY

Rosmarinus officinalis is another stalwart of Mediterranean cuisine. The needle-like leaves of this bushy herb are assertive and pungent, aromatic and resinous, and impart, for want of a better word, vitality to dishes. To prepare the leaves, pick a sprig and hold the stem at the base, then strip the leaves by plucking them in an upward direction. The leaves dry quite well, but from my perspective, there is no comparison with the fresh herb. They must be finely chopped before using (always a pleasure), although entire sprigs are quite acceptable when scattered over roasting vegetables. Rosemary is quite happy being the sole herb in a dish, and its flavour is robust enough to stand shoulder to shoulder with salty and sour tastes; however, it really shines with onion and garlic, it has an affinity with pine nuts and can act as a counterpoint to sweet, nutty vegetables such as potatoes, and it is almost essential to counteract the sweetness of butternut squash. Try making a flavoured oil by crushing rosemary leaves, with a little sea salt and black pepper, in some olive oil, until the leaves soften and the oil begins to take on a green tinge – wonderful drizzled over a white bean and garlic purée!

Q: What is rosemary? A: *Joie de vivre*.

SAGE

The downy leaves of *Salvia officinalis* (of which there are several subspecies or varieties, including the lovely purple sage) are just as assertive as rosemary but in a very different way! In my view, sage is far better when fresh. Sage is strong, pungent, penetrating and highly aromatic, with a fresh bitterness. Its flavour is made distinctive by the presence of a ketone called thujone – this gives the head-clearing effect – but pinene, 1,8-cineole and camphor back this up while adding a piney freshness. Nothing flowery, pretty or delicate here! Sage is best suited to dishes with big, robust flavours and textures, and where you need something to counteract oiliness or heaviness. Just like rosemary, it can counteract the sweetness of butternut squash, and the deep-fried whole leaves make an aromatic and attractive garnish. Sage is very good when used with other herbs too – just watch your quantities – and it will add an interesting dimension to a combination of marjoram and thyme, and a depth to lighter herbs such as parsley.

SUMMER SAVORY

Known as *throubi* in Greece, the small oval leaves of *Satureja hortensis* can be used fresh or dried. They have a peppery, fragrant herbal aspect, but summer savory has a nonetheless robust character. McGee suggests that it is a bit like a combination of oregano and thyme – not a bad thing at all – and although it is not nearly as well known as this pair, it definitely has a niche because of its affinity for all sorts of beans – see Gigantes Plaki – and also peas and lentils. In Germany, it is known as *Bohnenkraut*, which translates as 'bean herb'! It might even be the ancestor of oregano... There is also a winter savory (*Satureja montana*), although you probably will need to grow your own! Both types are characterised by the phenols carvacrol (oregano) and thymol (thyme).

SORREL

This herb fell into my 'Do I include this and if so where?' conundrum. Sorrel is not the easiest ingredient to obtain, and then only in the spring, and more commonly in France, and more often than not is treated as a vegetable (like spinach) rather than a herb. It eventually found its place here because it has a defining flavour quality – and that is sourness! The smooth oval leaves belong to a plant known as *Rumex acetosa* (or *scutatus* or *acetosella*) – a relative of the also-sour rhubarb, and, like rhubarb, sorrel contains oxalic acid. This has led some to caution that it should not be eaten frequently and only in moderation. Iron and aluminium react with its acid content too, so preparation and cooking requires care. In the past, it was highly valued as a pot herb and as an appetite stimulant – often being added to salad leaves to give a sensory surprise – and for this, I recommend using the French sorrel because it is more lemony than acidic. Sorrel does not cook well – its texture becomes mushy and the beautiful green colour fades – although some writers suggest that you can reserve and purée some raw leaves to restore the vibrancy to a cooked dish.

TARRAGON

Like sorrel, tarragon is associated with France and French cuisine. The small, long narrow leaves of *Artemisia dracunculus* (the name really does have dragon connotations) have a distinctive aroma and flavour thanks to the presence of estragole (a phenolic ether, related to anethole, which we encountered in fennel) in its volatile oil. This imparts the unmistakable sweet, herbaceous aromatic and anise character that we can instantly recognise in *fines herbes* blends and in mustards, and it is often said that in the kitchen the most useful herbal vinegar is – yes – tarragon! Probably the best-known tarragon-flavoured classic is Béarnaise sauce, where it is paired with lemon juice and shallots (and sometimes chervil). Now, this is off limits – being made with butter and eggs – but we can enjoy tarragon in a salsa, maybe with some parsley and garlic, and in salad dressings made with tarragon vinegar. Tarragon works well with the complexity of mushrooms – see Alison's Tarragon and Garlic Mushrooms – and the sweetness of peas.

THYME

There are many, many species of *Thymus*, and many have culinary use. The common thyme is called *Thymus vulgaris* and it is characterised by thymol – a phenol that is sweeter and gentler in flavour than the carvacrol that is found in oregano. Thyme is associated with the Mediterranean but most especially Greece. We use the small oval grey-green leaves fresh or dried in herb mixes, perhaps along with marjoram and sage, or in a *bouquet garni*, or *herbes de Provence*, with tomatoes, garlic and onions, or simply scattered over vegetables before roasting... Thyme is guaranteed to add an aromatic quality and very slight hint of bitterness which really complements savoury dishes – see Lemon and Thyme Radiatori Potatoes. The different varieties all have their merits – lemon thyme is rather good with garlic, lemon zest and breadcrumbs as a stuffing for large flat portobello mushrooms. In Middle Eastern cuisine, *za'atar* sometimes refers to thyme itself, but more often to a spice blend of thyme, marjoram, oregano, sesame seeds, sumac and salt.

EDIBLE FLOWERS

Many flowers are edible and can give a lovely visual impact to dishes if used congruently and sparingly as a garnish – for example, the flowers of chives can enliven salads, and tiny vivid rosemary flowers can look stunning if sprinkled over a drizzle of rosemary-infused oil on a white bean purée. Some, such as hibiscus, can give a major flavour impact, while others, such as courgette flowers, can be treated like a vegetable. For the record, the following are edible – apple blossoms, begonia, citrus blossoms (but if you are tempted, watch out for the faecal nuance

in their aroma), daylily (*Hemerocallis* species), elderflowers, gardenia, geranium, jasmine, lilac, linden blossoms, lotus, marigold, orchids, pear blossoms and peony.

However, here we will mention just a handful of the more commonly encountered edible flowers and their potential in plant kingdom cuisine.

BORAGE FLOWERS

These stunning star-like blue flowers have five petals. These can add beauty and delicacy to plates of food and cooling summer beverages. In Roman times, borage flowers were floated in drinks – they were thought to confer courage before combat. Borage and strawberries are often cultivated together as it is believed that they enhance one another's growth. So, why not add some beautiful borage flowers to a strawberry salad?

CAPERS

Capers are the unopened flower buds of *Capparis spinosa*, a bush that is native to the Mediterranean region, and distantly related to the cabbage family. Capers are most often preserved in brine or vinegars, or are dry-salted, and are one of the most useful ingredients for imparting a salty, sharp, sour frisson to a wide range of dishes. The cabbage family's sulphur-pungent aroma signature can be detected in the freshly picked buds, but this disappears when they are dry-salted and is replaced by the aroma of violets (ionone) and raspberries (raspberry ketone). Capers should always be rinsed and dried before using, and they can also be marinated in wine before adding to dishes and dressings. Capers do vary in size, from the tiny *nonpareil* to the larger, seed-filled caperberries. Caperberries have a milder flavour, but the seeds make for a completely different texture and eating experience – you might like to try capers in Prosecco with your aperitif.

COURGETTE FLOWERS

Courgette flowers and squash blossoms have an interesting and complex aroma – green, spicy, violet-like and musky! They are sometimes stuffed and deep-fried or fried tempura-style. This works very well with an Asian-style dipping sauce.

ELDERFLOWERS

From species of *Sambucus* (shrubby trees and bushes), and best picked when almost but not all of the tiny creamy flowers have opened, these can give a honeyed, slightly delicate and musky aroma to macerated strawberries. Hugh Fearnley-Whittingstall suggests macerating hulled and thickly sliced strawberries in fresh lemon juice and sugar, then leaving some downturned flower heads over the fruit to impart their aroma – and I can confirm that this is a simple yet beautiful dish (visually and flavourwise) to make when they are in season (in Scotland this would be in late June). They can also be prepared tempura-style – just like courgette flowers.

HIBISCUS FLOWER

This is not actually a flower, but the calyx which covers the smaller true flower. The scarlet colour is due to anthocyanins; they are tart and aromatic, and when dried are often found in herbal and fruit tea blends. Sometimes whole flowers are preserved by drying for use in sparkling wine-based aperitifs, where they give a dramatic visual impact when they rehydrate.

PANSIES AND VIOLETS

These undeniably pretty flowers can be added to salads, used as garnishes or even crystallised in sugar syrup for use in pastries.

ROSE BUDS AND PETALS

From *Rosa damascena* and other species, rose buds and petals are often dried and used in Middle Eastern cuisine – in sweet dishes and as an attractive garnish, but also in savoury and spice mixes, such as the Moroccan *ras el hanout*. This complex mixture includes cardamom, cassia (related to cinnamon), mace, clove bud, cumin seed, chilli and rose petals. Some versions of the better-known *harissa* contain rose petals. The aroma of rose is due to the so-called rose alcohols that are present in its volatile oil – citronellol and geraniol. Rose scent is often described as sweet – hence its affinity with desserts – but it is also delicately aromatic and equally at home in combination with spices.

NASTURTIUM FLOWERS

The flowers, leaves and immature fruits are all edible and have a similar flavour – pungent and aromatic, almost peppery. The stunning forms of its vivid orange-yellow-dark-red flowers, and rounded, succulent, veined green leaves, add colour, texture, flavour and visual appeal to a mix of summer salad leaves.

SPICES

If herbs add intrigue to dishes, then spices add excitement and drama! Spices are usually seeds, barks, roots and underground stems – plant materials that are much more robust than herbs. This means that their keeping qualities are better – they are less likely to lose their volatile oils so quickly, and they can withstand the process of drying and transport. Now, this is not the place to delve deep into the history of spices, but suffice it to say that they were crucial in developing early trade routes and at the heart of bloody and brutal wars – such was their desirability and value. Spices mirror our cultural histories more than any other food!

Because of the ancient and extensive spice trade, we find that many of the exotic spices of the East found their way into Mediterranean and European cuisines, as did spices from the Americas. So, although spices fall readily into categories depending on their origins, they are to be found in diverse regional cuisines. Here, we will look at several loose groups, based on region and flavour!

But before we begin, a word or two about

cooking with spices. Always purchase small quantities and store in tightly capped glass jars in a cool, dark and moisture-free place. Many spices, including the expensive saffron, will lose their flavour and colour over time. Raw spices in a dish are often unpleasant. So, if they are not to be cooked as part of the recipe, it is best to toast and crush or grind them before using. I like to do this by hand, in a mortar and pestle – very therapeutic. The aroma will really connect you to the dish you are preparing, and it is good to get physical! If spices are being fried as part of the process, don't let them colour or burn, or the result will be bitter. If you think this is about to happen, just add a little water or a moist ingredient – that will stop them burning and it will not affect flavour development. You will also need to keep stirring, because many will tend to stick to the base of the pan, increasing the potential for burning. Treat them gently and with respect and you will be amply rewarded!

The Tropical East
CARDAMOM

Cardamom (*Elettaria cardamomum*) belongs to the same family as ginger, and originated in Southwest Asia. It came as a surprise to me to learn that cardamom is the third most expensive spice after saffron and vanilla, but when I learned that the capsules must be harvested by hand, just before ripe, and that they all ripen at different stages, I understood why! The fibrous capsules contain tiny seeds which have a uniquely complex flavour. They are warming, and the aroma is due to floral-fruity linalool and esters, and the contrasting eucalyptus-like 1,8-cineole, which we have already met in bay and sage. Two types of cardamom are available – the small spherical sun-bleached capsules from Malabar are more floral in character, whereas the green, angular Mysore type contains more of the piney and eucalyptus-like aromatics. We might not have a choice when purchasing cardamom, but it is always good to match the variety with the cuisine! In Arabic

countries, cardamom coffee is made with freshly cracked green capsules, and cardamom is widely used in baked goods in Nordic countries. In spiced dishes, it will impart a uniquely warming and penetrating flavour. It is found in several classic spice blends, including the Moroccan *ras el hanout*, the Middle Eastern *zhug* (cumin, cardamom, garlic and chilli) and the Indian *garam masala* (cumin, coriander, cardamom, black pepper, clove, mace and cinnamon).

Nepal cardamom is related (*Amomum subulatum*) – it has a reddish coloured capsule that is usually smoke-dried. Its aroma-flavour is dominated by cineole and camphor, so, as you might expect, it is quite pungent and well suited to savoury dishes and pickles.

CINNAMON

The inner bark of *Cinnamomum* trees can be cut and peeled away from the underlying younger growth, forming long, curled quills or 'sticks'. Sri Lankan cinnamon forms a single spiral and is lighter in colour, with a delicate, sweet flavour (floral nuances are due to linalool and it is clove-like due to eugenol), and Chinese cinnamon (sometimes called cassia) forms a double spiral and is thicker, harder and darker, with a more robust aroma-flavour due to higher levels of a compound named cinnamaldehyde. We can purchase it in stick form (which is my personal preference for savoury dishes) or ground. A lot of cinnamon is used in desserts and confectionery – indeed, one of its old names was 'pudding stick'. It has a real affinity with apples and cloves, and with oranges.

Cinnamon also finds its way into many savoury dishes. Cinnamon's flavour profile is warming and sweet, and it is important in tagines and *dals*. It is also found in traditional spice mixes such as *garam masala* and the French *quatre épices* (with black pepper, nutmeg and clove); cassia is used in *ras el hanout* and the Chinese 'five-spice' mixture (with star anise, Szechuan pepper, clove and fennel seeds).

CLOVES

Cloves are the dried unopened flower buds of a tree belonging to the myrtle family, which rejoices in the botanical name of *Syzygium aromaticum*, and they are one of the strongest-flavoured spices on the planet! They contain up to 17% of aromatic oil, and most of the oil is composed of a chemical called eugenol, which rather unsurprisingly smells of cloves! Eugenol has numbing properties – think of the old-fashioned remedy for toothache: chewing a clove bud! It is also an excellent antibacterial. The name clove is derived from the Latin *clavus*, meaning 'nail', because of the practice of using a clove to pin a bay leaf to an onion for use in stewed dishes, and early scented pomanders were composed of an orange studded with cloves. Indeed, clove is rarely used on its own, probably because it is so overpowering, and is more often found along with cinnamon and ginger, and often in desserts and baked goods. However, it does form an important flavour element in *quatre épices, ras el hanout, garam masala* and five-spice.

CORIANDER

We are very familiar with the aromatic leaves of *Coriandrum sativum*, but in fact it is the dried fruits (seeds) that have the longest history of use. There are two types on the market. The European one is small and has a floral (linalool) aroma, whereas the Indian coriander is larger and contains less linalool and more pinene, citral (lemony) and some camphor, which gives a more penetrating quality. What we view as the seed is actually a husk that contains the seeds, and this is useful because when ground or crushed it helps thicken cooking liquids. However, it is the beautiful aroma and flavour of coriander seed that makes it indispensable in the kitchen. It has a lovely mild, elegant floral-citrus quality that blends so very well with other spices – especially the earthy cumin – and especially in curries; and for curries, see if you can obtain the Rajasthan variety, which is said to be the best. But its

lemony-orange citrus aroma means that it is versatile, finding its way into a whole manner of dishes – try it with orange zest in carrot or squash soups, in pickling spice and in *garam masala*. We must also mention its presence as a botanical flavouring in gin, where it adds an aromatic spiciness that complements all of the others, including juniper, angelica and citrus.

Coriander seeds can be toasted and ground before adding to your dish, and it is one of the spices that can be added at the beginning of the cooking process – it will be less likely to burn and catch like cumin – and this, along with its thickening qualities, makes it one of the stars in our kitchens.

CUMIN

If coriander seed is elegant, refined and fragrant, cumin is earthy and sweaty and assertive! Cumin is the seeds of *Cuminum cyminum*, an annual herb closely related to coriander. It was loved by the ancient Greeks, who used it as we would use black pepper at the table, and who maintained that cumin symbolised greed! In Roman times, it represented cheapness – and eating excess cumin was said to make a person 'tight' with money or a bit mean! For this reason, Marcus Aurelius was nicknamed Marcus *Cuminus*... Now, this is not the reason why we say that cumin should be used sparingly, and that as far as cumin is concerned 'less is more'! Its powerful, earthy and, yes, sweaty armpit aroma-flavour is imparted by the potent aromatic chemical called cuminaldehyde. Cumin is fundamental in many regional spice mixes, such as Indian *garam masala* and *panch phora*, Moroccan *chermoula* and Mexican *recado roja*, where it is paired with annatto (an aromatic bright red-orange colourant and a flavouring from the seeds of the tropical bush *Bixa orellana*), Mexican oregano, clove, cinnamon, black pepper, allspice, garlic and salt. I really do love cumin, and do not find the sweaty aspect off-putting at all – but a little really does go a long way, so be careful with its presence in a dish, and its balance with other spices. Usually, freshly ground cumin seeds are added to curries, but remember that cumin will burn fairly quickly, even within 30 seconds, so ensure that it is treated gently to avoid creating bitterness. Whole seeds can be used when roasting vegetables – especially carrots, beetroot and cauliflower.

BLACK CUMIN

Black cumin (*Nigella sativa*) belongs to the buttercup family and is unrelated to cumin, but it was well known in the same regions as cumin, and was cultivated for its small, dark, angular aromatic seeds which have been used since antiquity in traditional medicine and to flavour breads and cheeses, and as a spice in many other dishes. Its volatile aromatic oil contains thymoquinone, which is anti-inflammatory and antioxidant; this might explain its therapeutic benefits and value as both a medicine and a spice. It does contain some cuminaldehyde, but relax, it has a much more restrained and complex flavour! Rather like a fusion of herbs-oregano-caraway, aromatic black cumin seeds are often used in the breads of Southwest Asia and India.

STAR ANISE

A tree belonging to the magnolia family of South China and Indochina is the source of the pretty star-shaped, woody fruits that we know as star anise. It is not related to the anise that gives us aniseed (see below) – but they share a significant component called *trans*-anethole which imparts the instantly recognisable, sweet-spicy aroma-flavour. Star anise is wonderful when used with other spices for roasting vegetables, adding a delicacy and sweetness as well as visual appeal. McGee tells us that when it is used in a *shoyu* and onion simmering or poaching broth, it forms sulphur-phenolic compounds which he describes as having a 'meaty' characteristic – and here we could maybe substitute the 'meaty' word with umami! Star anise is also very good in sweet liquors for poaching fruits – especially pears.

TAMARIND

For me, this was difficult to categorise as it is not a seed or bark or root – so is it strictly speaking a spice? It is the sticky pulp that surrounds seeds in the pods of a bean tree (*Tamarindus indica*). The pulp is usually extracted with water, or processed into a thick paste. Tamarind is very sour indeed – being composed of tartaric acid and sugars – but it also has layers of savoury and roasted flavours. Its main use is in Asian cuisine, as a souring agent in sweet-sour and savoury dishes. In the West, we find it in the spicy, sweet and sour condiment Worcestershire sauce. As an aside, research has identified an appetite suppressant – alpha hydroxy citrate – which can be extracted from Malabar tamarind (*Garcinia cambogia*, related to the mangosteen). It is thought that this compound stops the body storing calories from carbohydrates as fat, and instead stores them in the liver in the form of glycogen – and suppresses appetite because it fools the brain into thinking that you have just eaten a large meal!

TURMERIC

Turmeric is a warming spice which is obtained from the deep golden yellow rhizomes of *Curcuma longa* – a member of the ginger family. It is native to Eastern India, the East Indies, Madagascar and the Pacific Islands, and is also cultivated in China. The main use of turmeric is as a dye. It contains a yellow pigment called curcumin, and traditionally has been used for body painting in the Pacific Islands, and in India followers of Vishnu use it to make a perpendicular mark on their foreheads. It also imparts a beautiful yellow colour to acidic dishes, and an orange-red colour to alkaline dishes, and it is a major ingredient in commercial curry powders. Although it is warming, it is not particularly pungent. Turmeric has a woody, earthy aroma, and a mild flavour. It will stick when frying, but does not burn readily, and it does not take long for it to release its flavour. However, it is important to use it in the correct proportions with other spices, because liberal quantities can impart bitterness. In India, chefs will often prefer to use the fresh root, because of the risk of adulteration of the powdered type, and turmeric from Kerala is highly rated. Numerous health benefits have been attributed to turmeric. Research has indicated that turmeric (and its component curcumin) is an outstanding antioxidant, and can protect the lenses in our eyes and help prevent cataracts, combat skin ageing, block the formation of damaging nitrous oxide radicals, detoxify carcinogens, help prevent the formation of tumours, and provide relief from inflammation associated with asthma and arthritis.

The New World

A visit to the botanical gardens of Barbados – the spectacular Andromeda Gardens and the stunning Flower Forest – sent my senses spinning. For a scent enthusiast, it was paradise. I held beautiful nutmegs in my hands, stroked gorgeous ginger plants, smelled heady, fragrant orange blossoms, and met graceful and exotic ylang ylang trees. Here we will look at some spices which have strong associations with the New World...

ALLSPICE

Allspice got its name because it was described as having the characteristics of several spices in one! It is the dried berry (often found in ground form) of the tropical tree *Pimenta dioica*. And yes, in the fresh, woody allspice we can detect the characteristics of clove (eugenol), cinnamon and nutmeg! Its main culinary uses are in pickling, and in sweet spice mixes along with ginger, cinnamon, clove and nutmeg – which are destined for cakes and sweet pies.

GINGER

Ginger is one of the most important spices, and has been since prehistoric times in Southern Asia. It is the starchy, warming, aromatic, pungent rhizome of the beautiful herbaceous plant called *Zingiber officinale*, and we cannot underestimate its importance in world cuisine and in our own kitchens. We probably have all heard of the fine Jamaican ginger, but great quality ginger can also come from Hawaii. We may well associate it with gingerbread, ginger ale and ginger beer, but may be unaware that much of the dried ginger produced is added to coffee in Yemen.

Fresh ginger has a unique aroma-flavour profile. You can detect sparkling lemony-citrus aspects, a floral quality, a clean-woody nuance and a peppery warmth. Yes, it is pungent, due to the presence of components called gingerols, but it is not overwhelming, and that is why it can add layers of complexity and flavour. McGee explains that its flavour is influence by its source, explaining that the Chinese type is the most pungent, South Indian rhizomes are more lemony, the Jamaican sort is delicate and sweet, and African-sourced ginger from Nigeria and Sierra Leone is penetrating and slightly eucalyptus-like. The pungency is altered by processing, so that dried ginger is more pungent, and if fresh ginger is cooked, the gingerols are converted into the sweet and spicy chemical called zingerone! Now we know...

The number of dishes that incorporate ginger is simply overwhelming – and here we have insufficient space to do it justice. It is compatible with many flavours – savoury and sweet, citrus (lemons, oranges and limes) and fruits (mangoes and melons and rhubarb), onions and garlic, chillies and peppers, earthy roots (carrots and beets) and delicate greens (cabbages and scallions), and numerous spices (especially its relatives cardamom and turmeric, and also cinnamon and clove). It is indispensable in many Asian-inspired dishes, from slowly cooked curries to fast and fresh stir-fries. And if all of this is not enough to convince you to keep some fresh ginger in your fridge, we could mention its health benefits. It is an excellent antioxidant and anti-inflammatory; clinical trials have demonstrated that its flavonoids can reduce swelling and pain in arthritis. Some nutritional experts maintain that consuming ginger with turmeric on a regular basis could block the formation of key inflammatory compounds and combat arthritis – especially in conjunction with plant sterols/sterolins (micronutrients which can help prevent our immune systems from overreacting to stressors) found in unrefined seeds (sesame, sunflower, pumpkin, avocado).

NUTMEG AND MACE

Warm, sweet and aromatic, nutmeg was central in the horrific conflicts of the spice trade. Nutmeg is the fruit of the *Myristica* species – evergreen rainforest trees native to the Moluccas and cultivated widely in India, the Caribbean, Brazil and Réunion. It was said that the scent of the 'Nutmeg Islands' was so pervasive that even the birds of paradise become intoxicated! The fruit is around the size of a walnut; when opened, a bright red, lacy covering known as the aril is revealed – this contains sugars, and attracts birds so that the seed can be consumed and distributed. The aril is removed to give the spice we call mace; the kernel is the nutmeg, and their flavours are similar, although mace is said to be 'rounder'. The aromatic compounds, along with starches, oils and tannins, are distributed through the nutmeg kernel. We associate nutmeg with milky drinks, and the classic béchamel sauce, where the fresh, gentle, woody-spicy flavours add depth and warmth to the bland background. However, nutmeg also contains a peppery-flavoured component called myristicin, and it is this that has been associated with nutmeg's alleged aphrodisiac and mood-altering effects. Yes, this is indeed a well-founded reputation, but we would really need to consume piles of nutmeg, by which time the dose would have become toxic anyway!

In Indian cuisine, nutmeg is used sparingly – and it is never ever fried. Powdered mace is more commonly used – and again it is sprinkled in at the end of cooking *kormas* and *pulao* dishes.

Seeds

Here we will explore seeds from the East, the West and the North, and their impact on regional cuisines and specialities.

ANISE

Anise is the small seed of the Asian herb, *Pimpinella anisum*. Its distinctive aroma is described as 'anise' and is given by a constituent called *trans*-anethole – which is also found in star anise and fennel seed. These botanicals are used as flavours in a class of alcoholic beverages known as 'aniseed aperitifs', which includes *arquebuse, ouzo, tsipouro, raki, sambuca* and *pastis*. The French aperitif *pastis* is flavoured with anise, star anise and fennel seeds, and also with liquorice roots and stolons, which contribute an additional sweetness and their own distinctive flavour. *Pastis* has a relatively high alcoholic strength of 40–45%, and so it is usually consumed with the addition of water, which produces a cloudy yellow haze. In French, this phenomenon is known as *louchissement*. This is because anethole is insoluble in water, and forms tiny droplets which scatter light, producing cloudiness. *Ouzo*, a Greek/Eastern Mediterranean aperitif, is produced by the distillation of alcohol with anise, star anise and other botanicals such as cardamom, the choice being made by the individual producers. *Tsipouro* is a Greek aperitif that is made by the distillation of the grape pomace after fermentation. The fermented pomace is then distilled twice with herbs and seeds, including anise. *Tsipouro* is more alcoholic, with a stronger odour, and it is less sweet than *ouzo*. I like to use aniseed aperitifs to flavour rich tomato-based sauces – which are excellent with roasted aubergines, courgettes and mushrooms – and, of course, fennel! See Warm and Waxy Potato Salad, which also includes tarragon.

CARAWAY

Caraway is the seed of a small herb known as *Carum carvi* which belongs to the carrot family.

It is very much associated with the North and East of Europe, where over the centuries it has become embedded in regional cuisines and specialities such as the Scandinavian *aquavit*. It has a distinctive aroma-flavour – you will easily find the lemony and the spicy dill-like aspects which are attributed to the ketone called *d*-carvone. Caraway has a particular affinity with beetroot (see Beetroot and Coconut Dip), white cabbage, potatoes, lentils and baked goods, including breads. So, next time you are braising cabbage or roasting potatoes, or even making some lentil soup, think about adding a little caraway for an aromatic change of scene.

CELERY

Celery seeds can be used to give the distinctive celery flavour to many dishes. They have been used in pickles and dressings since ancient times, especially in the Mediterranean regions. Today, celery salt – which is the ground seeds mixed with salt – is a most useful ingredient to have on salads – and, of course, a Bloody Mary would just not be right without a tiny pinch!

DILL

Just like caraway and celery seeds, dill belongs to the carrot family, and it too is like a concentrated version of the herb – fresh and spicy, with lemony notes. In terms of aroma and flavour, it is reminiscent of caraway, because they both contain carvone. It is inextricably linked with pickled cucumber!

FENNEL

Fennel seeds taste and smell like a concentrated version of fennel which belongs to the carrot family. Yes, there is a pattern emerging here… You will find sweet and anisic fennel seeds in some Indian spice mixtures, and they can be chewed to freshen the breath. They feature in Kashmiri cuisine, and it is interesting to note that, unlike most spices, they do not need to be fried before adding to a dish, because they are

so aromatic! I like to use coarsely ground fennel seeds and sea salt to season vegetables before roasting. As a matter of interest, McGee tells us that the fine yellow pollen from fennel flowers has an anise and floral aroma, and in Italy this is sprinkled on to dishes just before serving!

FENUGREEK

Now, this is a difficult spice for me to write about! This is because I love using its oil in natural perfumery, where it gives a warm, rich, walnut-like note, but I do not use it much in the kitchen. Fenugreek seeds are brown, oblong and rhomboidal, with a deep furrow which divides them into unequal lobes. Dried fenugreek seeds are very hard, but when soaked and cooked, they yield mucilage, which gives a slippery texture. To me, they smell as though they are going to be sweet, but then they taste rather bitter, and are reminiscent of lovage and celery – flavours that I love. In Southern India, whole fenugreek seeds are used, but only in a very few recipes. They are usually fried for a few seconds after black mustard seeds, and then the other spices will be added. They are also roasted and ground and added to a chilli-spice mix called *muligapuri*. Elsewhere, ground fenugreek seeds are used to impart a maple-caramel flavour (given by a component called stoloton) to confectionery, so maybe the sweet impression is not so far off the mark after all!

POPPY

The seeds of the West Asian *Papaver somniferum* (the opium poppy) really do contain tiny traces of the alkaloids found in opium. They are tiny and appear blue-black, and have a delightful nutty, peppery flavour and crunchy texture. Poppy seeds can be used in salad dressings and in baked goods – especially breads. The only hazard is of the cosmetic variety – they do stick between the teeth, giving an alarming appearance should you smile, unaware that they are lurking at the junction between your front teeth and gums, and look as if you are wearing a dental brace made for a fairy. In Indian cuisine, they are roasted and ground, and used to give a nutty flavour to curries, and as a thickening agent.

Pepper

Pepper has been an important spice for centuries – however, we often find ourselves restricted to the ubiquitous black pepper, lurking in pepper mills across continents. Even the verb 'season' usually refers to adding salt and ground black pepper. Here we hope to change this and open up a whole world of pepper for you!

BLACK PEPPER (AND WHITE, GREEN AND ROSE VARIANTS)

Black pepper is one of the most widely used seasoning peppers – it is moderately pungent, aromatic and spicy. It is the dried berries of the vine called *Piper nigrum*, and has been used for millennia. In the past, it commanded a high value and became one of the most widely traded spices. The pungency of pepper is imparted by an alkaloid called piperine, which is not nearly as pungent as, for example, the capsaicin in chillies. Its spiciness is due to many other aromatics including terpenes and their esters, resulting in an aroma-flavour profile which includes warmth, woodiness, citrus aspects and even floral nuances. We find pepper in its entire form as dried fruits called peppercorns, which are used whole or cracked, crushed or ground. Pepper must be used 'fresh' – once the corns have been exposed to air, they rapidly lose their aroma and flavour. Try to buy it in small, sealed packets, and use as quickly as possible after opening. The best way to use pepper is to grind it and add it directly into a dish. Like the other spices, the key element is respect. 'Tellicherry' peppercorns command a higher price. They are the same as regular black peppercorns, but they are the biggest of the crop – 4.25mm or larger.

Black pepper is harvested when the berries are mature but not fully ripe, because this is the stage when piperine is at its peak. Paradoxically,

they are green at this stage, but when blanched and then dried, they become black. White pepper is the seed after the outer fruit layer has been removed, and it retains the pungency and warmth of black pepper. It is sometimes preferred in white sauces, as it is less visible! Green pepper is harvested, as you might expect, before ripening begins – but it is then preserved via dehydration, or freeze-dried, or canned, or bottled in brine. It really is a very different product – but it is still pungent with peppery characteristics, and an added leafy-green nuance. *Poivre rose* is harvested when the berries are just ripe, when they turn red in colour – although by this stage they may contain just half of the piperine and the other aromatic chemicals. Rose pepper is usually preserved in brine and vinegar.

CUBEB PEPPER

Cubeb pepper is also called tailed pepper, because the berries have tail-like stems. It is related to black pepper, but obtained from *Piper cubeba*, and is pungent, woody, spicy and fresh. It is sometimes included in spiced gins.

LONG PEPPER

Also a relative – this time from *Piper longum* – long pepper is very much associated with India and Ayurvedic medicine, where it is one of the 'Three Pungents', along with black pepper and ginger, and used to increase 'digestive fire', for treating cold and fevers, and relieving respiratory congestion. It is elongated in appearance, because here we have a dried flower spike with little berries embedded on the surface. It contains more piperine and is more pungent and woody than black pepper, and less floral-citrus.

PINK PEPPER

Here we depart from the genus *Piper*, and we must not confuse this with rose pepper, *poivre rose* (see above)! Pink pepper is from *Schinus terebinthifolius* of Brazil or *Schinus molle* of Peru, and both contain an irritating phenolic compound called cardanol. The Peruvian variety contains less cardanol, and is more resinous and aromatic, with pine, citrus and sweet elements – thus it is much more useful! My friend Lora Cantele – a true expert on all things aromatic – makes a great vodka martini with cucumber, yuzu juice (citrus) and pink pepper!

SZECHUAN PEPPER

Szechuan pepper is very much associated with Chinese cuisine, and is obtained from the *Zanthoxylum* species – a member of the *Citrus* family. Rather than dried berries, Szechuan pepper is actually the dried rinds of the small fruits. It is actually quite unique in the flavour world! Yes, we have pungency, this time due to sanshools, which are related to piperine, but they have an added zingy factor, producing a tingling sensation in the mouth because they act on several different sensory nerves. In addition to this, Szechuan pepper is, as you might expect from its botanical origin, lemon-citrusy.

GRAINS OF PARADISE

If Szechuan pepper is fizzy lemon, then grains of paradise are gingery pepper! Sometimes known as alligator pepper, this spice is a member of the ginger family – it is the small seeds of *Aframomum melegueta*. The pungency is contributed by gingerol and its derivatives – so it is gingery, woody and aromatic. It really is a delight. If you are feeling adventurous, chew a little; it is hot and pungent, and your head is saying 'pepper', but you are experiencing ginger! It can be used just like black pepper if you feel in need of some gingery warmth!

Pungent

MUSTARD

Staying with the pungent theme, mustard is just as important in world cuisine as ginger and black pepper. Can you imagine life without these exciting and vibrant flavours?

Ancient and pungent, mustard had already found its way into Europe by Roman times, and since then we have tended to think of it as a condiment rather than a spice. There are three sorts of mustard seeds – all from the cabbage family – black mustard from *Brassica nigra*, brown mustard from *Brassica juncea* (a turnip hybrid) and yellow or white mustard from *Brassica hirta*. Of course, as you would expect, they each have a distinctive flavour profile. The most pungent is black, which has a high content of the pungent chemical called sinigrin, which excites the mouth as well as the nasal cavity because of its high volatility! This is followed by the more popular and less pungent brown type, and then the milder white or yellow, whose pungent compound is the less-volatile sinalbin, and so we experience the pungency in the mouth rather than the nasal passages.

In cooking – especially Southern Indian cooking – mustard seeds are often fried in oil for a few seconds until they 'pop', a process which deactivates the enzymes that form the pungent molecules, and so instead of a hot, irritating pungency, we create a nutty-bitter flavour. In the South, black mustard seeds are commonly used, and in the North and East, the brown types are used too. In Europe and the Western worlds, we treat mustard very differently – often using condiments made from the starchy powdered mustard flour and sometimes the dried seeds (most often the brown type). Once the flour and/or seeds are soaked – you guessed it – the enzymes are reactivated and the pungent chemicals are released, so we have a much more intense experience. This can, however, be tempered by acids such as vinegars and wines. Mustard condiments are always added at the end of the cooking process, so that the pungents are not replaced with unpleasant cabbage-aroma molecules.

There is a whole array of mustards to enjoy. The legendary Dijon mustard of the Burgundy region – where the seeds have been grown and harvested in Dijon – is superb. It is made with verjuice, which is the tart juice of unripe grapes. English mustard is usually yellow and often smooth, sharp-flavoured and with a real bite, while Irish mustard can be smooth or grainy and is often made with stout, or ale, or even Irish whiskey. Being a Scot, I am pleased to report that Scottish mustard is excellent, with full, rounded and bold flavours – smooth and grainy types are abundant, often with ales or Scottish whisky. Our Isle of Arran mustard is rightly famous, and a very good range comes from my home town of Moffat. German mustards vary from the sharp-flavoured and smooth-textured types, to the mild, sweet and delicate Bavarian types.

Often the best use of mustard condiment is in salad dressings. This is because we can appreciate its unique flavour and pungency, but also because it can stabilise and thicken oil and vinegar dressings – try adding a mix of Dijon mustard and wholegrain mustard to an olive oil and cider vinegar dressing, with just a pinch of salt and sugar to enhance the flavour. This thick and creamy dressing is delicious with a warm bean salad...

Hot
CHILLI

Now, here we are talking about a close relative of the bell pepper – the chilli. Green chillies are unripe, and are not dissimilar to their green bell pepper relatives. In Eastern cuisine – in Indian and Thai curries, for example – green chillies are used fresh; they do vary in size and pungency, and this must always be considered when using in a recipe – taste them first! Red chillies are sweeter and hotter. They are most pungent and fiery when used raw; cooking will reduce their heat and form a more mellow flavour. Here we will look at the hot red chillies.

Chilli peppers are the fruits of members of the *Capsicum* genus – often varieties of *Capsicum annuum* – which is native to Mexico. They are now the most widely consumed spice in the world – 20 times that of black pepper. Originating in South America more than 5000 years ago,

chillies are now found in recipes across the globe, although it is Mexican cuisine which exploits chilli to its full potential – often blending different varieties of chilli, as other cultures blend different spices. Chilli gives heat, but also flavour, colour (carotenoids) and texture. Think of the hot, thick Mexican *mole* sauces – *mole* means 'mix', and there are many recipes, but the common factor is chilli – where different types may be mixed along with hot and sweet spices such as black pepper, Mexican pepper leaf, cumin, cloves and anise; sometimes cacao; tomato and tomatino (a Mexican husked tomato) for sourness; dried fruits for sweetness; and ground nuts or seeds for thickening and body.

Chillies are characterised by the hot and pungent defence chemicals called capsaicins, which are distributed throughout the fruit, but concentrated in the seeds and the placenta – the pith-like tissue on which the seeds are formed. We have already discussed capsaicins; to recapitulate, this is the chemical group that causes the painful burning sensation that we learn to love! They are oily substances, so after preparing fresh chillies it is so important to ensure that your hands (and all utensils and chopping boards) are cleaned thoroughly in warm soapy water – and don't put your fingers anywhere near your nose or eyes after working with fresh chillies!

Growing conditions influence the levels of the capsaicins, and it is when the fruits begin to ripen from green to red that the maximum levels are reached. Now, we are talking here about the plural – yes, there are different versions of the chemical, and this means that we can experience different chilli sensations! Some chillies are milder and slow-acting, while others are fierce and instant; and some give a persistent heat over a 15-minute period, whereas others fade in a few minutes. Chilli can make us feel hot, and induce sweating to cool us down, and it increases our metabolic rate too. This means that it helps burn calories – and for some of us that is worth knowing. Even better, capsaicins can also fool our brains and trick us into a sense of satiation, so that we feel full and eat less!

Chilli heat is even measured on its own scale, in Scoville units. The hot chilli types include – in ascending order – *jalapeño*, *poblano* (fresh green), *ancho* (dried ripe red *poblano*), *seranno* and *cayenne* (all varieties of *Capsicum annuum*), *tabasco* (*Capsicum frutescens*), and the scotch bonnet or *habanero* chilli (*Capsicum chinense*) is the hottest, with its distinctive orange lantern appearance.

So, we can vary heat in several ways – by selecting the variety, by varying the amount and by preparation – and we can reduce heat by removing the seeds and pith, where the capsaicins are concentrated. And, of course, cooking will lessen the fire and introduce flavour.

In many cuisines, dried chillies are used. The processing (heat and moisture removal) will affect the flavour profile, and introduces layers of complexity. Raw chillies are fiery and fresh, but dried ones can have a plethora of flavours – from fruity, woody, earthy and even nutty. Sun-drying was the traditional method, and dried chillies produced this way are still on the market. Another traditional practice was to smoke-dry – for example, Mexican *chipotle* and some Spanish *pimentón* (see below) – and here the smoky aspect lends character and depth to the chilli flavour.

In India, red chillies are more commonly used in the dried form – sometimes cracked and sometimes powdered. Here, the varieties are not often specified – but you may well come across the vivid red and moderately hot Kashmiri chilli, the pungent Guntur and the Madras variety from Tamil Nadu.

It really is not possible to mention all of the dishes that contain chilli, or even begin to list its numerous culinary best friends! But some combinations deserve a few lines – such as chilli with garlic, tomatoes, aubergines, potatoes, cauliflower, butternut squash, avocados, almonds, olives, beans, coconut milk, mangoes, ginger, lemon, lime, and herbs such as oregano, coriander,

mint...and think of Mexican salsas and stews known as *chili*, the fabulous Spanish *patatas bravas*, the Italian *penne al'arrabiata*. Chilli is also useful in sweet dishes, desserts and beverages – in chocolate, in coconut milk 'ice cream' to give a hot/cold contrast, or even floated along with some lime in Indian spiced gin and tonic, where sliced red chilli amplifies the aromatic warmth of cubeb and black pepper, and contrasts wonderfully with the ice.

Unique and red

Now, paprika and *pimentón* could well have been included above with chilli, but, then, they have such a different nature that I felt they deserved their own space! Especially since Greg collects paprika tins...

Paprika is made from air-dried mature red bell peppers, and paprika powder is a vibrant red colour – thanks to the carotenoids (notably zeaxanthin) which may be present at more than 1%. Paprika also inherits red pepper's ability to act as a thickening agent – so paprika gives us colour, flavour and texture. Although it can be sprinkled over a dish as a garnish, to get the best out of its flavour we can cook it gently in oil. However, adding to the culinary joy that is paprika – there are several different types – each of which has its particular flavour characteristics and uses. We have Hungarian paprikas and Spanish *pimentóns* to explore in our kitchens.

HUNGARIAN PAPRIKAS

Paprika is very much associated with Hungarian and Eastern European cuisine. The stew popularly known as *goulash* often contains meat with vegetables and is seasoned with sweet paprika and other spices, and is the Hungarian 'national dish'. There is a bewildering range of Hungarian paprika, ranging from sweet and mild, and sweet and rich, to sharp, robust and pungent. Most recipes will call for the sweet, mild and flavoursome *csemege*, or the medium-sharp, spicier and slightly fiery *feldes*. It is easy to make a plant-based version of *goulash*, based on beans or chickpeas with an assortment of seasonal vegetables.

Originating in central Mexico, paprika reached Spain in the 16th century, where it was called *pimentón*. Again, as Greg will testify, there are many varieties and brands; however, the main categories are the mild *pimentón dulce* from sweet red bell peppers, the moderately spicy *pimentón agridulce* from long, dark red peppers, the hot *pimentón picante* from pungent long red varieties, the oak-smoked *pimentón de la vera* which is smoky, sweet and mild, and the hot and smoky *pimentón de la vera picante*. In Spanish cuisine, *pimentón* features in tapas dishes such as *patatas bravas* (with hot smoked *pimentón*), and *aceitunas à la madrileña* – olives marinated in olive oil, red wine vinegar, garlic, dried oregano and sweet *pimentón*.

PIMENT D'ESPELETTE

Piment d'Espelette is beautiful, mildly hot, with a fruity and briny sweetness – it is named after the town on Espelette in the Pyrenees-Atlantique – and *piment* from this specific area has AOC status (*appellation d'origine controlee*). However, this variety is also prevalent in the Basque country of Northern Spain and is featured in the cuisine of that region too. It is the authentic *piment* to use if you are making *piperade* – sautéed onions, garlic, green peppers and tomatoes – a delicious dish that can be enjoyed on its own, or blitzed to a coarse, salsa-like texture, piled on to slices of crusty bread and served as part of a tapas.

Multisensorial

SAFFRON

I confess to a saffron obsession. It all started when I was writing about scent in the natural world, and I ended up spending unhealthy amounts of time with my nose buried in a glass jar of saffron and encouraging others to do the same. It is one of our earliest aromatics and occupied a unique place in the realms of both fragrance and medicine – and we can see this in the beautiful Xeste 3 frescos at ancient Akrotiri, and in the astounding Blue Monkey frescos of Minoan Crete. Over the centuries, its reputation spread far and wide; by the 10th century, saffron was being cultivated in Spain, and by the 14th century considerable quantities were being grown in England. In 1728, the area between Saffron Walden and Cambridge was especially noted for the cultivation of *Crocus sativa*. My saffron trail took me back in time to the Middle Ages, when nuns scented their veils with it to enhance their prayers and singing and prevent fatigue (they must have been high as kites), and when in Europe it was a legal drug that enhanced the feeling of wellbeing. It heightened and altered sensorial perceptions and even induced hallucinations – but was socially controlled by its high price, and thus only used by elite members of society. Now, I was not aware of entering altered states of consciousness, but I did derive an inordinate amount of pleasure from its scent, and, of course, started to use it rather frequently in cooking! Any excuse, Derek said!

Saffron – the dried stigmas, which are the three dark red ends of the style of *Crocus sativa* – is the most expensive spice on the planet. This is because it takes 70,000 flowers to produce just 2.25kg of the fresh spice, or just 500g of the dried version. Each flower is harvested by hand and this must happen on the day that the flowers open in late autumn. OK, it is an expensive habit, but, as we shall see, it is worth it!

Saffron gives a glorious apricot-yellow colour to dishes thanks to its carotenoids – especially one called crocin, which is attached to a sugar molecule. This means that saffron has dual solubility in water and oil, but, more importantly, crocin is so intense that only traces are needed to give a noticeable colour. So our senses are excited by the colour of sunshine, but what of its flavour? This can only be described as, well, unique. The aroma (given by safranal which is formed during the drying process) is spicy, with a happy hay-like quality and a very slightly phenolic, medicinal note, and it has an astounding effect on other aromas: it softens them and makes them almost tactile. Its flavour is bitter but rounded, maybe a little medicinal but with sweetness too. As I said, it is unique. There is no substitute. Because of this, we often see it working solo in a sweet or savoury dish, or with mild and complementary spices such as rose, nutmeg, cardamom and cinnamon. It is very good with many vegetables – especially the pale fennel, cauliflower and potatoes – and of course rice or white beans, where we can fully appreciate its colour. It has a subtle flavour, but it is not so delicate that it cannot be used with other spices. Just think of the Spanish *paellas*, and Indian *biryanis* and *pulaos*! I often use it in tomato-based sauces, where it adds a real richness of colour and intrigue, sometimes with sweet or hot smoked *pimentón*, because this too gives a depth of colour, and sweetness and warmth, or a smokiness, which complements saffron's flavour profile.

And remember – a little goes a long way, mercifully, and we tend to use just a 'pinch' or a few strands. Some recipes ask that you rehydrate saffron in a little warm water before adding to the dish as this helps to extract flavour and colour.

Special

SUMAC

Sumac is the ground, dried red berry of a Southwest Asian tree known as *Rhus coriaria*. It has a unique flavour profile – sour-tart, astringent and aromatic. It is very much associated with Middle Eastern and North African cuisine. Sumac is used as a garnish – imparting an attractive vibrant maroon colour, and lemony-sour-citrus, pine and woody elements (contributed by limonene and pinene). It is also part of the traditional Middle Eastern spice mix *za'atar*. Enjoy sumac as a seasoning in salads, with tomatoes or over hummus.

Resins

Rarely used – but so interesting; we have included two spices from resins here.

ASAFOETIDA

Asafoetida is the ground, dried sap of the root of a fennel-like member of the carrot family – *Ferula asafoetida*. Also known as *hing*, it is possibly the most unusual spice you will ever encounter. Its flavour is given by sulphides, and, as you can imagine, it is pungent, sulphury, sweaty and cheesy! So, when might we want to use this? The answer is: when you would like umami with an onion-garlic-white-truffle element! It is widely used by the vegetarian Jains, who will not use onions or garlic, because these contain an inner bulb that would develop into a new plant.

Asafoetida is important in vegetarian South Indian cooking – a small pinch or two can transform bean, lentil and vegetable dishes and the flavoured oils known as *tarkas* – giving a marvellous savoury impact. To make a *tarka*, heat some vegetable ghee and add a pinch of asafoetida, and cook gently for about 15 seconds before adding your other spices – such as mustard seeds, chilli, curry leaves, garlic and ginger and then cumin – and when the spices are cooked, drizzle over *dal*, or a vegetable or pulse dish. Or you can add it as the first spice in your curry. Once you have used it, you will never look back!

MASTIC

Mastic gets its name from the word 'masticate', which gives us a clue – it was once used as a chewing gum! It is the dried and finely powdered gum-resin that exudes from the trunk of *Pistacia lentiscus* – a pistachio relative. Its flavour profile is dominated by pine-like and woody elements, and it is much more suited to sweet dishes – especially in Greek desserts and in *ouzo*. In Lebanon, it is called *miskeh* and is used mainly in milk-based puddings. You might like to try it in a coconut milk ice cream, with some rosewater and cardamom. Be warned – if you purchase the gum in its natural 'tear-drop' state, it is very sticky, and it will be difficult to remove from your mortar and pestle or spice grinder! The finely powdered type is easier to use; it is blended with flour and sugar, to help incorporate it into liquids.

Sweet (but only by association)
VANILLA

We are ending our foray into spices with the eternally popular vanilla – inextricably linked with sweetness. In reality, it is not particularly sweet – and if you don't believe me, just go and chew a vanilla pod. It is sweet by association, but can make dishes taste sweeter!

Vanilla comes from the pod or 'bean' of a climbing orchid. There are many species in the genus *Vanilla*, but much of the commercial vanilla flavour comes from *Vanilla planifolia*, native to Mexico. This is where it originally became associated with cacao and chocolate! Most vanilla is produced in Madagascar, Réunion and the Comoros islands – and this is known as Bourbon vanilla. It is very expensive, second only to saffron, and for the same reason: vanilla production is carried out by hand, and it is a very labour-intensive and slow process. Lengthy processing is necessary to develop its flavour. The pod is full of phenolic compounds – including the aromatic aldehyde called vanillin – along with sugars and amino acids. So when the pods are slowly sun-dried, the browning reaction is instigated, resulting in a unique, rich, deep flavour contributed by over 200 volatile aromatic compounds, with natural sugars and fats! In a vanilla pod, you will find lots of flavours – woody, floral, leafy, tobacco-like, fruity, clove-like, and caramel and smoky, phenolic notes. However, the source and variations in processing methods mean that several types of vanilla are commercially available – and these have subtly different flavour profiles. McGee explains that the Bourbon type is highly regarded, being very rich and with an astonishing depth of flavour. The Indonesian type

is less rich and smokier, whereas Mexican vanilla is fruity and wine-like, and the rare Tahitian vanilla is floral and sweetly aromatic.

The enduring love affair with vanilla is due to its unique flavour, which is perfectly suited to sweet foods and beverages, adding warmth, balance and harmony – it has a unique smoothing quality.

OILS, VINEGARS AND SALTS

The creative use of oils, vinegars and salts can transform mundane dishes, elevate the ordinary to the special, and even add intrigue!

Oils

Oils are fundamental to our cooking. It is important to use the right oil for a dish. I use cold-pressed olive oil for most basic culinary processes, but I will use others such as rapeseed if I am frying, and nut oils in salad dressings for their flavour. We can also purchase beautiful flavoured oils for augmenting and accentuating the presence of herbs and spices in our dishes, and explore the flavours of seed oils which can give wonderful accents and lift to everyday fare.

A word of caution...many oils, when heated, form large quantities of toxic aldehydes, including the carcinogenic acrolein (2-propanol), which are very harmful to our health. Sunflower seed oil is one of these, and so it is far better to avoid anything cooked (especially fried) in sunflower. For occasional frying and high-temperature cooking, it is best to use rapeseed or coconut oil, or vegetable ghee. I also recommend that excessive browning of carbohydrate-rich ingredients such as potatoes and cereals is avoided – because this forms carcinogenic acrylamides.

We do not advocate sunflower, safflower and corn oils for culinary use. Apart from the aldehyde issue, they also contain a high ratio of Omega 6 to Omega 3 fatty acids. Omega 6 fatty acids include linoleic acid (LA) which is converted in the body to gamma-linolenic acid (GLA) and helps to stimulate skin and hair growth, maintain bone health, regulate metabolism and support the reproductive system. Now, Omega 3 is used in the body to make anti-inflammatory eicosanoids, but Omega 6, if consumed in excess, produces pro-inflammatory eicosanoids. Paul Clayton and Colin Rose explain that it is the balance that is important, and that we are currently consuming far too many Omega 6 foods, including the ubiquitous sunflower oil – and the ratio may be between 10:1 and 100:1, depending on consumption. The ideal ratio is 1:1 or 2:1! To redress this, we can avoid eating foods cooked in sunflower oil, avoid sunflower spreads and take an Omega 3 supplement to tip the balance towards a healthy ratio. See 'Some Important Plant Compounds and Their Role in Health Maintenance'.

AVOCADO OIL

Thick and a bit unctuous, rather like the avocado itself, the oil is often reserved for salad dressings, where it will impart a very mild pleasant green-grassy flavour. However, it can withstand some heating, and can be brushed over vegetables before grilling. Always buy unrefined and cold-pressed avocado oil; it looks cloudy but the flavour is far superior. Keep it cool and in the dark, and enjoy it before it goes off!

COCONUT OIL

In the past, this was the most important commercially produced vegetable oil. It is very stable, and solid at cool temperatures. However, it is rich in saturated fats – at around 90% – meaning that it can raise LDL cholesterol in the blood. However, it is thought that if it is consumed in moderation as part of a balanced plant-based diet, along with cholesterol-lowering vegetables and seeds, this will afford protection. It can be used very successfully in baking – performing well as a functional ingredient in place of butter or margarine, and its mild flavour is very good in chocolate cake and carrot cake.

HAZELNUT OIL

Hazelnut oil is beautiful and distinctive, and so very sweet and nutty. It works well in salad dressings – especially for salads that feature nuts (try carrot, pear and hazelnut or beetroot, apple and hazelnut). Like walnut oil, it can be used in cakes as an alternative to butter and margarine. It does not keep well, so store it in the fridge and use it or lose it!

HEMP SEED OIL

Hemp seed oil contains 25 times more Omega 3 than olive oil and 40% less saturated fat; because of this it is considered to be a useful addition to a healthy diet. It can be used in cooking in much the same way as olive oil: great for salads and roasted vegetables – especially potatoes – but not for deep frying. It has a pleasant, nutty taste. It is best to use the organic, cold-pressed types.

OLIVE OIL

Extracted from a fleshy fruit rather than seeds or nuts, olive oil is unique. For me, it has to be organic cold-pressed extra virgin for everyday cooking, but it is good to have a special bottle (or two) of extra virgin for salads or where you would like its distinctive flavour to feature. It has a low 'smoke point' and so it is not suited for heating at high temperatures, such as in deep frying.

The best oils are pressed from newly harvested olives, and are unrefined and fresh. Olive oil is characterised by its monounsaturated fatty acids, notably oleic. This means that it is very stable, and it does not raise cholesterol. Olive oil contains a hefty dose of antioxidants in the form of phenolic compounds, carotenoids and vitamin E, so it does have considerable health benefits as well as excellent keeping qualities – but it must be stored in the dark to prevent photo-oxidation.

Olive oil is pale yellow-green in colour – due to chlorophyll, beta-carotene and lutein. Words used to describe its flavour include pungent, peppery, fruity, grassy and green. However, the flavour profile depends on the variety of olive and the geographical source. Some oils are more pungent than others, and this depends on the content of phenolic compounds. Their fruity (apple, melon) character is given by esters, while terpenes confer subtle floral (linalool) and citrus (limonene) elements. Fragments of fatty acids, generated by enzymes during the olive-grinding process, give us the typical grassy and green aspects, while other molecules are peppery, nutty, earthy and hay-like. When you have the opportunity, match the source of the ingredients to the cuisine – and with olive oil we have many to choose from, including oils from Italy, Spain, the South of France and Greece, and all offering their own delights.

PUMPKIN SEED OIL

For me, this is indispensable in the kitchen. Popular as a salad dressing in Central and Northern Europe, it is rich in polyunsaturated linoleic acid and monounsaturated oleic acid. It has a stunning, intense, rich, toasted, nutty aroma and flavour which is great not only in salad dressings but also when sparingly drizzled over soups and stews – adding both flavour and colour. The cold-pressed oil from raw seeds is deep olive-green because of chlorophyll and lutein. If the seeds are heat-treated before extraction to increase the yield, the oil will contain more carotenoids than chlorophyll and it will look brown in the bottle, but you will still have a greenish hue when it is sprinkled over food. As with all oils, quality is paramount, so buy the best that you can afford.

RAPESEED OIL

Rapeseed oil has been the subject of much discussion and controversy in recent times! The industrial oil extracted from the seeds of a relative of the turnip (*rapa*, hence the name) can contain high levels of erucic acid (54%) which is cardiotoxic. However, the so-called 'canola' cultivars (a contraction of 'Canada' and 'oil') have a very low erucic acid content, and have become popular in cooking. It would seem that organic,

'virgin', cold-pressed rapeseed oils from these cultivars are indeed safe for cooking, including frying and roasting, because they do not form much in the way of toxic aldehydes at high temperatures. They have a high smoke point and a delicate and light flavour. They contain a lot of Omega 3 – ten times more than olive oil! All good.

SESAME OIL

Sesame oil is remarkably resistant to oxidation thanks to the presence of lignans (antioxidant phenolic compounds), vitamin E and some more antioxidants formed from the toasting process! It is used as flavouring rather than a cooking oil – perfect added to stir-fries at the last moment to give a delicate toasted flavour, or drizzled over broccoli or green beans followed by a sprinkle of toasted sesame seeds.

WALNUT OIL

Walnut oil must be kept in the fridge and used quickly or it will oxidise and become rancid (and oh, what a waste!). It makes a beautiful salad dressing, and carries the aroma and flavour of walnuts so very well that it can be used in baking too, in place of conventional butters or margarines, when you would like to augment a walnut element. It is perfect for sautéing mushrooms!

Vinegar

'Vinegar is alcohol's fate...' (McGee 2004, p.771).

I just could not resist quoting Harold McGee here – he does have a delightful way with words. *Vin aigre* is, literally, 'acidic wine', fermented by the *Acetobacter* and *Gluconobacter* species. I had the privilege of knowing these fascinating bacteria in my days working with fermented foods. We have a lovely array of these acidic ingredients to choose from, when we need a sour or tart accent. We do not usually use white or distilled vinegars – unless we are making some natural cleaning products (for which they are wonderful!). Culinary vinegars include...

Asian rice vinegars are made from fermented rice wine. The microbial helpers include moulds and yeasts and lactic acid bacteria, and so rice vinegars can be packed with umami. There are several varieties and flavours, ranging from light to dark – but they are always delicate in flavour.

BALSAMIC VINEGAR

Balsamic vinegar – or *aceto balsamico* – is in a class of its own. It has been made in Emilia-Romagna since the Middle Ages. It is the product of decades of fermentation before ageing and maturing in wood casks. Classically, it is made from red Lambrusco or white Trebbiano grapes, although in modern times several other varieties are also used. It is a long and slow process, resulting in such a high concentration of sugars and acids that only specially adapted yeasts can survive and complete the fermentation, while the product ages and matures. The final vinegar is almost syrupy, thanks to almost 12% glycerol and unfermented sugars. In the old days, it was a balsamic medicine – used to soothe the throat – and so it is very sweet and palatable. A spoonful of balsamic is quite delicious – it has a perfect smooth, aromatic, savoury, sweet and sour balance. Buy the very best – the cheaper 'condiment' types are quite nasty in comparison – sometimes these are simply sweetened wine vinegars coloured with caramel. In the case of balsamic vinegar, you get what you pay for, and the best is certainly not cheap!

CIDER VINEGAR

From yeast-fermented apples, cider vinegar does retain an aromatic reference to apples with its volatile phenols and ethers, and it is not overly acidic. Cider vinegar is very good in salad dressings of the vinaigrette type, especially with wholegrain mustard. Sometimes it is cloudy, but this is simply the precipitation of tannin-protein complexes.

MALT VINEGAR

Malt vinegar is the fermented fate of unhopped beer, which is made largely from malted barley. It has been used in the British Isles for a very long time indeed – in the olden days, it was called *alegar*. See Greg's innovative recipe for Pickled Chips, where 'chips with salt and malt vinegar' is given a complete makeover!

SHERRY VINEGAR

Vinagre de Jerez from Cadiz, Spain, is made from young, immature sherry from the Palomino grape, which is then blended and aged and matured in wood barrels. This is aged using the *solera* process – where it is blended with older products, so that over the years, the average age increases. Over time, this ensures quality and consistency. Sherry vinegars are richer and have a more fulsome flavour than wine vinegars, but they are not as sweet and syrupy as balsamic. However, they have body, they are wonderfully intense and savoury, with a raisin-like quality, and have a good glycerol content, giving a very pleasant mouth-feel. If you are making a dish inspired by Spanish cuisine, this is the only type to use! Buy the best – *vinagre de Jerez Gran Reserva* is aged in wood for a minimum of ten years. If you would like a slightly sweeter sherry vinegar, choose *al Pedro Ximénez* which will really deliver a fruity, raisin-like punch. Wonderful flavours – the result of history, great ingredients and real craftsmanship.

WINE VINEGARS

Wine vinegars are made from wine or yeast-fermented grape juice. This initial fermentation results in some beautiful aromatic flavour compounds being formed, and the subsequent fermentation will develop savoury, umami compounds. We can find both red and white wine vinegars – both serve well in classic vinaigrettes, but they can also be used to add acidity to sauces and cooking liquors if enhanced piquancy is needed.

Salt

The culinary world would be a much duller place without salt – our most basic and important seasoning. It is often said that judicious salting transforms a dish from the mundane to the sublime. Of course, over-salting is certainly unpleasant, but if we are careful and restrained, and know when to stop, we have mastered one of the most important lessons in flavour creation. Salt is a unique taste enhancer and modifier; it emphasises aromas, and suppresses bitterness. It can draw water out of plant tissues – and thus can be used for preservation.

Salt features in most of the recipes in this book – and we use it for so many culinary processes. If salt is added to water, to the level of sea water – which is around 3.5% or 35g per litre – it will raise the boiling point by around 1°C. This means that as well as enhancing flavour, the cooking process will be quicker!

Nowadays, there are many types of salt to choose from – compared with my youth when all we had in the house was granulated 'table salt' – some iodised fine grains in a large plastic bottle that was decanted into intricately designed containers destined for gracing our dinner table! These table salts often have additives (aluminium, silicon, sodium compounds and calcium compounds) to keep the cubic crystals from absorbing water and clumping, and additives to prevent the additives from drying out!

Broadly speaking, we have sea salts and rock salts. As always, buy the very best that you can afford. And don't use the fine granulated sort with iodine in the plastic bottle. Here are some of our favourites...and some oddities that you might like to explore!

FLAKE SEA SALT

Flake sea salt is made by surface evaporation of brine. We use Maldon sea salt most often; from the Essex coast of England, it is minimally processed and has large hollow pyramid crystals with a soft, crunchy texture. Isle of Skye sea salt is another favourite – you will find that the crystals are smaller, crisper and crunchier. The Cornish Sea Salt Company produces both crystal and flake forms.

FLEUR DE SEL

Fleur de sel – the 'flower of the sea' – is fine and delicate. It hails from the extensive sea salt beds off the Southwest coast of France. The crystals accumulate at the surface of the saltpans under specific climatic conditions of temperature and humidity. It might contain traces of algae, but this just adds to the aroma and flavour. The aroma of sea salt has been investigated and many compounds have been implicated including alcohols, phenols, aldehydes, ketones, esters, other terpenoids and norisoprenoids, which are molecules formed by the degradation of carotenoids in plants and algae. These are considered to be 'biomarkers' of the marine environment, and, if measured, can give a 'fingerprint' of the marine salt. People who work in saltpans in regions such as Aveiro in Portugal and Guérande in France have reported smelling a violet-like odour on occasions. Now, β-carotene can be degraded to β-ionone, a violet-scented compound that is present in many fruits, wines and the volatile oils of many flowers! A recent study indicated that β-ionone might even have health benefits, including chemopreventative and anti-tumour properties. It is present at trace levels in marine salt from Aveiro and Guérande, but it has not been found in saltpans in the Algarve, in the south of Portugal, possibly because of the drier environment and Mediterranean influence.

HAWAIIAN SALT

Hawaiian salt – or *alaea* salt – is a pinkish-brown-red unrefined sea salt that has been mixed with iron oxide-rich red volcanic clay known as *alae*. Little used in the West, it is, however, important in traditional Hawaiian cuisine, and it has sacred uses too.

Himalayan pink salt is a rock salt, mined by hand from the Khewra Salt Mine in Pakistan. The caves were formed millions of years ago when a shallow sea evaporated and a geological movement trapped the salt in pockets – this is now known as a 'salt range'. The salt is unprocessed other than by stone grinding. It is a very pretty salt – tinged with pink – and it is often claimed that its minerals have health benefits. This is unsubstantiated, but I enjoy using it purely for its colour and flavour, and when I want to grind salt, rather than use flakes! It can also be used for baking potatoes – see Black Cardamom Salt-Baked Potatoes.

INDIAN BLACK SALT

Indian black salt has a brown-pink to deep violet colour. It is another rock salt, and in Urdu it is called *kala namak*. It is very pungent because of its sulphur content, and its colour is due to an iron sulphide called greigite. When ground, it appears purple or pink. You might come across it in the Indian spice blend known as *chaat masala* where it imparts an aroma of hard-boiled eggs!

SEAWEED-FLAVOURED SALT

The Cornish Sea Salt Company produces a seaweed-infused variety. This is a delight – mild, savoury and slightly peppery.

SMOKED SALT

Both Maldon and the Cornish Sea Salt companies produce smoked salts. These can be used to add another dimension to sauces and seasonings. Both are gently smoky, not overpowering; the Cornish one is smoked with cherry and apple wood, giving a savoury, smoky tang, and the Maldon one is made using a cold smoking method.

CONDIMENTS, SPICE MIXES AND SAUCES – INSPIRATION AT A GLANCE

For reference or inspiration, here are the ingredients in the classic herb and spice blends from across the globe.

Advieh (Persia) – powdered dried rose petals, cardamom, cinnamon and cumin, sometimes black pepper, caraway, cloves, coriander, dried lime, ginger, nutmeg, pistachio and saffron.

Adobo (Latin America and the Caribbean) – garlic, oregano, pepper and other spices; used as an all-purpose seasoning.

Berbere (Ethiopia) – hot peppers, black pepper, fenugreek, ginger, cardamom, coriander, cinnamon and cloves, sometimes cumin, allspice, nutmeg, paprika, onion, garlic.

Bharat (Lebanon) – bay leaves, dried or ground ginger, cinnamon sticks, nutmeg, cloves, allspice, black peppercorns, white peppercorns and cardamom.

Bouquet garni (France) – bay, thyme and parsley.

Chermoula (Morocco and Middle East) – onion, garlic, coriander, chilli, cumin, black pepper and saffron, made into a loose paste with olive oil and sometimes lemon juice.

Chilli powder (Latin America) – ancho chillies, paprika, cumin and Mexican oregano, sometimes coriander, cayenne and dried, powdered garlic.

Chimichurri verde (Central and South America, Argentina) – parsley, garlic, red pepper flakes, fresh oregano, with oil and vinegar; sometimes with coriander leaves, cumin seeds, thyme, basil, lemon; *chimichurri roja* contains red bell pepper and tomato; a raw sauce or marinade with finely chopped fresh herbs.

Dukkah (Egypt) – cumin seeds, coriander seeds, sesame seeds, pepper, salt (with olive oil and bread).

Fines herbes (France) – tarragon, chervil and chive.

Five-spice (China) – star anise, Szechuan pepper, cassia, clove and fennel seed.

Garam masala (India) – coriander seed, cumin, cardamom, black pepper, clove, mace and cinnamon.

Gomashio (Japan) – toasted sesame seeds ground with coarse salt.

Gremolata (Spain) – parsley, garlic, lemon rind and juice.

Harissa (Tunisia) – roasted red pepper, chilli, garlic, coriander seed, saffron, sometimes rose petals, and sometimes caraway.

Herbes de Provence (France) – thyme, marjoram, fennel seeds, basil, rosemary and sometimes lavender.

Khmeli suneli (Georgia) – fenugreek seeds and leaves, coriander, savory and black peppercorns, sometimes dill, bay leaves, mint, dried marigold petals.

Muligapuri (India) – fenugreek seeds and chilli, with others (variable).

Panch phora (Eastern India and Bangladesh) – brown or yellow mustard seeds, nigella (black cumin) seeds, cumin seeds, fenugreek seeds and fennel seeds (the name means 'five-spice').

Pesto alla Genovese (Italy) – Ligurian basil, garlic, pine nuts, salt and olive oil, and traditionally Parmesan cheese.

Pesto alla Siciliana (Italy) – tomato, almonds, basil, salt and olive oil, and traditionally Parmesan cheese.

Picada (Catalonia) – garlic, parsley, nuts (almonds, walnuts, hazelnuts or pine nuts, or a mixture), sometimes breadcrumbs, salt and olive oil (it is used to flavour and thicken cooking liquids).

Pistou (France) – basil, garlic, salt and olive oil.

Quatre épices (France) – black pepper, nutmeg, clove and cinnamon.

Ras el hanout (Morocco) – cardamom, cassia, mace, clove, cumin, chilli and rose petals.

Recado roja (Mexico) – annatto, Mexican oregano, cumin, clove, cinnamon, black pepper, allspice, garlic and salt.

Romesco (Spain) – roasted red pepper, garlic, almonds or hazelnuts, tomato paste, sherry vinegar, smoked *pimentón*, cayenne pepper, salt and olive oil.

Shichimi togarashi (Japan) – coarsely ground chillies with Szechuan pepper, dried citrus peel, sesame seeds, poppy seeds, hemp seeds, ginger, garlic, shiso mint and nori (used as a condiment).

Tapenade (Southern France) – olives, capers, vinegar (often anchovies).

Tarator (Eastern Europe, Bulgaria) – walnuts, garlic, tahini, olive oil, lemon juice and sometimes breadcrumbs.

Za'atar (Middle East) – thyme, marjoram, oregano, sesame seeds, sumac and salt.

Zhug (Middle East) – cumin, cardamom, garlic and chilli.

DAIRY SUBSTITUTES

Possibly due to the increasing number of vegans and people following a dairy-free diet for health reasons, there has been an exponential growth in milk, cream, yogurt and butter substitutes on the market.

Plant milks

It is difficult to keep up with developments in this area, but examples include almond milk (good in coffee, it gives an enhanced roasted aroma and flavour); cashew milk (good body, mild flavour and good for sauces); coconut milk (a strong flavour, best used when you actually want your dish to taste of coconut, and certainly not in coffee); hemp milk (rich in linolenic acid which the body uses to make Omega 3 fatty acids, so it may well have anti-inflammatory actions too); oat milk (bland and with little aftertaste, it is useful for making sauces and in coffee); rice milk (bland but often has a thin texture and lacks body); and soya milk (a good source of protein, it is long established, and commercial products have improved much over the years – it dominates the market).

Plant creams

Plant creams have the texture and viscosity of dairy single cream. In this category, we find oat cream and oat crème fraiche, almond cream and soya cream, and we can make cashew cream (see page 248).

Plant yogurts

Coconut yogurt is very thick and has a good creamy texture; it is pleasantly tart and has a tangy coconut flavour. It is quite intense. Soya yogurts are also widely available.

Dairy-free spreads and plant-based butter substitutes

The main features to look out for are how they taste, and how they behave when used as spreads and when heated. You may find that some have better cooking characteristics than others – for example, some brands split (and spit!) when heated. They are made from a variety of vegetable oils, such as sunflower (perhaps best avoided because of the Omega 6 issue and potential to cause inflammation) and soya, but recently avocado and rapeseed spreads have become available, and these are excellent. Vegetable ghee is usually made with soya oil and is good in Indian dishes, and when you want a glossy finish.

However, it is also worth mentioning 'trans-fats' at this point. Plant oils are modified to make the product spreadable, and this was originally achieved via hydrogenation. The process of hydrogenation hardens liquid oils, but changes the structure of their fatty acids into trans-fatty acids by straightening out the kinks in the molecular chains. These are thought to be cardiotoxic, and they can raise blood LDL cholesterol, behaving more like saturated fats than unsaturated fats. More recently, dairy-free spreads are being produced by alternative processes which minimise or eliminate trans-fat formation, so look for words to this effect on the label. As an aside, some of my acquaintances use the presence of trans-fats as a reason to consume dairy butter rather than margarines...perhaps unaware that the microbes in the cow's rumen also produce trans-fats, and that the fat in milk, butter and cheese is actually around 5% trans-fats!

Food Preparation

You will find, throughout this book, discussion on preparation and cooking methods, and a fair amount of kitchen science. So, we do need to look at one more thing that will make your time in the kitchen easier and more productive – great utensils.

UTENSILS

Knives and cutting utensils

Most food preparation starts with washing or cleaning debris off the ingredients, and then cutting them in some manner. It is vital that your knives are sharp and appropriate for the task. You will find that you have a favourite – mine is a short-bladed utility knife, followed by a longer version of the same for tackling larger root vegetables, squashes and melon. Contrary to popular belief, you are more likely to cut yourself with a blunt knife! Blunt knives will also tear and damage plant tissues, compared with the clean cut of a sharp knife. Very few of us have expert knife skills, so to achieve thin slices a mandolin is a good investment.

What about peeling? Again, you will find a utensil that suits you – but it too must have a sharp blade. I use a swivel blade for everything from peeling potatoes to taking the skin off butternut squash.

Cookware

Yes, it *does* matter what your casserole dishes, pots and pans are made of! Different materials have different heat conduction properties.

Ceramics include earthenware, stoneware and porcelain. Earthenware is ancient and made from porous clay; it was invented in China before 1500 BCE. Stoneware is stronger and less porous because it contains more silica, and porcelain is stoneware that contains kaolin and silicates. It became known as 'chinaware' and then simply 'china'. Ceramics are very stable and unreactive; they retain heat very well, but do not respond well to high temperatures – so they are reserved for slow, gentle oven cooking.

Enamelware is the name given to cookware made from steel or iron with a layer of powdered glass fused on to the surface. They diffuse heat evenly and they are durable and unreactive. Enamelware does need care – the surface can become damaged by careless use of utensils and also by immersing cookware and bakeware into cold water. But if you are happy to take special care, enamelware is an excellent choice.

Aluminium – if you have old aluminium pots and pans nearing the end of their life, then replace them! They are made from aluminium alloys and are cheap, light and have very good conductivity. But aluminium is reactive – both the pan and foods can be discoloured by acids. Most modern aluminium utensils are anodised or are given a nonstick coating.

Nonstick pots and pans are usually coated with Teflon – a carbon-fluorine material with plasticity – and this gives a slippery surface which stops food sticking. Teflon is fine at low to moderate temperatures, but above 250°C or 500°F it will give off toxic gases, so it is vital that Teflon is not overheated – and it often is. It can also become scratched and flake off. Food-grade silicons can also provide nonstick surfaces – but again these do not do well at high temperatures. So, if you have old or scratched Teflon-coated utensils – ditch them now! Thankfully, we can now buy ceramic-coated utensils that are nonstick – kinder to the environment and healthier to use!

Copper is expensive and beautiful, and has great conductivity, but food cooked in copperware can contain toxic copper ions that have been leached out! Modern copperware is lined with stainless steel.

Cast iron is heavy; it retains heat well but it is easily corroded and needs to be seasoned by coating in oil and heating for several hours. The down side is that polyunsaturated oils can oxidise and become smelly and unpleasant, and cast iron needs careful cleaning and drying. I prefer cast iron enamelware, especially for griddle pans and casserole dishes.

Stainless steel is more expensive than the others, but it is chemically stable and unreactive. On its own, it is not the best conductor of heat, but modern pots and pans have copper or aluminium layers in the base, meaning that they are more responsive. It is, in my opinion, by far the best choice! There are nonstick ceramic-coated options too.

Mortar and pestle

This is indispensable. We use a large, heavy granite one for making *pistou*, for grinding spice mixes and making aromatic pastes and oils. Apart from anything else, the aroma while you are working is incredible! A medium-sized version is useful too, especially for small amounts of spice.

Blenders and processors

These are also very useful. A hand blender is a good choice for soups, whereas a processor is better for purées.

Ice cream and sorbet maker

A luxury, but it does the job!

The Recipe
Collection

Preface

My undertaking was to provide recipes that could help
illustrate neurogastronomy and to promote plant-based
recipes to everyone – *including myself*. Whether you are
vegan, vegetarian or neither, and whether you are an inquisitive
home cook or devoted food lover, my ambition was to provide
recipes that were enjoyable to make and would 'eat well', without
over-elaborating and without compromising flavour – dishes that
everyone could utilise as often or as infrequently as desired, and
recipes that stood up for themselves.

I have discovered that plant ingredients are a wonderful source
of inspiring food – an addition or alternative on our table that can
be one meal or a complete choice of lifestyle.

What I advocate here is adopting these plant-based recipes as a
permanent option in your diet or more – should you wish to follow
the principles of plant-based food entirely. I'm a real 'foodie' food
lover, so my natural curiosity drives me some way along the path,
but I hope that these recipes will work for anyone who appreciates
variety and above all great flavour in great food.

As a general rule, the fewer ingredients in a recipe, the more
those ingredients must perform, but it really matters everywhere.
I cannot stress enough the worth of sourcing good-quality
ingredients when and wherever possible. Use the very best you can.
Above all, I hope you enjoy the recipes and I hope you make them
as often as I now do.

Cook happy,
Greg

Small Plates

What do I really mean by small plates? Well, apart from the obvious, I mean recipes for adaptation and choice and for time and place. You can alter them to suit your larder or preference, but mostly they are versatile in that they can be made without too much preparation and can be eaten as a group of dishes or as a single one if need be. I think my favourite way to eat is *mezze* or *tapas* or *thali*...in fact, I don't think – I *know* it is. I also think it has become a favourite of many people who love food – I actually wonder how many of us still serve friends at home with a straight three-course dinner, or with the rising love of Eastern, Middle Eastern and Mediterranean food, do we eat in a fashion more akin to *mezze* and *tapas*, with the inclusion of wonderful salads and dips alongside roasted peppers and breads? I hope so – it is what I've been doing for many years now. I hope my friends were pleased – they said they were!

There is something fantastic about a spread of food rather than a plate of food, don't you think? It appeals to all the senses – the sight of different dishes reflecting the colourful recipes of a cuisine, the smell of warming spices and the range of different flavours and textures on offer. One of the great advantages is trying a dish you don't expect to like because it's not the whole meal – only one part of it. I know many people who have tried a Middle Eastern carrot dish having avoided carrots since childhood, but discover they really like them 'done that way'.

I believe that's the great joy of varied dishes – you discover what you may never have otherwise tried, whether it is sumac in a fresh salad for the first time, or returning to cauliflower because this time it has been roasted with spices rather than being boiled.

I tasted sumac for the first time when I was 20 (many years ago) in a local Turkish restaurant. I knew the Turkish owner and I remember asking him if I could have some of 'that stuff in the salad that made it taste so good'. I still have a vivid memory of sitting in the restaurant when I tasted it. I was managing a health club at the time, and on his next visit the owner presented me with some in a little bag – I've been using sumac in salads ever since. Thank you again, Haluk!

The real point of small plates is to give friends and family (and especially children) choice – let them try things and tempt them out of their preconceptions with all their senses...the sight of different ingredients...the sound of people cooking in alternative ways...the smell of exotic spices...the feel of eating different textures...and the taste of new food. It's OK not to like something, because in a *mezze* nothing is the main dish, and there will be others you do like – but not to try is a real shame.

Many years ago, a Chinese restaurateur friend of mine once told me over Dim Sum, 'The more mess on the table cloth the better – it shows people have been reaching over and trying all the dishes.'

Med Deli Ribbons

4 large carrots

2 tsp chermoula (see recipe on page 284)

1 tsp olive oil

handful of chopped black olives

handful of toasted pine nuts

ground tellicherry black peppercorns

Mediterranean Delicatessen Ribbons are almost too simple. They are delicious and require very little work. The heat brings out the sweetness in the carrots, and the *chermoula* provides the punch. You get a very satisfying texture from ribboned vegetables, and because of their elongated surface area they cling on to lots of flavour too. This will work with several other vegetables from which you can create long ribbons, but I favour carrots as they give such a great visual colour contrast and natural sweetness.

❋ Wash and peel the carrots before trimming the tops and tails off. Discard the peel and trimmings. Hold firmly on a secure work surface and peel the carrots into long ribbons from top to bottom. Toss the chermoula through the ribbons to coat them thoroughly. Heat the olive oil in a wide frying pan and pan-fry the carrot ribbons for 6–7 minutes until you see them begin to give and take on a slight colour. Remove from the heat and serve immediately with a few chopped black olives and the pine nuts scattered over. Sprinkle over some ground black pepper according to taste.

Alison's Tarragon and Garlic Mushrooms

handful of fresh tarragon leaves, chopped

small handful of flat-leaf parsley, chopped

2 large garlic cloves, crushed

30g (¼ cup) dairy-free butter, warmed to soften

200g (½lb) chestnut mushrooms, quartered

sea salt and ground black pepper to season

some good artisan bread, cut thick for toasting

Introducing variation in recipes doesn't always work. It relies on some consideration being given to the balance of flavours and textures involved, but it can be an inspirational way to enjoy a dish again in an alternative way.

This just works completely. There's something about the aroma of fresh tarragon that draws me in over the familiar smell of hot garlic. It's a herb I avoided in my early years of cooking because I developed the belief that it didn't agree with me – like so many of us, though, it was just that I'd eaten a dish which happened to have tarragon in it and I subsequently blamed its distinctive aroma for years. I'm sure there's a moral in there somewhere. Never say never – there's almost always a way back! Thank you, Alison!

❋ Mix the herbs, garlic and dairy-free butter together in a bowl. Add to a large frying pan and heat through until just beginning to sizzle. Add the mushrooms and toss through the hot butter. Fry on a medium heat for 5–6 minutes until just cooked through, then increase the heat to high for the last 2–3 minutes to gain a caramelised edge on the mushrooms. Season with salt and pepper as required.

Serve immediately on your favourite toasted bread.

Beetroot and Coconut Dip

Spiced with Toasted Caraway Seeds and Chilli

1 tsp caraway seeds

250g (9oz) pack pre-cooked beetroot

110ml (½ cup) coconut milk yogurt

pinch of chilli flakes

juice of ½ lemon

pinch of sea salt, crushed

I love this dish for its great flavour, but also for its visual impact on the table. It is another perfect example of the senses working in union. You can't hide the wonderful visual effect of the dish and then the joy of eating the textural contrast between the pieces of beetroot and the smooth yogurt. The chilli provides a background lift while the toasted caraway provides a second tier of bready flavour over the beetroot's earthy sweetness.

❋ Toast the caraway seeds in a dry frying pan for a few minutes until gently toasted and aromatic. Cool and grind in a pestle and mortar.

Blitz all but one of the cooked beetroot in a food processor and combine with the yogurt, chilli flakes, lemon juice and the ground caraway. You're looking for a very slightly coarse mixture, not a smooth cream. Check for seasoning and add a pinch of crushed sea salt if necessary. Place the dip mixture into the serving bowl you wish to use and finely dice the remaining whole beetroot. Add to the top of the dip in the centre. Finish with a thin zig-zag drizzle of coconut yogurt over the top.

Serve with toasted pitta breads or the flatbreads from page 274.

White Beans with Smoked Chilli and Lime Pickle

and Mexican Oregano

½ onion, finely chopped

2 tsp rapeseed oil

1 garlic clove, crushed

½ tsp chilli powder

½ tsp cumin seeds, ground

300ml (1¼ cups) light vegetable stock

1 x 400g (15oz) tin of cannellini beans, drained and rinsed

1 tbsp fresh coriander stalks, very finely chopped

1 tsp Mexican oregano

1 tsp Gran Luchito smoked chilli and lime pickle

squeeze of lime juice

small handful of fresh coriander leaves, roughly chopped

sea salt

some favourite bread for toasting

Sometimes it just has to be beans! I wanted a *chili* dish, but I'm not a fan of meat replacement for the sake of it, so I had to find something else to satisfy. White beans, like many varieties, are well established in many comforting European dishes, but not so often with the added warmth of chilli to accompany them.

The beans deliver a wonderful texture somewhere between comfort and ease of eating. Visually, you expect a mild dish despite the name, so the heat is less anticipated, and the inclusion of the lime provides a fresh counterpoint. The Mexican oregano is perfect here – adding a herby, peppery warmth and depth that you don't get from normal oregano. It really is worth seeking out, although it is technically not oregano.

❊ Sauté the chopped onion gently in rapeseed oil for 6 minutes. Add the crushed garlic and cook for a further 2 minutes. Add the spices and cook out for 1–2 minutes, stirring occasionally. Add the stock, beans, coriander stalks, oregano and pickle and simmer again until the sauce has reduced by half and is coating the beans. Add the lime juice and season to taste with sea salt. Serve sprinkled with fresh coriander leaves on your favourite toasted bread.

Maftoul House Salad

with Roasted Cauliflower, Pomegranate and Soft Herbs

1 small cauliflower, broken into small florets

1 tbsp olive oil

100g (½ cup) maftoul

1 litre (4 cups) mild vegetable stock

2 tsp finely diced preserved lemon

2 tbsp dried cranberries

90g (⅓ cup) tinned chickpeas, drained

small handful of fresh dill, chopped

small handful of fresh mint, chopped

small handful of fresh coriander, chopped

1 tsp sumac

seeds of ½ ripe pomegranate

freshly ground black pepper

small handful of toasted pine nuts

squeeze of lemon juice

drizzle of extra virgin olive oil

Maftoul (meaning 'hand rolled') is a traditional Palestinian large grain couscous made from bulgur wheat that is sun-dried before being rolled in freshly ground wheat flour. It is cooked and eaten in much the same way as its cousins fregola, mograbiah and other variants of couscous.

Maftoul is a wonderful vehicle for all sorts of flavours and has a texture and mouth-feel all of its own – one that surpasses any average couscous. You can really adapt it to suit what you have in your larder, as long as you follow a few rules. You need varying texture and flavour in a salad like this and balanced seasoning, of course. Get that right with what you have available to you and it all adds up to a dish that's interesting and will therefore 'eat well'.

❋ Preheat the oven to 220°C (425°F).

Blanch the cauliflower florets for 2–3 minutes in lightly salted boiling water. Drain and place in a bowl. Drizzle them with the olive oil and season with salt and pepper before laying them out on a baking tray. Roast in the oven for 10–15 minutes until just tender and lightly golden at the edges.

Meanwhile, cook the maftoul in light vegetable stock for 6–7 minutes according to the packet instructions. Drain and set aside to cool a little.

In a fresh bowl, add the remaining ingredients, except the pine nuts, to the cooled maftoul and mix gently through to combine.

Depending on the ripeness of the pomegranate seeds, the maftoul may turn a little pink, but that's a great sign, as it will spread wonderful sweet ripe pomegranate flavour throughout the dish.

Once the cauliflower is ready, allow to cool for 5 minutes or so and then combine with the salad. Place the salad into your serving dish and check for seasoning, adding a little ground black pepper if required. Sprinkle the salad with the toasted pine nuts and finish with a squeeze of lemon juice and a drizzle of extra virgin olive oil on top. Serve warm as a light lunch to allow all the flavours to be at their best, or chilled among other picnic dishes.

Green Beans with Chermoula and Tomato

150g (¾ cup) chopped tinned tomatoes, plus a little water

1 tsp chermoula paste (page 284)

pinch of sea salt

pinch of sugar

400g (16oz) packet green beans, trimmed

Eating green beans with tomato really isn't a new idea. I've done it many times before, as I'm sure you have, but the addition here of the *chermoula* takes it somewhere else – I think it's safe to say, Morocco. I could call it a twist on an Italian idea, but somehow that doesn't cover it – the *chermoula* elevates the dish to quite another level, making it a stand-out dish among a spread of any small plates. You watch – people will try it and then keep going back. The combination of Mediterranean flavours in the *chermoula* is really allowed to perform, transferring the humble green bean into a modern comfort food.

❋ Combine all the ingredients, except the green beans, in a small pan and cook through for about 10–15 minutes on a low to medium heat until the tomatoes start to break down in the sauce. You want to amalgamate everything well but be careful not to allow the sauce to dry out – use another splash of water if you think it's getting too dry.

Meanwhile, cook the beans in lightly salted boiling water for about 6 minutes until tender. Drain. Place on a warm plate and combine with the hot sauce. Serve with toasted pitta breads on its own or as part of a *mezze*-style meal.

Mushroom Ceviche

120g (1 cup) shiitake mushrooms

100g (1 cup) closed-cup mushrooms

5–6 chestnut mushrooms

4 tbsp extra virgin rapeseed oil

juice of ½ large lemon

1 tsp rosemary sea salt

1 tsp freshly ground tellicherry black peppercorns

I love cooked mushrooms in many ways, and I do like raw mushrooms – so this is the best of both worlds! There isn't much work here and the result is bordering on addictive. As with all things raw or served this way, you have to get the best quality you can; this is essential – otherwise, it is unforgiving. The aromas of the marinade and the sharp zing of flavours against the creamy texture of the mushroom are superb. You really feel as if you're eating a treat, yet you know it is a healthy option.

It is worth highlighting that whatever mushrooms you do use, do include some shiitake. They add a texture that creates a contrast – you don't really want all the same. Also I find it worth slicing the shiitake just a little bit thicker than the others. Seek out the tellicherry peppercorns – they're not hard to find now and you won't go back.

If you wish, you can use different flavoured sea salts – chipotle chilli sea salt works really well if you want a little heat, as does wild garlic sea salt and truffle salt. I feel a plain oil is best, though, as you don't want to mask the flavour of the mushrooms.

❊ Make sure all your mushrooms are clean. Slice them about 2mm thick, remembering to slice the shiitake slightly thicker. Make sure you slice through the stalks too. Mix them all gently together in a bowl.

Combine the rapeseed oil with the lemon juice, the rosemary salt and ground tellicherry pepper in a separate bowl and whisk together to create a dressing. Taste the dressing to check for seasoning – adjust if necessary to balance. Pour the dressing over the mixed mushrooms and once again gently fold together to coat the mushrooms with the dressing. Cover and chill in the fridge for at least an hour or two. Serve with freshly toasted ciabatta or your favourite bread.

Indian-Inspired Kale and Kasuri Methi Potato Cakes

with Tomato and Mint Spiced Chutney

500g (1lb) white floury potatoes

1 tsp turmeric

5 or 6 large leaves of cavolo nero, stems removed and chopped

1 shallot, finely chopped

1 tsp olive oil

1 tsp cumin seeds

1 tsp mustard seeds

2 dried bird's eye chillies

1 tsp kasuri methi (dried fenugreek leaves)

1 tsp ginger paste

a little ground Keralan green pepper (black pepper is also fine)

sea salt to taste

Spiced Tomato and Mint Chutney (page 264)

More than most things in food, I love spices, contrasting flavour and texture. So Indian food is never far from my thoughts. I've kept the chilli heat low to medium here, to suit most and to balance the cakes better – but you can easily add an extra chilli if you like your chillies the way I do.

The contrast between the hot potato cakes and the cold tangy chutney is really rewarding, as is the contrast in texture between the crushed potato and soft kale and the occasional pop of a mustard seed or two. It is important to still have some textural bite to the kale, so be careful not to overcook it.

I learned the cooking rule 'less is more' a long time ago, particularly with turmeric and saffron – and it's good advice – but I'd like to apply a further caveat to spices such as cumin, fenugreek and mustard seeds...and that is 'less is enough'. By that I mean they aren't totally dominating flavours, in the way that turmeric and saffron can taste medicinal if overused, but some spices will dominate if you allow one to override the others...so use with some generosity in Indian cooking as they are a joy to cook with, but always take care to balance.

❋ Still with the skin on, dice the potatoes into roughly 2cm-sized pieces (they will cook quicker and be easier to crush). Cook in slightly salted water with ½ tsp of turmeric for about 12–14 minutes, depending on the potatoes. You are looking for a tender firmness, as you want to retain some good texture for the cakes in the final mix. Drain and leave to cool a little before removing the skins. (You can peel them before cooking, but as a rule I take the view that cooking with the skin on is always better unless it is really not convenient for a particular recipe.)

Meanwhile, cook the cavolo nero also in slightly salted gently boiling water for 5–6 minutes. Drain and press in a sieve to push out excess retained water. Set both aside while you fry off the onion and spices.

Gently fry the shallots in a little oil for 5 minutes. Add the cumin seeds, mustard seeds and chilli, and continue to fry on a low heat for 3 minutes. Add the ginger paste and cook for a final 3–4 minutes, stirring occasionally to combine everything and to ensure nothing catches in the pan. Add a little dash of water if you feel it is too dry and at risk of catching. Burnt spices are bitter and irreversible and you don't want them in your dish!

Once cooled, combine everything in a bowl, including the kasuri methi, and gently crush everything together. You are looking to retain little pieces of soft potato within the cakes – not mash. Add a little ground Keralan pepper and season with sea salt to taste before combining gently one last time.

Hand mould into 6–8 cakes depending on your preference and cover and chill until you are ready to use them.

Fry gently in a nonstick pan for 3–4 minutes each side – in a little oil, or even better if you have some flavoured oil like coriander, chilli, mint or ginger.

Serve with the Spiced Tomato and Mint Chutney as suggested or a very simple salad of chopped tomatoes mixed with coriander leaves, a pinch of salt and pepper and a dash of red wine vinegar.

Lemon and Thyme Radiatori Potatoes

These are inspired by the pasta shape of the same name which, as you may already know, takes its name from its resemblance to a radiator. It is, of course, essentially roasted potatoes with some herbs, but it proves a point that presentation always contributes to a dish no matter how simple, and I get a tremendous childlike joy from eating the potatoes this way, carving piece by piece as I go. For those who were taught not to play with their food...go ahead and play.

There is a serious side too, of course. Cutting the potatoes like this allows whatever you put on them to get in and around the potato better and distribute the flavours. The first bite 'with the eye' creates curiosity and interest while the contours deliver enhanced flavour due to the increased surface area in contact with your ingredients. All backed up by the comforting, familiar texture of waxy roast potatoes.

❋ Preheat the oven to 220°C (425°F). Carefully cut slits in the potatoes but don't cut through – about two-thirds of the way is ideal. It sounds strange to say, but use a sharp table knife instead of the more usual kitchen knife. The extra width of a standard table knife will give you a wider cut and a better final appearance. Please don't use a blunt knife, though!

Combine the ingredients for the flavoured oil.

Place the potatoes in a roasting tin and coat with the flavoured oil, particularly in the cuts, before roasting for approximately 1 hour. Baste the potatoes at 20-minute intervals, covering loosely with foil after the first 30 minutes. Once ready, remove and scatter them with thyme leaves, a final drizzle of olive oil and rosemary sea salt before serving.

10 small–medium waxy potatoes

For the flavoured oil

juice of 2 small lemons

2 tbsp olive oil

handful of chopped thyme leaves

sea salt

1 garlic clove, finely chopped

For finishing

extra olive oil

extra thyme leaves

rosemary sea salt (chilli sea salt or plain sea salt also works well)

As some of you will have already noticed, these are, of course, a variation of the Swedish-inspired hasselback potato, which incidentally takes its name from the Hasselbacken Hotel in Stockholm where it was created. There is so much history in food.

Gigantes Escabeche

1 banana shallot, peeled, halved lengthways and finely sliced into half moons

2 spring onions, whites finely sliced into discs

200ml (¾ cup) white wine vinegar

400ml (1½ cups) extra virgin olive oil

1 tsp dried oregano or summer savory

1 roasted red pepper, diced – from a good-quality jar is fine

sea salt and pepper to taste

1 x 400g (15oz) tin of butter beans, drained and rinsed

2 tsp fresh lemon juice

This is a Greek-style dish using an old Spanish method of cooking – a true 'Mediterranean' recipe that might not be the first in the book you reach to make but, put among a *mezze* or included in a picnic, it will stand out as a dish people will ask about and return to.

I love pickles, but this way of cooking is mellower, and allows the beans to maintain their taste and texture while the escabeche adds flavour and prolongs their shelf life. It's also a wonderful dish to incorporate into salads.

❋ Combine all the ingredients, except the beans, in a pan and briefly bring to the boil before reducing the heat and simmering gently for 30 minutes to cook the onions and allow the flavours to develop. Remove from the heat and add the beans, mixing together gently to combine everything. Squeeze in some fresh lemon juice and chill for 12 hours or overnight in a sealed container before using. Store in the fridge and use within 2–3 weeks. They are best eaten at room temperature when you want them and particularly good as part of a *mezze* or picnic on a hot summer day. Just lift some out and allow most of the oil to drain back. Eat on bread, toast or in a salad.

Pane e Olio e Sal e Pomodoro

(Bread and Oil and Salt and Tomato)

bread – seek out a quality artisan bread or make your own

oil – the best you can afford (I like Colonna from Italy, but it is your choice that matters)

salt – sea salt flakes

tomatoes – on the vine, as fresh as you can get, the best that you can find

It is timeless and it's simple – and, let's be honest, it is almost not even a recipe – but it truly deserves celebrating – and for good reason. These four ingredients combined like this reflect the essence of what plant-based food really represents – quality ingredients from natural sources combining, creating something simple and delicious to enjoy.

What I really want to convey here is how something so basic can be turned into something so good to eat, with almost no thought other than the quality of ingredients. Good ingredients are the building blocks of any good food, whether plant-based or not, and they matter a great deal.

Fresh homemade or artisan bread...your favourite regional extra virgin olive oil, according to your taste...good sea salt 'flakes'...and the best-quality fresh vine tomatoes you can source. I often have this when I need to reset my taste buds – it reminds me to think without complication and have faith in the character of great produce.

❉ Cut a thick slice of bread, drizzle with a little oil, crush or chop a tomato on top and sprinkle on some sea salt.

Smile and remember how good the simple life can taste.

Retro Roasted Onions

in Herb-Infused Sunshine Tomato Sauce

100ml (⅓ cup) olive oil

1 medium onion, chopped

approximately 20 shallots, peeled, keeping the base intact

1 tbsp good dried oregano (Mexican oregano is ideal)

sea salt

freshly ground black peppercorns (tellicherry are ideal)

350ml (1½ cups) crushed tomato passata

pinch of saffron strands

handful of toasted pine nuts

I have a very kind and generous mother-in-law. Among the many acts of kindness in any given year is an annual gift of a large recycled supermarket bag of homegrown shallots. I always want to do them justice and not simply use them up as chopped onions... and this is the recipe I have settled on. The brand of supermarket bag varies each year but not the quality of the shallots. Thank you, Valerie!

I saw someone eating whole baked onions and was immediately taken with the question of why we don't eat them like that more often. Onions are far more than an ingredient or base to a recipe, but we often forget to enjoy them as a vegetable in their own right. As with one or two other recipes I have written, this is an out-of-favour dish that has great flavour and truly deserves to be reunited with us all. Done well, they are delicious and very satisfying – not to mention easy to make and very cheap...especially when the shallots are free!

❀ Select a deep-sided ovenproof frying pan that will hold the shallots snuggly when in the sauce – 24cm diameter is about right. This is important as you want the shallots to stay upright as much as possible in the cooking and not roll about too much.

Warm the oil in the frying pan and add the chopped onion. Gently cook the onion on a low–medium heat for 10 minutes or so until soft and translucent. Add the shallots and cook on a medium heat for 4–5 minutes, carefully turning them over, before adding the oregano, black pepper and ½ tsp of sea salt. Add the crushed tomato passata and the saffron. Pour about 100ml (⅓ cup) of water on top – it is a very good idea to use the empty passata bottle and swirl the water around to get the last remains of the passata...also the bottle being 350ml means a third of the bottle is naturally close enough to 100ml.

Gently turn the onions over in the sauce to combine everything before positioning each shallot with the base facing up. Bring to a

brief boil before reducing the heat to minimal and simmering for 10 minutes. Transfer to the oven for a further 20–25 minutes at 180°C (350°F) until the onions are soft and tender.

Serve either in the pan or carefully transferred to a serving dish, sprinkled generously with toasted pine nuts. This is ideal as a slightly larger small plate for several to share and also very enjoyable as a sharing dish for two with some toasted pittas and a glass of good red wine.

Black Cardamom Salt-Baked Potatoes

5–6 black cardamom pods

2 x 500g packets (or 4 cups) rock salt

6 medium-sized waxy potatoes, skin on

Cooking potatoes under salt like this gives them an extra dimension in flavour. They cook in their own moisture, locking in the true flavour that boiling can lose so easily. It's a wonderful way to cook. The salt seasons without penetrating the potato, leaving a waxy, buttery, delicious end result that makes you appreciate the humble potato all over again. You can use aromatics such as fennel seeds or hard herbs to similar effect, but I love the dark smoky notes that black cardamom delivers. It's useful to have extra dishes in which to use up your herbs and spices, as you want to always have them at their best. Dried herbs and spices have an essential place in the kitchen, but not in the same place for months and years!

A deep, round ovenproof dish is ideal for this.

❄ Preheat the oven to 220°C (425°F). Crush the cardamom pods in a pestle and mortar and combine with the rock salt. Place a layer of half of the rock salt in the bottom of an ovenproof dish and place the potatoes on top. Cover with the remaining salt and sprinkle a little water over the top to help the salt form a crust. You don't want to dissolve any of the salt, just wet it very slightly so it hardens up quickly in the oven. Bake for 40–50 minutes until the potatoes are tender in the middle. Insert a skewer if you want to check. Carefully crack open the salt crust and dig out the potatoes. They should lift out without difficulty, but you might need to brush the odd bit of rock salt off the skin.

Pimientos de Padron

1 tsp olive oil plus a little for drizzling

250g (9oz) packet padron peppers

sea salt

It is amazing what a little risk will do for your appetite. I buy and make these whenever I see them. Named after the municipality they come from in Galicia in Northwest Spain, they are not uncommon in certain supermarkets here in the UK.

These mild little green peppers are delicious pan-fried in a little good olive oil and sea salt – a true Spanish tapas classic – and every now and again you get a chilli hot one that lights up the palate. It's like Russian roulette with green peppers. They say it's approximately 1 in 12, but frankly I've eaten plates of these and often missed out – it's not guaranteed. It depends on whatever water-to-sun ratio the pepper has had during its growth, so you just can't tell in advance. Use good sea salt and a good olive oil, and eat them as soon as they are ready. Cold beer on standby.

If you're impatient for the chilli hit, then you could, of course, serve them with a good chilli sauce on the side, but I prefer to eat them simply with olive oil and sea salt and wait for the hidden hot one.

❄ Heat the olive oil in a frying pan on a medium heat and add the peppers. Toss over in the pan until they blister and darken a little. Remove to a warm serving plate and drizzle with a little more extra virgin olive oil and a sprinkle of sea salt.

Roasted Piquillo Peppers

Stuffed with Saffron and Caper Skordalia with Migas de Pan and Mojo Verde Sauce

500g (1lb) floury potatoes, quartered

pinch of saffron strands

2 tbsp almond milk

1½ tbsp salted capers

approximately 10 piquillo peppers from a good-quality branded jar

1 tsp garlic paste

Migas de Pan (page 282)

Mojo Verde Sauce (page 265)

Piquillo peppers are actually a variety of chilli, predominantly from Northern Spain, that have no heat. What they have instead is a delicious sweet flavour enhanced by their traditional preparation method – roasted over embers and then peeled and deseeded before packing. Piquillos get their name from the Spanish for 'little beak' and it's not difficult to see why.

These stuffed peppers are a derivation of the Spanish tapas classic with the welcome addition of *migas* (breadcrumbs) and a very classic green chilli sauce. I have to be honest and say this dish is one of my absolute favourites in the book, and I make this every time I come across the slightly elusive jars of *piquillo* peppers. What's not to like? Soft sweet peppers with creamy garlicky saffron-hued mashed potato, spiked with salty capers and topped with nutty, crunchy, smoky *migas* and a herby chilli sauce.

❋ Cook the potatoes in lightly salted water for 15–20 minutes until tender.

Combine the saffron with the milk and leave to infuse. Soak the capers in cold water for 10–15 minutes to wash the excess salt off before drying them on kitchen paper and roughly chopping them.

Once the potatoes are cooked, drain and set aside until cool enough to peel the skins off. Drain the piquillo peppers and set out on a plate.

Stir the saffron milk to combine well. Crush the skinned potatoes together a little before adding the saffron milk, caper and garlic paste. Now gently mash everything with a potato masher to form the *skordalia* stuffing.

Preheat the oven to 200°C (400°F).

Stuff each pepper individually with the *skordalia* by holding it as you would an ice cream cone and spooning the mash in carefully with a teaspoon. Lay each completed pepper in a round Spanish *cassuela* or similar-shaped ovenproof dish, 'beaks' facing in to form a cartwheel effect.

Sprinkle with some of the *migas de pan*, drizzle with some good extra virgin olive oil and cook uncovered in the oven for 25–30 minutes until the peppers are just beginning to get a roasted edge to them.

Finish by sprinkling the remaining *migas* on top just before serving and place the mojo verde sauce on the table for people to serve themselves.

Simple
Turkish Salad

with Sumac and Pul Biber

3 good-quality medium
tomatoes, finely diced

1 small or ½ large red onion,
finely diced

½ cucumber, deseeded and
finely diced

1 small sweet red pepper,
deseeded and finely diced

6 sprigs of fresh mint, leaves
finely chopped

½ tbsp sumac

½ tbsp pul biber (Turkish red
pepper flakes)

1 tbsp extra virgin olive oil

freshly ground black pepper

pinch of sea salt

squeeze of lemon juice

I couldn't leave this salad out, really. It's the natural progression from the salad in Haluk's Turkish restaurant all those years ago (see chapter introduction). All I have done is add my experience to it. There are only two rules I can think of: it must be served freshly made and it works best with food that has a little chilli kick to it.

❁ Place all the ingredients in a large bowl and gently mix through to combine well. Leave to stand for 5–10 minutes. Taste for seasoning and only add a further pinch of salt or squeeze of lemon juice if you feel it needs it. Serve immediately.

Corallini Paella in Tapas Pans

200g (1 cup) corallini pasta

600ml (2⅓ cups) hot vegetable stock

pinch of saffron strands

1 tsp sweet paprika (dulce)

2 garlic cloves, crushed

1 tbsp of very finely chopped onion

ground black pepper

pinch of crushed chillies

4 roasted piquillo peppers from a jar

I spend far too much time on holiday raking around in markets, and that does occasionally include supermarkets. It's quite interesting what you can find, as it inevitably demonstrates the popular tastes of the country.

Without having seen it, I'm not sure I would have thought it acceptable to make paella with small pasta shapes (*fideo* aside) – but it works very well. The tiny shapes, more often used in soups, make a very interesting textural change and I find making it this way an enjoyable alternative to the traditional rice.

The supermarket had it on display, naturally in a huge paella pan, next to the standard paella, and it was this version that was running out. I've simplified it to work as an attractive tapas dish here, but you could elaborate it if you wish in a larger pan with other small vegetables.

It's not always easy to get particular shapes of pasta, and pasta manufacturers often have different names for similar shapes...so if you can't get corallini, then look for other very small pasta shapes like conchigliette lisce, cinesine or another favourite of mine, mezze tubettini.

❊ Add all the ingredients, except the peppers and pasta, to the hot stock and leave to stand for 5–10 minutes to infuse.

Cook the pasta in the stock on a medium heat for 9 minutes, stirring occasionally. The actual timing will depend on the pasta you use, of course, so add a little extra stock if it looks like drying out too soon during the cooking.

Preheat the oven to 180°C (350°F).

Once cooked, transfer the pasta into four individual pans or tapas dishes and lay a piquillo pepper on the top of each dish. Transfer to the oven and bake for 10 minutes to form a slight crust on the top and heat the pepper through.

Serve as part of a spread of small dishes.

Roast Saag Aloo

400g (1lb) waxy potatoes

1 tbsp vegetable ghee

1 small onion, chopped

2 garlic cloves, very finely chopped

1 green chilli, finely chopped

1 tbsp ginger, finely chopped

1 tsp Kashmiri chilli powder

1 tsp turmeric

200g (7oz) packet of fresh spinach

1 tsp garam masala

sea salt

I have ordered many plates of saag aloo in my time. It is quite a favourite, but all too often it is underwhelming – swamped in an average sauce or with undercooked potato in it, and I don't concur with the use of frozen spinach here either. Simple dishes are not an excuse for lazy cooking – they are an opportunity to let the simple ingredients stand out.

I wanted to create a side dish that was worthy of the main table. What I achieved was a great meal that can be downsized to be a small plate or upscaled to a main dish as required. There is a dryness to this dish that I really like, which allows the potato and spinach to be seen and heard, if you get my meaning. Whatever you do, don't make too little of it...it's very, very moreish.

❀ Boil the potatoes for about 7–8 minutes in lightly salted water until they are partially cooked. Once cool enough to handle, dice into roughly equal pieces (about 6–8 pieces depending on the size of the potato).

Preheat the oven to 220°C (425°F). Warm the ghee in a roasting tin for a few minutes while it reaches temperature, then remove the tin and add the diced potato. Turn the potato over in the tin to coat well.

Place the roasting tin with the potatoes in the oven and roast for 20–25 minutes, turning them around in the oil halfway through. Once the potatoes have some roasting colour, turn off the oven and keep the potatoes warm. Heat a little ghee in a high-sided frying pan and fry the onions, garlic, ginger and green chilli together for 10 minutes before adding the chilli powder and turmeric and frying together for a further minute or two. Add the spinach and allow to wilt in the heat. Just as it's fully wilted, add in the potatoes and the garam masala and mix gently to combine. Check for seasoning and serve in a warmed Indian-style dish with *parathas* or *rotis*.

Pickled Chips

3 potatoes (Maris Piper or King Edward are ideal), peeled and cut into chips

125ml (½ cup) malt vinegar

1 tbsp rapeseed oil

a little polenta for dusting

sea salt

You might read this recipe and think, why not just put the vinegar on afterwards? Well, this way the chips don't get moisture on them when hot, so they stay crisp and still have that wonderful malt vinegar flavour. You get a kind of second sense of the vinegar without it being full-on. It's a bit of fun really, but it does work.

�֍ Place the cut chips in the vinegar and allow to marinate for 10 minutes. Preheat the oven to 200°C (400°F). Remove the chips from the vinegar, thinly coat with oil and dust with a little polenta before placing on a baking tray. Roast for 30–40 minutes, turning occasionally. Serve hot, sprinkled with a little sea salt.

Warm and Waxy Potato Salad

with Tarragon and Shallot Dressing

- 400g (1lb) waxy new potatoes, washed, with skin on
- 2–3 small shallots, finely chopped
- 2 tsp Dijon mustard
- 1 tsp light soya sauce
- 2 tbsp chopped tarragon leaves
- 100ml (½ cup) extra virgin olive oil
- 1 tsp Pernod or ouzo
- 1 tsp lemon juice
- sea salt flakes for seasoning
- 1 tsp freshly ground black pepper for seasoning

I'm willing to bet that the vast majority of everyone loves potatoes, but that a lot of people aren't so fond of tarragon. I have to admit it's a herb I had to grow into, if that makes sense, which compels me to offer some advice. Like many new or infrequently used ingredients, if you think you don't like them, it's possibly down to a bad experience at the hands of others – cook with these ingredients yourself, and to your own taste, and you'll often find you do like them, just not when others have been overly generous with them. I found the same with cumin many years ago, and with cinnamon.

Here, tarragon really gives a wonderful lift of originality to what is a fairly 'grown-up' potato salad, by the time you boost it with a little Pernod or ouzo. Some further advice – it's worth spending the time getting the shallots finely chopped – it really helps the final dish.

Boil the potatoes in lightly salted water until just tender in the middle – approximately 10–15 minutes depending on the potatoes. Combine the remaining ingredients in a bowl (except the seasoning) and whisk together to create the dressing. Now add seasoning to taste.

Once the potatoes are ready, drain and cut in half lengthways before adding the dressing and mixing through gently to coat the potatoes. Serve warm as a small plate or a simple but delicious summer lunch for two.

Griddled Sweetcorn Cobs

with Urfa Biber and Lime Butter

30g (¼ cup) dairy-free butter

zest of 1 lime

juice of ½ lime

1 tbsp urfa biber pepper flakes

1 Indonesian long pepper, crushed

4 corn cobs

olive oil

pinch or two of chipotle sea salt

Urfa biber is a Turkish red pepper that's been exposed to two natural processes. By day it is sun-dried before being wrapped up at night to infuse in its own moisture. The result is beautifully rich but mild pepper flakes that have undertones of chocolate and sweet raisin with a smoky chilli note. Perfect for this recipe or simply sprinkled on a host of other dishes too.

These corn cobs are bordering on addictive, eaten hot off the griddle pan with an extra pinch (or two) of sea salt or chipotle sea salt if you have it. The sweetness of the corn just marries so beautifully with the sharp lime juice, while the smoked chilli notes of the Turkish pepper flakes work to intensify the already smoky charred edge that griddling delivers.

I know it's not reinventing the wheel here as far as corn on the cob goes, but, as I've said elsewhere, we sometimes forget just how great some of the familiar things are and we don't revisit them often enough.

❋ Soften the dairy-free butter and combine it well with the lime zest, lime juice, urfa biber and crushed pepper. Set aside to infuse.

Coat each corn cob lightly with some olive oil and cook on a hot griddle or barbecue for approximately 15–20 minutes, moving each cob around regularly to ensure they cook through evenly and get a little colour all over.

Once ready, spread each one with the flavoured butter and enjoy!

Romanesco

with Citrus-Infused Salsa Verde and Toasted Flaked Almonds

2 tsp quality salted capers, rinsed and roughly chopped

2 cloves garlic, crushed and finely chopped

handful of fresh coriander leaves, chopped

6 or 7 fresh mint leaves, chopped

6 tbsp extra virgin olive oil

1 tbsp sweet pickled gherkins, finely chopped

grated zest of ½ lemon

juice of ½ lime

1 tbsp orange wine vinegar (or 2 tsp red wine vinegar)

a few twists of freshly ground black pepper

1 very fresh Romanesco brassica

handful of toasted flaked almonds

Romanesco is a wonderful and sadly underused vegetable that encapsulates many of the principles of neurogastronomy discussed in the book. It's visually striking in both colour and its unusual fractal form, and it has a wonderful texture and a gentle nutty taste. Adding the freshly made and uplifting citrus-infused *salsa verde* simply completes the picture by contributing a delicious aroma and greater layers of flavour.

Romanesco is not all that commonly found in UK markets and grocers, so you'll need to keep an eye out for it, although you won't struggle to recognise it when you do see it. Buy it as fresh and unblemished as you can and use it quickly. The little chartreuse florets damage and discolour easily if abused, but in its best form it's a stunning addition to the table.

❉ First make the citrus-infused *salsa verde*.

Combine all the ingredients other than the romanesco in a pestle and mortar and crush together to form the salsa. You want a fairly rough-textured finish that will deliver little spikes of flavour throughout the dish. Taste for seasoning and adjust accordingly with freshly ground black pepper and sea salt to balance. The salsa needs to be slightly viscous, but loose enough to pour over and coat the romanesco well. Set aside to rest for 30–60 minutes to allow the flavours to marry well.

Trim all the leaves and stem from under the romanesco and break it carefully into its natural florets, keeping each individual floret as intact as possible.

Cook the florets in lightly salted boiling water for 10–12 minutes until just tender but retaining a reasonable bite. Drain and immediately arrange in the middle of a serving dish. Spoon over the *salsa verde* and turn everything over gently to coat well. If you want to be fussy, then adjust as many florets as you can to face upwards to maximise the visual effect of the colour and shape of the romanesco. Serve immediately scattered with toasted flaked almonds.

Carrot and Lime Leaf Kebabs

with Lemongrass and Caraway Seeds

4 large carrots, peeled and sliced widthways at an angle into 16 thick pieces

60ml (¼ cup) lemongrass-flavoured rapeseed oil

pinch of chilli flakes

1 tsp caraway seeds

½ tsp ground turmeric

pinch of sea salt

2–3 grinds of black pepper

kaffir lime leaves, fresh or frozen and thawed (16 double leaves)

4 long bamboo skewers, soaked in water

These are so delicious! You can leave out the chilli if you prefer – they still work really well. Ideal hot or cold as a *mezze* dish, starter, snack or spicy picnic addition.

Lime leaves are commonly used in Thai, Indonesian, Cambodian, Malaysian and Vietnamese cooking and can be sourced in frozen form quite easily from Asian stores. They impart a very distinct citrus note unlike any other ingredient I know – just their aroma makes me hungry.

Inevitably, lemongrass goes very well with them, but the sweetness of roasted carrot and the slightly bready caraway seeds just make this irresistible. The leaves are double-shaped, making them perfect to wrap around things for cooking. Otherwise, wrap a large single leaf around each carrot piece. You don't eat the leaves by the way...but you knew that, right?

❋ Parboil the carrots in lightly salted boiling water for 10 minutes. While the carrots are cooking, make the marinade by combining the oil, chilli, caraway seeds, turmeric and salt and pepper.

Drain the carrots and add to the marinade and allow to sit for 10–15 minutes, tossing them around occasionally.

Wrap each carrot piece between a lime leaf and skewer – repeat till you have skewered all the carrot pieces equally between the four bamboo skewers.

Lay the skewers across a small roasting dish so the carrot pieces are suspended. Drizzle with the remaining marinade and roast for 20–25 minutes at 200°C (400°F) or until tender and lightly charred.

Brunches and Lunches and Picnics

I absolutely adore eating outside. It really has to be abroad, though – not because of any foodie snobbery, but simply because, sadly, I have never outgrown my childhood phobia of wasps (another unwanted primary school experience, at the will of an overtly disciplinarian school mistress – and a little more serious than badly over-boiled butter beans). Oh well – they say talking about these things is good for the soul.

I tried eating outside again at home recently only to discover I was sitting over a small wasps' nest, which explained the relentless attention two were paying me. For years, I believed that if you opened up a nest, you'd see a 'wanted' picture of me inside.

Happily, my fear abates to mild apprehension in most other countries, so eating outside is still a wonderful pleasure whether it is brunch, lunch or an impromptu picnic. I do think people worry too much about what goes with what, though – the best picnic I have ever had was an eclectic spread of delicious items bought from a wonderful delicatessen in the Cotswolds. I just bought a bundle of things I liked the look and sound of and we ate them in no particular order sitting outside Longborough Opera House during the interval of *Le Nozze di Figaro*, miraculously undisturbed by insects of any kind.

I'm not an opera expert in any way, but I do love great live music and the atmosphere it generates. You really do know when you're properly relaxed – time seems to be on your side and any food involved tastes even better. All my senses seem to work in unison to record the experience in high definition, and I never struggle to recall the memories.

Like so many things now in modern life, food is a very emotive subject and I realise not everyone has the time to constantly stop and 'smell the strawberries', but I believe with a little effort and a little more attention to our senses we can all benefit.

So, where and when you can, enjoy these recipes as much as you can. Allow your senses to work overtime...and not work overtime out of your senses!

Alison's Breakfast Avocado

with Orange Pepper Seasoning and 'Green' Tabasco Dressing on Toasted Porridge Bread

Serves 4

2 tbsp lime juice

1 tsp green jalapeño Tabasco

2 tbsp extra virgin olive oil

½ tsp sea salt

2 ripe avocados

4 slices My 'Isle of Skye' Porridge Bread (page 256)

1 tsp orange pepper seasoning

The breakfast world is split, I think. There are those who habitually and happily eat the same breakfast every morning, and then there are those of us who need constant change and choice. I am without doubt a member of the latter camp, but I do have regular favourites. I'm willing to bet that avocado isn't on most people's breakfast list, but having had this one Sunday morning, it's absolutely on mine now. Green Tabasco is a milder jalapeño chilli pepper sauce that goes perfectly with the creamy soft texture and flavour of avocado – leave it out if a little chilli in the morning isn't your thing, but I recommend that you give it a go!

❋ Whisk the lime juice, green Tabasco, olive oil and salt together to create the dressing. Peel and cut each avocado into 8 slices and immediately coat with the dressing to prevent discolouration. Toast four thick slices of porridge bread and top with equal portions of the avocado quarters. Sprinkle each with orange pepper seasoning and serve.

Black Kale Bubble and Squeak

Serves 4–6

750g (1½lb) potatoes (Maris Piper, King Edward or similar), quartered, skin on

5–6 large cavolo nero leaves, stalks removed and roughly chopped

1 medium onion, chopped

1 tbsp dairy-free butter

1–2 tsp mild curry powder mix (see page 280)

½ tsp freshly ground black pepper

sea salt to taste

Tabasco sauce (optional)

Bubble and squeak is a favourite comfort food for many people, and especially for Sunday brunch. On a Saturday night when we have friends over, I will very often do the cooking – which usually includes some Saturday afternoon 'seeking solace' preparation time in the kitchen and some playing of favourite vinyl through the evening. When Sunday morning comes round, with a few 'delicate heads' about, Alison often takes over the kitchen to provide us all with some restorative breakfast/brunch. I pick the cavolo nero from the garden and prepare it, then get out of her way!

The dark cavolo nero provides just the right texture and inky taste against the sweet waxy potato and soft curried spice notes. Staying up late with friends and listening to old vinyl is completely optional though!

❉ Cook the potatoes in lightly salted water until tender but not falling apart, then drain and allow to steam off until cool enough to peel (it's a good idea to do this part the day before).

Cook the cavolo nero in lightly salted water for 5–6 minutes and drain well.

Fry the chopped onions in the dairy-free butter for 5 minutes before adding the curry powder and cooking for a further 2 minutes. Now add the cavolo nero and continue frying everything together for a further 5–6 minutes. A little colouring on the cavolo nero is a good thing.

Crush the peeled potatoes but don't mash them. Add a second knob of dairy-free butter to the pan and add the potatoes, stirring as you fry for a further 2–3 minutes.

Now flatten everything down in the pan with a spatula and gently brown the bubble and squeak on one side before turning and browning the other side. Take care here not to overdo it – you just want a nice fried edge to all the cooked ingredients and for everything to be piping hot throughout before serving.

Like me, you might want a wee dash or two of Tabasco sauce on yours...but that is *very* optional!

Fennel Vichyssoise

with White Grapes and Dill Oil

Serves 4

2 large fennel bulbs, trimmed

1 large onion

3 medium-large potatoes, peeled

30g (¼ cup) dairy-free butter

1 tsp olive oil

1 litre (4 cups) good-quality vegetable stock

sea salt

white pepper

2 tbsp Pernod

50ml (¼ cup) dairy-free cream (optional)

handful of white seedless grapes

dill oil (page 285)

Vichyssoise is a classic French soup traditionally served cold. Needless to say, it's most delicious on hot summer days when its cooling influence has greatest effect. It's another example of a world-famous dish that can rely entirely on plant ingredients – you only need to adapt the cream you are using (if you're using it at all).

I first experienced this, not surprisingly, in France. Not, though, in a fine-dining city restaurant but in Terminal 2 of Charles De Gaulle Airport. With hours to wait for our connecting flight, we walked almost the entire length of the sweltering airport looking for something more appealing to eat than fast food and found a French brasserie* serving classic French fare – and doing very well out of a long lunchtime. We waited for a table and were seated by our waiter, who subsequently brought food fit for any Parisian restaurant.

It was like an oasis in the desert – and this recipe is my memory of my first course, albeit slightly embellished with grapes and a little dill oil.

❋ Slice the fennel, onion and potatoes thinly on a mandolin or with a sharp knife. Melt the butter and olive oil together in a large pan, add the fennel and onion, and gently cook down for 10–15 minutes until soft and only just colouring. Add the potato and stock, bring to the boil, then reduce the heat and cook for a further 30 minutes. Remove from the heat, check for seasoning and add a little sea salt if required plus a little white pepper. Add the Pernod and stir through, before allowing to cool. Blend the soup and pass through a fine sieve, pushing it gently through with a ladle. Allow to cool completely before covering and refrigerating. Serve well chilled (cream stirred through if using) with a few halved white grapes in the centre and dots of dill oil.

It's called Brasserie Flo.

Carpaccio of Beetroot and Kohlrabi

with White Truffle Oil, Crisp Fried Capers and Dill

Serves 4

1 tbsp salted capers, rinsed and dried

olive oil

1 medium raw beetroot, trimmed but not peeled

sea salt

1 small raw kohlrabi, trimmed and peeled

1 tbsp white truffle oil

1 tbsp dill, roughly chopped

squeeze of lemon juice

OK, first off, you will need a mandolin for this as the kohlrabi really needs to be paper-thin. Too thick and it loses its delicate raw appeal – too few neat circles and it looks untidy. This is a slightly chefy dish, but it does deliver flavour and style as a perfect formal first course or summer lunch in the garden with a glass of chilled white wine. In particular, the dark sweet flavour of the roasted beetroot contrasting with the bright raw earthiness of the kohlrabi is delicious, and the fried capers are a little addictive too.

❋ Fry off the capers in a little olive oil in a pan for about 3–4 minutes until crisp and slightly puffed up. Set aside to cool.

Trim the beetroot of stalks and root. Wash and coat with a little olive oil and a pinch of sea salt before roasting in a hot oven at 200°C (400°F) for about an hour until the beetroot is only just tender in the middle. Set aside to cool completely. Using a mandolin, slice the kohlrabi into fine paper-thin slices and set aside. Once the beetroot has cooled, peel the skin off, leaving the beetroot as 'barrel-shaped' as you can – it will look less edgy in the final dish.

Very carefully, slice the beetroot on the mandolin or with a sharp knife to achieve thin discs but not as paper-thin as the kohlrabi. Layer the beetroot discs around the outside of your serving plate, followed by the kohlrabi discs in the centre. Wash your hands between discs or you will stain the kohlrabi. Drizzle with white truffle oil and scatter with the fried capers and fresh dill. Just before serving, squeeze a little lemon juice over the dish.

Freekeh and Fresh Herb Salad

Serves 2

200g (1 cup) freekeh

1 tsp sea salt

3 spring onions, finely sliced

equal amounts of chopped coriander, mint and flat-leaf parsley (approximately 50g/2oz each)

100g (½ cup) pistachios, shelled and coarsely chopped

seeds of 1 ripe pomegranate

1 tsp sumac

½ tsp orange pepper seasoning

For the dressing

1 tbsp pomegranate molasses

4 tbsp extra virgin olive oil

sea salt to taste

For those who haven't yet discovered freekeh, it's sun-dried green wheat with a wonderful texture that's enhanced by fresh vibrant flavours such as mint and pomegranate. It must be one of the healthiest comfort foods, and has the ability to convert the hardiest of the 'anti-green food' brigade.

As with many recipes, you can adjust the level of some of the ingredients to suit your taste – up the pistachios a little, down the mint a little – but be mindful not to swamp the freekeh. It makes a really satisfying work-day lunch if you have time to put it together in the morning, but it's really best freshly made and served as a stand-out part of a *mezze* or weekend lunch, perhaps with some additional roasted vegetables.

�֍ Cook the freekeh according to the packet instructions – approximately 14 minutes. Drain and cool.

Combine with the remaining ingredients, reserving a few pistachios. Whisk the dressing ingredients together and mix gently through the freekeh. Top with the reserved pistachios.

Gentle Indian Soup

Serves 4

1 small butternut squash, peeled and cut into 2cm (1 inch) dice

1 courgette, sliced into ½cm (¼ inch) discs

2 tsp olive oil

sea salt

1 onion, roughly chopped

1 tsp vegetable ghee or olive oil

1 garlic clove, chopped

1 handful of curry leaves

1 litre (4 cups) vegetable stock

2 tbsp finely chopped coriander stalks

1 x 400g (15oz) tin of chickpeas, drained and rinsed

1 tsp ground Keralan green peppercorns or ground black pepper

2 tsp dried fenugreek leaves

½ tsp turmeric

fresh coriander leaves

I believe it's true to say that most Indian food does not actually require chilli heat or dominant spicing. It's really more common to eat mildly spiced dishes that are balanced for flavour and to suit the ingredients, especially in Northern India. Many of us, including me, still make and adore curries on the hotter side of the scale, but I have learned over the years to appreciate the subtlety of Indian spicing. It's a wonderful cuisine which the word 'curry' doesn't even begin to explore.

The only Indian spices I am using here are turmeric, fenugreek leaves and some curry leaves. To increase the authenticity of the flavour, I've also used Keralan green peppercorns (which are really not that difficult to get now), but that's the limit of my heat spicing here. I genuinely feel very strongly about peppercorns – we just don't give the varieties and their unique flavours enough consideration or recognition.

❋ Coat the squash and courgette in 2 tsp of olive oil and a little sea salt, and roast in the oven at 200°C (400°F) for 10 minutes or so. Remove the courgettes and continue roasting the squash for a further 10 minutes until just tender.

While the vegetables are roasting, gently fry the onion in a little vegetable ghee or olive oil for 10 minutes until soft and translucent, adding the garlic and curry leaves halfway through. Add the stock, chopped coriander stalks and half the chickpeas, bring to the boil briefly and reduce the heat to simmer while the vegetables finish roasting. Once ready, add the courgette and squash, retaining eight larger pieces of each for later, followed by the Keralan pepper, fenugreek and turmeric. Leave to simmer for 10 minutes. Blend the soup and check for seasoning.

Warm four attractive soup bowls and place two pieces of squash and courgette in each bowl followed by the remaining chickpeas shared equally, then ladle the hot soup in on top. Finish with chopped fresh coriander leaves.

It's impossible to condense the history of the spice trade and its effect on the modern world today into a few simple sentences. It's an extraordinary history of what was, in its day, the world's biggest industry, responsible for both the creation and destruction of empires and the discovery of continents. Spices that are widely available and inexpensive today were once the reserve of the privileged and generated immense personal wealth for those who governed them. Many spices were even used as currency. There is a story of 16th-century London dockers being paid their bonuses in 'cloves'. Can you imagine it?

Sardinian Fregola

with Zucchini, Mixed Tomatoes and Gordal Olives

Serves 2 generously

200g (1 cup) Sardinian fregola

1 tbsp olive oil

1 medium pink onion (or red), cut into 1.5cm (½ inch) dice

1 romano pepper, deseeded and cut into 1.5cm (½ inch) dice

1 clove garlic, crushed

1 tsp oregano

1 courgette, cut into 1.5cm (½ inch) dice

handful of fresh basil leaves, chopped

handful of fresh mint leaves, chopped (reserve a few for finishing)

handful of pitted gordal olives, sliced widthways

handful of mixed-colour baby tomatoes, halved

pinch of chipotle salt or chilli salt

pinch of freshly ground tellicherry peppercorns

squeeze of lemon juice (optional)

Fregola is a large couscous-like pasta originating from Sardinia, made typically from semolina dough and toasted in an oven. Like most pasta or pasta-orientated products, it's a vehicle for flavour and needs good ingredients to accompany it – and I'm willing to guess its tiny pearls of pasta texture might not appeal to everyone as it has quite a different mouth-feel, but pair it with contrasting textures and fresh flavours as I have here, and it makes a wonderful hot (or cold) salad. Texture, as I've said before, is very important in food – more than I think a lot of people realise.

❊ Cook the fregola in lightly salted water for 10–12 minutes or according to the packet. Drain and mix a little oil into the fregola to keep it loose. Set aside.

Heat the olive oil in a high-sided frying pan and add the onion and romano pepper. Cook for approximately 10 minutes on a medium heat before adding the garlic, oregano and courgette, and continue to fry gently until the courgette has some colour and is tender but holding its shape. You need the vegetables to have texture or the dish will lose its appeal.

Add the fregola and combine with the vegetables for 5 minutes to coat with the pan flavours and heat the fregola. Add the chopped herbs and olives and stir through. Remove from the heat and serve in wide pasta bowls topped with the tomato halves and seasoned with the chipotle salt and tellicherry pepper and a few chopped mint leaves, drizzled with a touch of your best olive oil. A squeeze of fresh lemon juice isn't a bad alternative here to salt if you're salt-conscious, or even if you just want to add it.

Dishes like these rely particularly on the flavour and quality of the vegetables you use – this is not a dish to 'use up' courgettes and tomatoes that have been around for a while.

If you can't get gordal olives, then good-quality large green olives will be fine, but I urge you to seek out the gordal ones – they are out there and they are wonderful.

Gigantes Plaki

with Moroccan 'Vichy' Carrots

Serves 2

For the gigantes beans

1 large onion, finely chopped

100ml (⅓ cup) extra virgin olive oil

2 garlic cloves, finely sliced

2 tsp tomato purée, mixed with a little water

1 x 400g (15oz) tin of chopped tomatoes

small handful of flat-leaf parsley, chopped

1 tbsp throubi (summer savory)

2 x 400g (15oz) tins of butter beans, drained and rinsed

For the Moroccan carrots

1 large carrot, peeled

200ml (1 cup) water

30g (¼ cup) dairy-free butter

2 tsp sugar

1 tbsp pomegranate molasses

1 tsp black peppercorns

1 tbsp oregano

1 tsp orange pepper seasoning

½ tsp sea salt

To serve

a little chopped parsley

a piece of thick bread, toasted, from which to cut a crouton shape

Greece > meets Morocco > meets France.

Gigantes Plaki or Gigandes Plaki, better known to us perhaps as giant baked beans (*gigantes* is from the Greek word for giant), is a popular Greek dish of white beans cooked in tomato sauce. Vichy is a classic French way of cooking carrots that lends itself to a multitude of other ingredients because it imparts flavour as it poaches – in this case, some favourite flavours from across the Mediterranean Sea in Morocco.

It took me a very long time to try butter beans again after my first experience of them in a miserable primary school dinner – boiled white butter beans with an indiscriminate white fish in a starchy white tasteless sauce served with what seemed like, at the time, a side order of extra fish bones! It would be unthinkable to offer that to seven-year-olds now. I can still picture the plate (pale hospital green) and where I was sitting in the school dining hall – sadly, not every food memory etched into me is a wonderful one!

✱ Sauté the onion in a pan with some of the olive oil on a medium-low heat for about 10 minutes until softened but not browning. Add the sliced garlic and cook for 1–2 minutes before adding the diluted tomato purée, chopped tinned tomatoes, half the parsley and the throubi. Cook for a further 10–15 minutes adding a little extra olive oil occasionally. Don't allow the sauce to dry out – add a little water if necessary.

Add the drained beans and gently combine through the sauce, heating through for a further 5 minutes. Finish by adding the remaining chopped parsley and the remaining olive oil. Season with sea salt to taste and keep warm for the flavours to infuse until ready to serve. Both the beans and sauce should have a slightly oily edge to them, hence the need to use an extra virgin olive oil here.

Gently scrub the carrot with a clean scourer to remove the peeler edges – it creates a better finished dish but it's not essential. Slice the carrot widthways at a diagonal angle into large

pieces about 2–3cm long and then halve these lengthways. You should have a diamond-like shape on the inner flat side.

Combine all the other Moroccan carrot ingredients in a pan and heat through to dissolve the sugar and amalgamate the pomegranate molasses.

Add the carrots to the poaching liquid and bring to the boil before reducing to simmer for

15–20 minutes until the carrots are just tender – you need a little bite to the carrots as the beans are quite soft and you want some contrast in texture.

Once ready, remove the carrots from the poaching liquid and serve on top of the hot beans with a little chopped parsley and a large crouton – the shape of which I leave entirely to you.

Isabella Panzanella

(Melon and Tomato Bread Salad)

with Prosecco-Soaked Caperberries and Isabella Basil

Serves 4–6

handful of caperberries, drained and rinsed

glass of Prosecco

½ gala melon

3 medium red tomatoes, each cut into 6 irregular-shaped pieces

3 small yellow tomatoes, halved

3 small green tomatoes, halved

1 tsp sea salt

2 tsp orange vinegar or red wine vinegar

½ loaf of ciabatta bread, torn into large bite-size pieces (stale bread if you have some left over is ideal)

large handful of fresh basil leaves – Isabella basil if you can get it

It's a slightly crazy world we live in now, isn't it? Many years ago the less financially fortunate of our Italian cousins would seek to make a simple meal from leftover stale bread by adding a few cheap and available ingredients in order to make something from very little. Did they know it was delicious or was it just necessity – the mother of invention, as they say? They were Italians...I think they knew!

And now we actually make stale bread, so we can replicate what they made from leftovers... Such are many of the world's great dishes – a derivation of circumstance or financial necessity. We could learn a lot from them today, I'm sure!

I have used the branded 'Isabella' basil here because of its particular intensity of aroma – a cultivation of herb crafted for a certain UK supermarket which I think is a worthy story in itself.

❋ Soak the caperberries in the glass of Prosecco for as long as you can – overnight or at least 2–3 hours. You can buy them already in Prosecco – if you can find them.

Cut the melon half into wedges, removing the seeds as you go. Remove the skin and dice the flesh into similar-sized pieces as the red tomatoes. In a bowl, combine all the tomatoes and the melon along with the sea salt and vinegar. Mix through very gently and leave to one side to allow the flavours to marry together. If you have bought fresh bread for the recipe, then you will need to dry it out. Place the torn pieces on a baking tray in a medium-hot oven for 10–15 minutes until the bread is dried out but not completely toasted. Allow to cool while the tomatoes and melon continue to marinate. Stir them through and check for seasoning – you can add a little ground pepper if you like.

Finally, add everything together in a large attractive serving bowl and gently turn over to allow the juices to coat the bread and the basil leaves to spread through the salad. Serve.

The story of Isabella and the basil pot

In Italy, basil was regarded as a token of love. This theme is explored in Keats' writings, when he tells Boccaccio's tale of 'Isabella, or the Pot of Basil'. This story was part of the Decameron, a mediaeval allegory set in Italy at the time of the Black Death. Keats' adaptation tells the story of Isabella, whose family was planning her marriage to 'some high noble and his olive trees', but she falls in love with Lorenzo, who works for her brothers. When the brothers learn of this, they murder Lorenzo. However, his ghost speaks to Isabella in a dream, so she exhumes his body, and his head is planted in a pot of basil. Isabella tends this pot, as she pines away. As well as the representation of love, this also associates basil with final resting places.

Taken from Fragrance and Wellbeing by Jennifer Peace Rhind (2014).

Smoky Tomato Soup

with Cavolo Nero and Butter Beans

Serves 4

1 tbsp olive oil

1 small onion, roughly chopped

800ml (3 cups) vegetable stock

2 x 400g (15oz) tins of tomatoes

1 x 400g (15oz) tin of butter beans, drained and rinsed

5 or 6 cavolo nero leaves, stems removed and roughly chopped, or kale

sea salt and pepper (orange pepper if you have it)

handful of basil leaves

smoked extra virgin olive oil

This soup recipe is simple and uncomplicated, but I found that I really liked the layered textures and fresh taste compared with some heavier, more complex soups – a place for everything, as they say.

It came about, like many good recipes do, from a wish to elevate something more ordinary to something more 'substantial'. The texture is very satisfying and the flavour is clean and appealing – and it's a little effort plus a little thought. The last touch of smoked olive oil just adds a subtle depth of aroma and taste and demonstrates a little further attention to detail.

✽ Gently fry the onion in the olive oil until translucent and add the stock. Cook on a medium heat for 5 minutes and then add the tomatoes. Bring to the boil, then reduce to a simmer for 10 minutes. Briefly pulse the soup with a hand blender (approximately 5–10 seconds – this will add a little body to the soup, but you want to keep most of the chopped tomato), then add the beans and chopped cavolo nero. Cook for a further 5–10 minutes to cook the cavolo nero. Now season with salt and pepper to taste. Serve with torn basil leaves, a good drizzle of smoked olive oil on top and some good bread on the side.

Cavolo nero – I have a real love of this inky green member of the kale family. It's often found under aliases such as Italian kale or black kale, but whatever it's being called, it's truly delicious. It's also very, very easy to grow and returns many months of harvest – even in the colder months.

Cannellini Bean and Green Bean Warm Salad

with Harissa Dressing

Serves 2

Dressing

1 tsp fresh harissa (page 260)

2 tbsp extra virgin olive oil

1 tsp orange vinegar

pinch of caster sugar

1 x 400g (15oz) tin of good-quality cannellini beans, drained and rinsed

100g (4oz) packet green beans, trimmed

approximately 12 sweet mixed baby tomatoes, halved

sea salt

black pepper

This is a perfect dish when you don't want to compromise on freshness and flavour, but you have limited time. It can be assembled in 20 minutes or so and will leave you with both the satisfaction of eating well and, perhaps just as importantly, the feeling you didn't give in to something quick but much less rewarding.

✿ In a bowl, combine all the dressing ingredients and whisk together. Check for seasoning and set aside.

Place the drained and rinsed cannellini beans in a clean bowl. Cook the green beans in lightly salted water for 4–5 minutes. Once the green beans are done, drain them over the cannellini beans so the hot cooking water covers the cannellini beans and heats them through for a minute or two, returning the green beans to the pan to stay warm.

Drain the cannellini beans and divide between two warm pasta bowls. Arrange the warm green beans on top. Scatter mixed tomato halves in both bowls and drizzle each serving with the dressing. Add a pinch of sea salt and a grind of good black pepper and serve. It's a dish that's actually better warm than hot and would even serve well cold – in a picnic, for example.

Orecchiette con Pangrattato

(Pasta with Flavoured Breadcrumbs)

Serves 2

handful of coarse breadcrumbs

1 garlic clove, finely chopped

grated zest of ½ lemon

chilli flakes (optional)

1 tsp thyme leaves

sea salt

freshly ground black pepper
(tellicherry)

200g (2 cups) orecchiette

your best extra virgin olive oil
for drizzling

Orecchiette – or 'little ears' as the name translates – is a
wonderfully versatile pasta that 'cups' flavour within its shape and
helps deliver perfect mouthfuls every time. Do buy the best quality
you can find, and that means 'bronze die', as I find cheaper versions
can be particularly disappointing.

Pangrattato is simply flavoured Italian breadcrumbs, often
referred to as 'poor man's parmesan' as they were commonly used
in place of the cheese when it was unavailable or, more likely,
unaffordable.

This is a very easy, quick and satisfying dish where the pasta
is given flavour, texture and seasoning – all from the pangrattato.
You can, of course, embellish it by adding some peas, broccoli or
asparagus, which would be delicious, but do try the poor man's
version first and spare a thought for the ingenuity of those who
had much less than we do now.

❁ Mix the breadcrumbs with the chopped garlic and toast them
in a hot oven for 4–5 minutes until crisp and golden brown. Once
cooled a little, combine the toasted crumbs with the lemon zest,
chilli flakes and thyme leaves, and season with sea salt and the
black pepper. Set aside.

Cook the orecchiette according to the packet instructions in
lightly salted water. It should require approximately 10–11 minutes
and still retain some good texture.

Divide the orecchiette into warmed pasta bowls and scatter
each bowl with the pangrattato. Drizzle with a little extra virgin
olive oil and serve.

*It's wonderful how far the world
of food has travelled, but just
occasionally it's very rewarding to
sit down and be humble.*

Ribollita

(Tuscan Peasant Soup of Cannellini Beans, Cavolo Nero and Bread)

Serves 4

2 tbsp extra virgin olive oil

1 medium onion, chopped

1 carrot, diced

1 small fennel bulb, diced

3–4 garlic cloves, finely chopped

2 tsp sea salt flakes

2 tsp freshly ground peppercorns

½ tsp chilli flakes

3 small tomatoes, chopped

½ glass of white wine (optional)

200g (½lb) bunch cavolo nero, stalks removed and roughly chopped

1 litre (4 cups) good-quality vegetable stock

1 tsp porcini powder (optional)

400g (15oz) tin of cannellini beans, rinsed and drained

1 tbsp lemon and thyme oil (see below)

Note – I specifically listed tinned beans here because I felt they suited better. If you think about it – they are in keeping with the 'reboiled' tradition of the soup.

I have been fortunate enough to visit Italy on many occasions and I've come away with the same notion every time. The Italians really do know food. They adore food and have an astonishing respect for it. In particular, they respect *all food* and therefore inevitably plant-based dishes are everywhere by default. They are there because they are great dishes and everyone and anyone orders them. I find the same, if not more so, with traditional Indian food.

Cavolo nero is a particular favourite of mine. Black cabbage, by literal translation, has a beautifully strong texture, robust colour and wonderful flavour, making it perfect to accompany the white beans here.

I'm almost tempted to call this a stew as it's quite a hearty and filling soup, but soup by tradition it is. Use your best extra virgin olive oil here and the best bread you can find to eat with it – preferably homemade.

❋ To make the soup

Heat 1 tbsp of olive oil in a large pot – big enough to accommodate the stock and bulk ingredients you're using. Fry the chopped onion, diced carrot and fennel with the garlic, salt, pepper and chilli flakes until the vegetables are translucent and softened. Add the tomatoes and the wine and continue to cook for 2–3 minutes before adding the cavolo nero. Stir together. Now add the stock and the porcini powder and bring to the boil before decreasing the heat and simmering. Separate about a quarter of the beans and mash them up a little – this will act to help thicken the soup when you add them and create a slightly silky stock. Add the beans along with the mashed ones and stir through. Leave to simmer for 10 minutes to allow the beans to warm through and for all the flavours to marry well. Serve in individual bowls topped with small pieces of rustic broken bread and drizzled with the lemon and thyme oil.

To make the lemon and thyme oil

Place 3–4 sprigs of thyme and the zest of a small lemon in 150ml (5fl oz) of extra virgin olive oil. Heat through gently for 5 minutes and then leave to cool completely. Remove the thyme, refrigerate and use within 1–2 weeks.

Most food, if not all, has a history, but none more so than peasant food and often none more delicious!

Ribollita (literally translated as 'reboiled') is a famous Tuscan soup made with bread and vegetables. There are without doubt many variations, but the main ingredients always include leftover bread and beans and vegetables such as cabbage, kale, carrots and onion.

Like much of Tuscan cuisine, the soup has peasant origins, stemming from the reboiling of leftover minestrone or vegetable soup from the day before. It is suggested that it originated in the Middle Ages when servants may have gathered up other people's discarded food-soaked 'trenchers' (bowls made from bread) and recooked them for their own meal.

It makes you very grateful for a few beans and some 'fresh' bread and vegetables of your own now, doesn't it?

Zita 'Puttanesca'

with Seared Aubergine and Sorrento Lemon

Serves 2 generously

1 large aubergine, cut lengthways into approximately 6 thin slices

3 tbsp olive oil

250g (9oz) zita (No. 18) pasta, or alternatively a long pasta such as bucatini

2 cloves garlic, finely chopped

300g (1¼ cups) 'Mutti' Datterini tomato passata or other good-quality passata

pinch of chilli flakes

2 tsp salted capers, rinsed of excess salt

1 tsp dried oregano

70g (½ cup) pitted black olives

a little freshly ground black pepper

small handful of fresh flat-leaf parsley, chopped

a Sorrento lemon – but other lemons will suffice

If you don't already know what *puttanesca* in the name of this pasta dish refers to, then let me gently enlighten you. It is said to refer to the ladies of the night – the working girls – the oldest trade in the world – who required something simple, quick and inexpensive to make between 'clients'.

Whatever its history, this is a great-tasting pasta dish that anyone can enjoy and one that can rely solely on store cupboard ingredients, plus or minus what you have available. Hence my addition of seared aubergine. It's also quite common to use anchovies in this dish, although I've discovered that's not the case everywhere – in and around Naples, for example. So the Naples version it is, which sits very neatly with the historically Neapolitan 'zita' pasta.

You could be fanciful and cook down fresh plum tomatoes instead of using passata to make the sauce, but really its heritage is a dish of little fuss, and after all that's what passata is for, isn't it?

❉ First brush the aubergine slices with olive oil on both sides before searing on a hot griddle for 2 minutes each side to get good distinct bar marks. Remove and set aside.

Set the pasta to cook in lightly salted boiling water, giving it the full designated cooking time on the packet as this is one pasta you don't really want too al dente. It should be about 10 minutes, but equally take care not to *over*cook it.

Meanwhile, gently heat 2 tbsp of the olive oil in a wide saucepan with high sides and sauté the garlic for a minute without browning, before adding the passata, chilli, capers, oregano, olives and black pepper.

Cook everything through on a medium heat until the pasta is ready. If the sauce begins to look too dry, simply add a splash of water to loosen it up. I always find it useful to add a little water to any empty passata jar or tomato tin and swill it around to catch any remaining tomato sauce and form a sort of weak tomato water.

Check for seasoning and add salt or additional pepper if you require, but remember the capers were salted. Add the last tbsp of olive oil and stir through.

Drain the pasta as soon as it's ready and add to the sauce in the pan, gently folding through to coat the pasta generously while still on the heat.

Slice each piece of seared aubergine into three strips and gently fold them through the dish before serving, scattered with chopped parsley and a final brief squeeze of Sorrento lemon...or the best lemon you can find.

Roasted Kuri Squash and Coriander Soup

with Ginger and Pumpkin Seed Oil

Serves 4

1 whole kuri squash, approximately 1kg (2lb)

unflavoured rapeseed oil

1 tsp caraway seeds

sea salt and black pepper

1 tbsp ginger-infused rapeseed oil or oil with ½ tsp ginger paste added

1 shallot, chopped

2–3 tbsp finely chopped coriander stalks

800ml (3 cups) vegetable stock

pumpkin seed oil to finish

ginger-infused rapeseed oil to finish

Everyone makes soup with squash, so I know I'm not revolutionising cooking here. But take the time to find kuri squash and you will be rewarded. I bought it by happy accident at a local market, attracted by its vibrant colour and manageable size.

I have purposely kept the ingredients simple, purposefully avoiding chilli or garlic because when I tasted the roasted squash I felt it was quite rightly the star and only required complementing rather than accompanying. The caraway seeds add a comforting bready note, while the ginger in the oil gives a sense of depth and warmth. Be very sparing with any pumpkin seed oil – it's visually wonderful and adds a truly interesting flavour contrast, but it's a powerful flavour so less is definitely more.

✿ Preheat the oven to 220°C (425°F). Cut the squash into quarters and remove all seeds. Quarter each of the four pieces into wedges – you should now have 16 roughly equal wedges. Coat all the wedges with a little unflavoured rapeseed oil and arrange on a roasting tray. Sprinkle the caraway seeds over each wedge, season with sea salt and freshly ground black pepper, and roast in the oven for 20–25 minutes until soft and colouring at the edges.

On a medium heat, gently fry the shallots in the ginger oil for 5–10 minutes until softened and add the chopped coriander stalks and vegetable stock. Bring to the boil and turn down the heat to a simmer.

Once the squash is ready and cooled a little – remove the skin and break the roasted squash wedges into the stock. Stir through on a low heat for 5 minutes before carefully blending with a hand blender. Check the seasoning and adjust if required with sea salt and ground black pepper.

Pour into bowls and finish with a final drizzle of ginger oil and *a few drops* of pumpkin oil.

Marrow Boat to France

Serves 4

Ratatouille with Black Garlic (page 206)

1 marrow

basil-infused rapeseed oil

sea salt

freshly ground black pepper

20g (approximately ¼ cup) toasted pine nuts

handful of basil leaves, shredded

An average marrow is not a small vegetable and can put people off using it...other than in soup maybe. So I devised this easy sharing dish and it really works. It's up to you what you serve it with – penne pasta, perhaps – but we ate it with fresh warm crusty bread and some good red wine. I filled this one with my Ratatouille with Black Garlic but go with what you have or want – it's a very simple idea, but the roasted marrow adds a really nice fresh and, more importantly, tasty vehicle to your choice. The recipe is probably best for four diners as each marrow half will serve two sharing; otherwise, the other half can be used for soup the next day, of course.

❀ Make the ratatouille.

Preheat the oven to 220°C (425°F). Carefully cut the marrow lengthways into equal halves. Remove all seeds from the middle. Rub the half you are using with basil oil, particularly on the inside flesh. Season with sea salt and black pepper and roast on a baking tray for 20–30 minutes until just beginning to colour and the flesh is tender when pierced with a sharp knife. Remove from the oven and place on a sharing plate. Fill with hot ratatouille and top with toasted pine nuts and shredded basil leaves before finishing with a last drizzle of the basil oil.

Pissaladière

For the green tapenade

70g (½ cup) green olives, pitted

30g (approximately ¼ cup) capers, rinsed

80ml (⅓ cup) olive oil

½ tbsp of fresh lemon juice

freshly ground black pepper

For the base

270g (1¼ cups) strong plain white flour

15g (1 tbsp) dried active yeast or 2 tsp easy blend yeast

1 tsp salt

250ml (1 cup) warm water

2 tsp olive oil or rapeseed oil

For the onions

4 tbsp olive oil or rapeseed oil

30g (¼ cup) dairy-free butter

1kg (2lb) white onions, peeled and sliced

pinch of sea salt

pinch of black pepper

1 tsp herbs de Provence or thyme

approximately 24 black olives, pitted

2 garlic cloves

It's worth taking time and great care over cooking the onions as they are a principal player here – so buy the best you can and be patient.

Pissaladière is historically from Nice in Southern France, most likely taking its etymology primarily from the 'salty fish' or anchovies that would traditionally be included – the very thing we're taking out...sorry France.

So, naturally this is an alternative pissaladière – but in the true nature of many recipes there is always room for adaptation, within reason – especially if the reason is a fundamental one – and tapenade is still very in keeping with Southern France.

Pissaladière is a great idea – lots of sweet slow-roasted onions with a contrasting salty punch and a wonderful texture underneath. I'll be honest – it beats a lot of pizza for me. The lattice effect adds a great 'visual bite' too.

✿ To make the green tapenade
Blend the green olives, capers, garlic and half the olive oil together to form a rough paste. Add the remaining olive oil, lemon juice and black pepper, and pulse again for a few moments to finish. You need a thickish blended style of mixture similar to pesto in order to pipe it on the pissaladière. Set aside. What you don't use is wonderful on toast!

To make the dough for the base
Mix the flour, yeast and salt in a bowl, forming a well in the centre. Pour in the water and olive oil and combine into a soft dough. Tip out onto a lightly floured surface and knead for 5–6 minutes to create a smooth, pliant dough. Place in a clean, well-oiled bowl and cover with oiled clingfilm in a warm place for approximately 1 hour or until doubled in size.

For the onions
Heat the olive oil and dairy-free butter on a low heat, then add the sliced onions, sea salt, ground pepper and herbs. Cover and cook them gently for approximately 40 minutes, stirring occasionally,

until really well softened. Uncover and continue to cook gently for 15–20 minutes, allowing the moisture to cook off and the onions to go golden and sweet. Set aside to cool.

Once the dough has risen, knock back and knead again for a few minutes. Roll it out into a rectangle approximately 25 × 35cm (10 × 14 inches) and place it on an oiled baking sheet. Spread the cooked onions over the dough, leaving a gap around the edge. Spoon or pipe the caper mix in thin diagonal lines criss-crossing the onions to form a wide lattice effect and dot the black olives in each small triangle you create. If you wish, season a little more with freshly ground pepper and leave to prove again for a further 20 minutes before baking in a hot oven, preheated to 220°C (425°F), for 15–20 minutes.

Serve warm, cut into squares.

All out of 'Waldorf' Salad

Serves 4

100g (approximately ½ cup) macadamia nuts

1 tbsp brown sugar

1 tbsp water

1 tbsp agave syrup

1 tbsp walnut oil

4–5 tbsp natural coconut milk yogurt

juice of ½ lemon

1 stick fresh celery, de-stringed

1 crisp fresh red apple

1 crisp fresh green apple

1 tsp cider vinegar

salt and pepper

1 gem lettuce – red gem if you can get it

Waldorf salad is further evidence of a worldwide classic dish that relies on plant ingredients. It's very common to take out the mayonnaise and replace it with yogurt, so there really is no tweaking to be done – it's just a matter of personal choice.

To that effect, I have used coconut yogurt let down with a little lemon juice, and opted for toasted macadamia nuts rather than walnuts, but you could use almost any nut or mix of nuts you fancy – the original walnuts are very good. In fact, if you check out the history of the dish below, you'll see that nuts themselves were actually a tweak to the original.

✻ Place the nuts on a tray and roast in the oven at 190°C (375°F) for 5–6 minutes until toasted. Combine the brown sugar, water, agave syrup and walnut oil in a warm pan, ensuring everything dissolves, and coat the warm nuts in the syrup mixture before returning to the oven for 2–3 minutes to set the glaze. Spread out on baking paper and allow to cool completely.

Combine the yogurt and lemon juice thoroughly.

Finely slice the celery crossways. Core and dice the red apple. Core, quarter and slice the green apple lengthways. Place them all in the yogurt to prevent the apples discolouring. Add the cider vinegar and a pinch of salt and pepper (not a strong pepper – tellicherry is fine here).

Combine the mixture well and chill until you are ready to add the cooled nuts. Add the nuts and mix through well. Lay out the gem lettuce leaves in a star shape on a large circular serving plate and build the salad in the centre. Serve immediately.

Advice on variation... You could use a crisp pear or other crisp fruit instead of the green apple – it's fine to peel the apples if you wish, but you'll lose colour in the finished dish. Use whatever roasted nuts you prefer (sweet-coated or not), but they should be of a reasonable size – walnut, peanut, cashew, hazelnut, almond – because you need a good crunch. Likewise with the salad leaves – they need a crisp texture, which is why the gem lettuce works so well.

The original Waldorf salad story...

*For those who didn't already know – including those
among you who have never had a Waldorf salad before,
or never needed to know what one was, or have never
watched* Fawlty Towers (*the well-known British TV sitcom
to which this dish owes its title*) *– this classic salad dish
was first presented at the Waldorf Hotel in New York
City between 1893 and 1896, prior to the hotel becoming
the Waldorf Astoria when it merged with its neighbour,*

*The Astoria, in 1897. The person credited as the creator
of the salad was Oscar Tschirky, the maître d'hôtel at the
time, who was also responsible for many of the hotel's
other dishes. First published in the cookbook* Oscar of the
Waldorf, *the original recipe list did not include nuts. They
didn't make an appearance until a publication in 1928.
Which means this salad was already on the go for several
years before my 'Papa' (my father's father) was even born!
And it's worth every printed word to publish again now.*

Petit Pois à la Française

Serves 4

4 spring onions

4 shallots

4 small gem lettuce

4 fresh prepared and cooked artichokes or artichoke hearts from a jar, drained of any oil

2 tbsp rapeseed oil

30g (¼ cup) dairy-free butter

1 clove garlic, sliced

750g (4 cups) fresh or frozen petit pois

120ml (½ cup) water

sea salt

½ tsp sugar

freshly ground black pepper

1 tbsp fresh mint or chervil, roughly

You might be drinking wine, but nobody's going to tell you that you aren't eating well.

There are some dishes that are, and always were, vegan-friendly anyway. Classic dishes that the world has loved without ever needing to classify – therefore creating 'classics'. A moment's work to adopt an alternative to the ubiquitous dairy butter and you're done. I have also included artichoke hearts because they work here, and I really enjoy them, but you can easily omit them if you wish. I know a lot of people who are content to eat artichokes, but almost nobody that ever serves them. They are perceived as a bit of a nuisance to prepare, and that's because they are, so you can use a quality brand of jarred if you like, but aim to use fresh when in season in spring/summer. Needless to say, do get the freshest peas and lettuce available – and the lettuce must be gem lettuce. For most of us, it's going to be good-quality frozen petit pois – but frozen peas are a success story.

✿ Trim and slice the spring onions at an angle into roughly 1cm-long pieces. Trim and peel the shallots and then halve them lengthways before cutting them lengthways again into long thick slices. Trim each lettuce by cutting the base away and, if necessary, removing the outer leaves. Now quarter each lettuce heart and quarter each artichoke heart, and set aside.

Combine the rapeseed oil and dairy-free butter in a large pan on a medium heat, add the shallots and gently cook to soften for 2–3 minutes but not to brown them. Add the sliced garlic for 1 minute followed by the peas, lettuce, spring onions, artichokes and the water. Stir through and add a little sea salt and the sugar and a good grinding of freshly ground black pepper. Stir through on the heat for 4–5 minutes and check for seasoning – it should now taste fresh and moreish with a slight sweet background note. Season to your taste, adding any of the herbs you wish. Serve with crusty French bread and, if you're like me, with a good red wine served in small old-fashioned 'French bistro' wine tumblers.

You Say Potato, I Say Tomato

Serves 4 as side dish or 2 as generous lunch or easy supper

For the red pepper paste

2–3 roasted red peppers from a jar

2 tsp tomato purée

½ tsp salt

1 tsp pul biber (Turkish red pepper flakes)

150ml (⅔ cup) olive oil

6–7 medium-sized waxy potatoes, approximately 800g (2lb)

4–5 best-quality medium-sized tomatoes, fairly ripe

4 tbsp rapeseed oil plus more to finish

handful of fresh flat-leaf parsley, chopped

pinch of crushed chilli seeds

1 garlic clove, crushed

squeeze of lemon juice

sea salt

freshly ground pepper

2 sprigs of rosemary

I created this thinking it would make a good side dish, but in fact it makes a great lunch dish or even a simple midweek supper. It looks really appetising because of the roasted overlapping tomatoes, which taste great because their wonderful ripe flavour has been concentrated in the oven, while the potatoes have naturally absorbed the combined elements of the dish, creating a real comforting texture. As foodies would say, this eats well.

❋ Make the red pepper paste by blending the roasted red peppers with the tomato purée, salt, *pul biber* and 150ml (⅔ cup) olive oil.

Preheat the oven to 220°C (425°F). Halve the potatoes and then boil them, skin on, in lightly salted water until just beginning to get tender (about 10–15 minutes). You don't want them to cook fully as you're going to cook them a little further with the tomatoes and you don't want them to fall apart. Once cool enough, either peel for a slightly more refined finish or not if it's just a rustic lunch – you decide. Slice them into roughly 5mm-thick discs and layer them in a lightly oiled dish such as a *cazuela*, as follows.

You ideally want three layers of the potato, and the tomatoes need to overlap and cover the top. Mix the oil, parsley, crushed chilli and garlic together and season with a little lemon juice and sea salt to create a dressing. Layer the potato, spreading 1 tbsp of the red pepper paste and 1 tbsp of dressing over each potato layer as you go, together with a brief grind of black pepper. Slice the tomatoes widthways approximately 5mm thick and layer them, overlapping, on top of the potatoes. Place the rosemary sprigs on top, followed by a good grind of fresh black pepper and a final sprinkle of sea salt. Pour the remaining dressing over the tomatoes and rosemary. Cover and bake in the oven for 20 minutes, then uncover and bake for a further 20 minutes until the tomatoes are beginning to darken around their roasted edges. Serve with some warm crusty bread and perhaps a glass of chilled good white wine.

Red Quinoa Bowl

with Butternut Squash, Toasted Cashews, Red Apple and Elderflower Curry Dressing

Serves 2

base of 1 butternut squash, peeled, hollowed and diced

1 tbsp ginger-flavoured rapeseed oil, or plain oil

sea salt

200g (1 cup) red quinoa

For the elderflower curry dressing

½ tsp mild curry powder (page 280)

1 tbsp cane vinegar or white wine vinegar

½ tbsp elderflower cordial

1 tbsp agave syrup

1½ tbsp extra virgin olive oil

pinch of sea salt

1 red apple

25g (¼ cup) toasted cashew nuts

1 tsp Keralan peppercorns, ground

4 lemon wedges

It's fair to say that quinoa hasn't commanded a lot of space at my dinner table. Like many people, I think I knew what it was, and that it had become a favourite with many of the particularly health-conscious among us, but I had never sought it out or cooked with it. I have to admit to probably being rather dismissive of it really – unjustified – but there you are. I think most of us are occasionally guilty of assuming we don't like something without ever trying it. What we actually do is box it away in our minds for future 'trial' and then never get it out. That same box can be happily broken open by a friend making it one day or ordering it at a restaurant and saying 'taste this'.

And so it was with red quinoa. I tasted a friend's lunch order some time ago and thought, oh, I do like that. You probably don't want to have lunch with me – I always want to taste everything.

✿ Coat the diced squash in the ginger oil and sea salt and roast on a roasting tray for 20–25 minutes at 200°C (400°F). You want just a little charring on the edges.

Prepare the quinoa according to your packet instructions and set aside to cool.

Combine the dressing ingredients and set aside to infuse well.

Once the squash has cooked and cooled slightly, core and dice the red apple and add to the cooled quinoa, along with the cooled squash, toasted cashew nuts and ground Keralan pepper. Mix through the dressing and gently stir to combine. Check for seasoning, adding a little salt if you wish. Serve with wedges of lemon.

How to speak Quinoa [Keen-Wha]

Quinoa is a more interesting product than you might think. First of all, it's not actually a grain you're eating – botanically speaking, it's a relative of spinach, beets and chard. We actually eat the seeds, which is why it's gluten-free. It's also a 'complete protein' due to the fact that it contains all nine essential amino acids that cannot be made by our bodies and which we therefore require from food. Impressed already, aren't you?

An Andean plant from South America, it was originally cultivated and used some 3000–4000 years ago before being somewhat sidelined by Spanish intervention in favour of cereals. There are over 100 varieties of quinoa, although the commercially available red, white and black are enough for most of us. It was celebrated with its own International Year of Quinoa in 2013 by the United Nations, and much deserved it was. Incidentally, as I write, we are currently in the International Year of Pulses. More silverware for the plant-based food trophy cabinet!

Black Venus Rice

with Tenderstem Broccoli, Toasted Almonds and Asian Dressing

Serves 2

100g (½ cup) black Venus rice

100g (4oz) packet tenderstem broccoli

For the dressing

1 tbsp sesame oil

2 tbsp good-quality soya sauce

1 tbsp rice vinegar

1 tsp rice mirin

1 small shallot, very finely sliced

2 tbsp rapeseed oil

1 clove garlic, sliced

red chilli, sliced diagonally and deseeded

handful of toasted flaked almonds

Black Venus rice was once cultivated for the sole use of Chinese emperors and the nobility, such was its high regard. I've even read that it was believed to have had aphrodisiac properties – hence the name Venus, Goddess of love...

It certainly has health properties, being higher in fibre, minerals and vitamins than many common rice varieties, and it boasts a fantastic nutty flavour. It will turn a rich purple colour when cooked, which looks quite striking on the plate with the right ingredients, but be patient – it does take 35–40 minutes to cook.

I wanted this dish to be fairly simple but also to show the rice as an equal and integral part of the flavours.

❋ Boil the black rice in lightly salted water for 35–40 minutes.

Meanwhile, prepare the broccoli by slicing each stem in half from top to bottom, creating twice the number of stems. Set aside.

Mix all the dressing ingredients together and whisk to combine. Set aside to infuse. When you come to use the dressing, you will be leaving most of the shallots behind.

Heat some rapeseed oil in a small frying pan and gently fry the garlic and chilli slices until the garlic begins to colour. Remove the chillies from the heat, placing them on a sheet of paper towel to drain and cool. Discard the garlic but keep the oil to use another day, perhaps as a spicy dressing.

Just before the rice is ready, blanch the broccoli stems in lightly salted boiling water for 4–5 minutes until tender but still retaining some bite. Drain the rice and the broccoli.

Serve immediately on warm plates, rice first, surrounded by layers of broccoli stems (broccoli heads to the centre), scattered toasted almond flakes and the chilli slices, drizzled with a few spoonfuls of the dressing, omitting the shallots. You can add a few thin shallot slices for additional texture and flavour, but don't serve too many or the onion flavour will overpower the dish.

Roasted Sweet Potatoes with Spiced Coconut Yogurt

Serves 2

2 medium-sized sweet potatoes

1 tsp olive oil

250g (1 cup) coconut milk yogurt

1 tsp fresh harissa (page 260)

freshly grated zest of 1 lime

pinch of sea salt

25g (approximately ¼ cup) ready-prepared mixed seed snack

handful of coriander leaves

freshly ground black pepper

You're thinking...ah, another baked potato dish! Stay with me, though... Don't just use potatoes here – it needs the sweetness of sweet potatoes to work. It's the sensory battle of sweet and spicy, combined with the cooling yogurt and contrasting crunch of the seeds that makes it all so enjoyable to eat. It's a great-tasting lunch that can be prepared while the potato is roasting. Again, you can adapt the spice in the yogurt to suit your chilli-meter, but you need at least enough to meet the sweetness of the roasted sweet potato.

✿ Preheat the oven to 200°C (400°F). Halve the sweet potatoes and rub all over with a little olive oil. Place on a baking tray and roast for 30–40 minutes until tender in the middle.

Meanwhile, prepare the other ingredients. Combine the coconut yogurt with the harissa and set aside. Chop the coriander leaves roughly and set aside.

Once the potato is ready, lay two halves per person on a plate and top with the harissa-flavoured coconut yogurt. Grate the fresh lime zest over along with a pinch of sea salt flakes. Sprinkle over with seed mix, coriander leaves and freshly ground black pepper.

Tomato, Orange, Harissa and Coriander Soup

Serves 4

1 tsp coriander seeds

1 onion, roughly chopped

handful of fresh coriander, chopped, and stalks finely chopped separately

500ml (2 cups) vegetable stock

juice of ½ small orange

1 tsp fresh harissa (page 260)

250ml (1 cup) chopped tinned tomatoes

250ml (1 cup) tomato passata

1 tsp orange pepper seasoning

1 tsp chilli salt

1 tbsp rapeseed oil

orange rapeseed oil to drizzle – if you have it

Soup is very versatile – everybody who likes soup knows that – but it's worth making the extra effort to lift great fresh flavours with the addition of some accessible but less common finishing touches. Here, the inclusion of orange pepper and the finishing with orange oil work particularly well because they are blind – by that I mean 'orange' is not visible in the soup, so it gently complements by adding aroma and flavour that's not anticipated.

I don't blend this soup at the end because I found I preferred the more rugged finish – I could say 'rustic' but I do mean rugged. I want the chunks of tomato to stand out, and when I hear rustic soup mentioned, I sometimes fear it's just a cook's way of leaving something unfinished. Truly rustic soup should not need blending and should be halfway to a main course for me.

Soup may be versatile and easy, but it still deserves care, attention and balance if you're going to do it justice.

❉ Toast the coriander seeds in a small dry frying pan until aromatic and then cool, crush to a powder and set aside. Fry the chopped onion gently in a saucepan on a low heat in a little oil for 10 minutes or until soft but not browned. Add the ground coriander seeds and chopped coriander stalks and stir through for 1 minute. Add the stock, orange juice, harissa, chopped tomatoes and tomato passata, and cook on a medium heat for 10 minutes. Add the orange pepper seasoning and chilli salt, and continue to simmer for a further 15–20 minutes. Add half the chopped coriander leaves and stir through. Serve in wide bowls finished with a little more coriander leaves and a generous drizzle of orange rapeseed oil on top.

Pizza Evolution

Makes 2 pizza bases

Basic dough base

1 tsp sugar

270ml (approximately 1 cup) warm water

15g (1 tbsp) dried active yeast or 2 tsp easy blend yeast

1 tsp smoked salt

500g (2 cups) strong white flour

60ml (¼ cup) smoked olive oil

Pizza – do you mess with it or simply serve a wonderful, authentic tomato and fresh basil one? Well, that's easy – you can do both!

I love pizza, but not the ones that reach your door in 30 minutes – with all the crisp texture of a damp towel. I want better than that. Like many of us, I've eaten pizza on little tables in side-street trattorias in Italy, and anyone who has will know pizza is 'special' there. Its great attraction is its simplicity and its versatility – you don't need lots of ingredients, just a few good ones. You can use contrasting ingredients, but just be mindful of the marriage of flavours.

I simply use great ingredients and my imagination. The list of bases you can create is endless as long as you don't overdo it and think about what you're going to top it with. For the record, I will always return to a wonderful tomato sauce and basil pizza as my favourite, sitting out in a very hot Piazza Erbe in Verona, with a glass of very chilled white wine.

❃ Activate the yeast by dissolving the sugar in 150g (approximately ⅔ cup) of warm water and then adding the yeast. Whisk briefly and set aside for 15 minutes until it's fully frothed up. Meanwhile, add the salt to the flour in a large bowl and measure out your oil and remaining warm water. Once the yeast is ready, combine all ingredients to form a dough and knead for at least 10 minutes* on an oiled or floured surface. Place in an oiled bowl, covered with a clean damp tea cloth, at room temperature to rise until doubled in size – about an hour but longer if necessary.

At this stage divide the dough into two and add your base flavours by kneading them in a little. (You can also wrap the dough in clingfilm and freeze at this stage for future use.)

Now leave to rise once more for 1–2 hours.

I usually create two alternative base flavours as below, but you could use your own alternatives such as dried rosemary, chilli flakes, dried oregano, sesame seeds, finely chopped olives...

*Kneading song – 'I Heard It Through the Grapevine' by Creedence Clearwater Revival from the album Cosmo's Factory *– 11.03 minutes.*

Just take care to consider what toppings go with the base flavour you've chosen.

At the risk of stating the obvious, here are a few experienced observations...

- Too much or too loose a sauce prevents the base cooking well.
- The base cooks better on a *preheated* tray/pizza stone.
- Sprinkle a little dry polenta on the tray before placing pizza on it.
- A little oil sprinkled over toppings helps them cook better.
- Most importantly, make it whatever shape you want – it's yours!

Caper Bread Base – with Tomato and Basil

This represents an interesting lift to my favourite. I love to use capers in cooking as they impart such a tremendous salty floral spike to anything they are added to, and this bread base is no exception. It builds another layer of flavour throughout and makes the base as interesting to eat as the top.

I know I have said this several times before but, given that so many ingredients have to 'stand up for themselves' in these recipes, it is so important to buy good-quality ingredients and not poor ones. I do think the dry 'sea-salted' capers are the only ones to buy. I even use the remaining sea salt as caper-flavoured salt on occasion.

1 tbsp salted capers, rinsed and chopped

Simple Pizza Sauce (page 285)

handful of fresh basil leaves

olive oil

polenta for dusting

�֍ Mix the capers through the base dough before the second rising.

On a lightly floured surface, roll the dough to your desired shape about 2–3mm thick, leaving the edges slightly thicker by pushing the dough out a little by hand. Transfer to a cold, lightly floured inverted baking tray to build the pizza on. Spread with 4–5 tbsp of pizza sauce and scatter with basil leaves. Drizzle with a little olive oil and slide it on to a preheated tray (dusted with a little polenta) or pizza stone and bake at 220°C (425°F) for 10–12 minutes until cooked through and golden around the edges. Lightly drizzle with good extra virgin olive oil again before serving.

Porcini Bread Base – with Cherry Tomatoes and Potato

There is a little more work involved in preparing this pizza but it is delicious. It's a luxury that you might not make every time, not because it's expensive – it's not – but due to the rich nature of the truffle and porcini flavours. You could, of course, just add sliced chestnut mushrooms to tomato sauce on the porcini bread base for a simpler version, but I urge you try the potato slices and intense porcini mushrooms drizzled with truffle oil.

10g (½ cup) dried porcini mushrooms, soaked in hot water for 30 minutes and drained

1 medium red skin potato, sliced on a mandolin 2mm thick

olive oil

1 tsp sea salt

freshly ground black pepper

5–6 red cherry tomatoes, halved horizontally

some truffle oil to drizzle

polenta for dusting

✖ Pick out 5g of the largest pieces of soaked porcini mushroom and reserve for the pizza top. Chop the remaining pieces and combine into the pizza base dough before the second rising.

Place the sliced potato in a bowl and drizzle in a little olive oil, tsp of sea salt and some ground black pepper. Mix through with your hands to ensure all the potato is coated. Spread out on a baking tray and roast in a hot oven at 200°C (400°F) for 5 minutes.

On a lightly floured surface, roll the dough to your desired shape, about 2–3mm thick, leaving the edges slightly thicker by pushing the dough out a little by hand. Transfer to a cold, lightly floured inverted baking tray to build the pizza on. Drizzle the truffle oil over and layer the pizza with the potato slices, dot with tomato halves and add the remaining larger pieces of porcini mushroom. Drizzle with a little more (plain) olive oil and slide it on to a preheated tray (dusted with a little polenta) or pizza stone and bake at 220°C (425°F) for 10–12 minutes until cooked through and golden around the edges.

Warm Mediterranean Potato Salad

Serves 2

5 or 6 medium-sized slightly waxy, buttery potatoes, peeled

pinch of saffron strands

Peperonata (page 276) or 1 good-quality jar of mixed roasted Mediterranean vegetables in olive oil

small handful of fresh dill, roughly chopped

Sometimes you have a craving for certain ingredients or you have something in your store cupboard you particularly want to use, so you naturally have to find a way to incorporate it into the dish you're making or otherwise make something around it – that is certainly how this simple dish evolved.

You could use a good-quality jar of roasted Mediterranean vegetables in olive oil for this – there are certainly some perfectly good ones to buy as store cupboard items – but making it from scratch when you have the time and inclination is definitely worthwhile too.

This makes a perfect pairing with Retro Roasted Onions. Just don't forget the bread and wine!

✿ Quarter the potatoes, cutting any larger ones into 6 if necessary to get them all about the same size. Place them in lightly salted boiling water and add the saffron strands. Cook for approximately 15 minutes until just tender. Drain and allow to steam and cool for a minute or two.

Pile the potatoes in the centre of a serving plate (one of a contrasting Mediterranean colour such as deep blue would be quite striking). Take about half the peperonata and drain it of most of its oil. Spread the peperonata evenly over the top of the potatoes and finish by scattering the dill over everything.

Ratatouille with Black Garlic

Serves 4 as a starter

1 medium onion

1 tbsp good extra virgin olive oil

1 courgette

1 small aubergine

2 fresh tomatoes

1 green pepper

1 red pepper

1 tsp fresh thyme leaves

3 black garlic bulbs, finely chopped

sea salt and ground black pepper

fresh basil leaves, shredded to finish

It's fair to say I'm messing with a classic here. But to be fair, only a little bit. Many people will view ratatouille as an old-fashioned dish, but all the more reason to revisit it really. It's not complicated – it just requires a little attention to detail and patience for such a simple recipe. It truly is worth buying good fresh vegetables – as always, it will show in the final flavours.

A small portion is ideal for a starter as the black garlic is memorable and creates quite a rich-tasting dish, but a larger portion eaten with some favourite fresh bread also makes a very moreish lunch or innocently indulgent supper in front of a good film.

The black garlic exudes a liquorice-like, almost truffle-like quality, while the fresh herbs lighten just enough to balance everything.

�֍ Sauté the onions in the oil until softened but not colouring. Dice the courgette, aubergine, tomatoes and peppers into 2cm pieces and add to the onions with the thyme leaves. Stir through and sauté on a medium heat for 5 minutes. Add the black garlic and stir through again. Now reduce the heat, cover and simmer for 15–20 minutes until the vegetables are cooked and softened. If you have a little too much moisture, just cook a little longer, uncovered, to quickly drive off the excess liquid. Season with salt and pepper and finish with shredded basil leaves.

Gnocchetti Sardi and Apple Pesto Salad

with Caramelised Walnuts

Serves 2

100g (1 cup) walnut halves

2 tbsp granulated white sugar

30g (¼ cup) dairy-free butter

100g (⅔ cup) gnocchetti sardi pasta

2 tbsp Apple Pesto (page 254)

I suppose what this represents is a take on a classic Italian dish really – pasta with pesto is, after all, a very familiar partnership. The apple pesto really plays with your common sense here, while the rest of your senses are busy anticipating a familiar favourite. The slightly less familiar pasta I have used, which hails from Sardinia, has a wonderful characteristic of catching flavour within it as well as on it and so delivering equally great taste with every mouthful. I do hope I haven't broken any unwritten rules with the apple pesto or offended any Italian traditionalists with my choice of pasta, but this does eat very well and I love the subtle sweetness the apple gives the pesto.

✻ Heat a nonstick frying pan and add the walnuts, sugar and dairy-free butter. Keeping the heat at medium, melt the sugar and stir through all the nuts for 4–5 minutes until they are all well coated, taking great care not to allow anything to burn. Transfer to parchment paper and, working quickly but carefully, separate all the nuts. Allow to cool completely for approximately 10 minutes so that the coating hardens and then store in a jar – except the ones you want for the dish...

Make the pesto according to the instructions on page 254.

Cook the pasta according to the packet instructions – it should take about 10 minutes. Mix through 2 tbsp of apple pesto and set aside to rest and cool, before refrigerating in a sealed container ready for when you want to serve it.

Roughly chop the caramelised walnuts and scatter over the pasta just before serving.

Mixed Tomato and Butter Bean Escabeche Salad

Serves 2

Gigantes Escabeche (page 132)

a selection of small salad or heritage tomatoes in different colours (red, orange, yellow, green – even striped if you can get them)

This is a wonderful way to adapt the Gigantes Escabeche recipe in 'Small Plates' into a perfect 'Gentle Plates' starter or delicious fresh lunch salad. Make more than you need of the small plates recipe and then, as it keeps very well, a day or so later change it up to this with minimal effort. I feel a little guilty putting this recipe in as all you are really doing is adding some fresh mixed tomatoes, but it elevates the beans to a very interesting, refreshingly sharp and satisfying salad dish that delivers contrasting textures and flavours...and friends will wonder how you did it in such a short time!

One word of advice: as it is a mildly pickled dish, it's a very good taste-bud awakener, but it is wise to be conservative with the portion size as too much is, well, too much...

❋ Slice the tomatoes in half, sprinkle a pinch of sea salt on them and leave them in a bowl for 10–20 minutes. Combine them gently with the beans and serve small portions in bowls as a fresh summer starter.

Cocas

1 quantity of cocas

Cocas are baked Spanish breads eaten with a variety of simple toppings, particularly typical of the Catalan, Valencia, Murcia and Aragon regions. They can be sweet or savoury, and range from simple picnic food to cocas named after saints specifically to celebrate holidays – a time of high demand for them.

They are one of those foods eaten by both rich and poor without distinction, and are a wonderfully versatile and delicious thing, not least due to the ease and enjoyment with which you eat them.

If you have ever made a pizza and thought leaving out the cheese meant it wasn't really a pizza, then here you are – to all intents and purposes, you were halfway to making a Spanish coca!

One important rule – never overload a coca: they are meant to be eaten with simple toppings.

They are commonly presented in one of four ways: open – the most common way, which I have used here; enclosed, which is not dissimilar in appearance to a calzone; with a central hole, commonly used as a sweet coca; and plain, served at the table to be topped as desired.

I've seen them in many shapes and sizes but I prefer the small round individual ones – done with alternative savoury toppings, eaten warm or cold, inside or out!

✳ Make a bread dough with strong white flour according to the recipe on page 274.

Prepare your chosen flavours.

Once the dough is proved/risen, knock it back and divide into eight equal pieces – each to be one coca. In turn, and on a floured surface, roll out each piece into a flat round about 15cm (6 inches) in diameter. With the tip of a knife, make short small scores in the top of the coca, without cutting all the way through.

The cocas are now ready to be topped. Once cooked, serve as a selection on one large serving platter.

Two Cocas with Spinach and Pine Nuts

- olive oil
- large handful of fresh spinach, shredded
- 1 garlic clove, finely sliced
- handful of toasted pine nuts
- sea salt

❋ Drizzle a little olive oil over the coca and then scatter on the shredded spinach followed by the garlic slices and pine nuts. Add a sprinkle of sea salt and a final drizzle of olive oil.

Leave to rise for an hour or so until roughly doubled in height before baking at 220°C (425°F) for approximately 10–12 minutes until cooked and pale golden brown in colour.

Two Cocas with Roasted Onion and Garlic

- olive oil
- 1 small sweet white Spanish onion or 1 small red onion, finely sliced in rings
- 1 clove of garlic, finely sliced
- sea salt

❋ Drizzle a little olive oil over the coca and then scatter on the sliced onion followed by the garlic slices. Add a sprinkle of sea salt and a final drizzle of olive oil.

Leave to rise for an hour or so until roughly doubled in height before baking at 220°C (425°F) for approximately 10–12 minutes until cooked and pale golden brown in colour.

Four Cocas with Peperonata

- approximately 4 tbsp Peperonata (page 276), oil drained off
- sea salt

❋ Place a spoonful of peperonata in the centre of each coca and spread it out just a little. There's no need to drizzle any oil on as the peperonata already contains oil.

Leave to rise for an hour or so until roughly doubled in height before baking at 220°C (425°F) for approximately 10–12 minutes until cooked and pale golden brown in colour.

Dinner Dates and Gentle Plates

I don't like cooking for myself...or is it more accurate to say that I don't like eating alone? I think it's by far the latter, actually. The pleasure you get from cooking is primarily the overwhelming high of making others happy – the hearing, seeing and knowing, above all, that you've made something between enjoyable and fascinating to eat, and, more importantly, the people important to you have enjoyed it. Most of us can follow a recipe and with a little care make something worth eating, but it's the quietly satisfying inner joy of presenting good food that's loved by others that drives a great home cook – and I suspect many of the most time-hardened professional chefs.

Whether we like it or not, as a species, we thrive on acceptance and positively glow at praise, but with cooking it's something else. We're not looking for applause, kind reviews or awards, although recognition is always uplifting, so why are we so hooked? Because we're giving rather than taking – simple as that.

The senses at a romantic dinner are undoubtedly heightened, are they not? Whether first date or fiftieth anniversary, it's all about the emotion at the table – the giving and sharing of food and the celebration of being together, or the hectic buzz of a family eating at the table, or the fun of friends 'breaking bread' together. That's probably an old-fashioned expression, but I like all the foodie connotations it brings in my head – it's all about satisfying senses in others and ourselves.

The recipes here are ideas for evening meals, whether romantic or platonic, families sharing or gentle suppers for one. The intention is to get us to eat together wherever possible, and, when we have to eat alone, not to shrink from the worth in cooking for ourselves.

Somebody once told me, or I read somewhere, that in order to truly love others, you must first learn to love yourself. I believe, likewise, if you can learn to like cooking for yourself, you'll love cooking for others more. (Somewhere inside me there is a little hippy trying very hard not to come out – he's very happy right where he is and he's got the record collection to prove it!)

Gnocchi

with Tomato Sauce and Fresh Garden Mint

Serves 2

extra virgin olive oil

½ onion, finely chopped

1 x 400g (15oz) tin of good-quality chopped tomatoes

2 tsp red wine vinegar

sea salt

ground tellicherry black pepper

Homemade Gnocchi (page 270) or 1 packet gnocchi

good handful of fresh mint leaves, shredded, but some left whole to finish the dish

I have a strange relationship with gnocchi. When it's on a menu or I'm offered it, I very often decline in favour of another dish, thinking it's a little heavy, or, more commonly, I don't feel in the mood for it, yet when it's served to me, I always love it. Go figure, as our American friends love to say!

It is up there among my favourite food memories, though. It was the first meal I had on my first visit to Florence, and I absolutely adored it. Tired from the day's long drive from the north of Italy, we arrived late in the day at our beautiful hotel 'Villa Cora' and simply ordered room service – and to this day it's the best room service I have ever eaten, which is probably not that surprising really, given the location.

It's a wonderful comfort food and also serves as a fantastic vehicle for flavour. The mint, however, is the star in this dish – straight from the garden in June when it's at its very best, it elevates this simple tomato sauce into a meal fit to be served in any Florentine restaurant – or hotel room!

❁ Warm the olive oil in a wide pan and gently fry off the onion until translucent and sweet. Add the tomatoes and a little water and cook on a medium heat for 10 minutes. Add half the shredded mint and continue to cook for 5 minutes. Add the red wine vinegar and cook down for a further 5 minutes before adding the remaining shredded mint leaves. Check for seasoning and adjust as required. Add a little olive oil and stir through. You are looking to create a sauce that is rich but not dry and has the glossy sheen that olive oil brings. Set aside and keep warm to marry all the flavours together.

Cook the gnocchi in lightly salted boiling water until they float to the surface or according to your packet instructions. Once ready, remove and drain and then add to the sauce. Return the sauce to the heat and stir everything through again gently to coat the gnocchi. Serve in warmed pasta bowls and grind on a little freshly ground black pepper.

Mushroom 'Open Lasagne'

with 'Black Truffle' Salsa Truffina

Serves 2 (for obvious reasons this is for a couple – but you can adapt as required)

8 good-quality medium-sized mushrooms

tbsp extra virgin olive oil

1 tbsp dairy-free butter

2 tsp chopped fresh marjoram

2 tsp L'Aquila salsa truffina (black truffle sauce)

4 sheets 'doppia riccia' lasagne

freshly ground black pepper

a little truffle oil

You might want to put a red rose in an empty Italian wine bottle on the table for a little nostalgic romantic fun!

You can buy black truffle sauce quite easily from various places and it's not that expensive, particularly considering you get a wonderful flavour from a small amount. Likewise, do try to source the 'Doppia Riccia' lasagne – it is aesthetically more appealing, and the curled edges catch a little more sauce too. 'Lasagne larga doppia riccia' simply translates as 'large double curled', but, of course, normal lasagne sheets will work perfectly well.

Truffles are a huge favourite of mine. They evoke flavour memories of Italy like no other ingredient – which for me are memories of a warm July evening sitting at a quiet outdoor restaurant table in Florence, on honeymoon.

This recipe is a great example of neurogastronomy at work. In the same way a song or scent of perfume can trigger a memory, I can still remember the sounds of the restaurant and the feel of the heat in the air, picture where we sat exactly...and, of course, recall the taste and smell of the black summer truffles.

❃ Chop four of the mushrooms into small equal pieces and then quarter the remaining four into thick slices. If your mushrooms vary in size slightly, then it's a good idea to chop the smaller ones and slice the larger ones.

Heat the olive oil and dairy-free butter in a sauté pan on a medium heat until the butter bubbles a little and then add the chopped mushrooms. Sauté for 3–4 minutes. You want them to retain some texture and not be too soft in the finished dish. Now add most of the chopped herbs and the black truffle sauce and stir through for a minute. Remove from the heat for now.

Cook your pasta sheets as instructed on the packet. They should take 8–10 minutes. Meanwhile, using a separate frying pan, add a little oil and on a medium-high heat sear the sliced mushrooms for 2 minutes on each side – you're looking for slightly caramelised edges. Take the mushroom slices off the heat and add them to the pan with the chopped mushrooms. As the pasta becomes ready,

place the mushrooms back on a medium heat in preparation for serving.

To plate, grind a little fresh black pepper into the chopped mushroom sauce and take off the heat. Lay a pasta sheet in the centre of a hot shallow pasta bowl – spoon half the mushroom sauce in the middle of the pasta, then lay the second sheet over the mushrooms in the opposite direction to form a cross. Repeat with the second serving plate and finish each bowl with some more freshly ground black pepper and the remaining chopped fresh thyme scattered over. Drizzle with a little extra truffle oil and serve immediately.

Linguine and Baby Turnips

with 'Black Truffle' Cream Sauce

Serves 2

6 baby turnips, scrubbed and trimmed

olive oil

200ml (1 cup) vegetable stock

1 tbsp fresh thyme leaves

2 tsp black truffle mushroom paste (I prefer the L'Aquila brand but there are others)

1–2 tbsp soya cream

freshly ground black pepper

200g (8oz) linguine

1 tbsp white truffle-flavoured extra virgin rapeseed oil

Many, many years ago I bought baby turnips from my local supermarket because and I thought, 'Great – some miniature turnips!' I had no idea what I was going to do with them. I still do it today – just buy something because I haven't seen it before and then worry about how to use it. I remember kohlrabi being one, many years ago, along with pomelo and romanesco. The turnip and black truffle complement each other particularly well here, as does the luxurious aroma of white truffle in the creamy sauce.

❊ Slice the turnips into thin discs (2–3mm/⅛ inch) using a mandolin or sharp knife, then blanch for 1 minute in boiling water. Drain and set aside.

Heat some olive oil in a large saucepan on a medium setting and gently sauté the turnip slices until they just start to look translucent and are picking up a little colour. Add the vegetable stock, thyme and truffle paste and stir through on the heat to combine. Now reduce the heat a little and add the cream and black pepper, stirring through while taking care not to break up the discs of turnip. Turn the heat to its lowest and keep warm to infuse the flavours while you cook the pasta according to the packet instructions – you want the sauce to be just reduced enough to coat the pasta when you add it, and the turnip to be only just tender and still holding its shape.

Do try to keep a little bite to the pasta (al dente, as I'm sure you know the Italians call it) – perhaps cooking a minute or so less than the packet suggests...

Once cooked, add the pasta to the sauce and gently turn it through to combine everything. Now serve on bold coloured plates that contrast with the pasta and drizzle each serving with white truffle oil accompanied by hot bread and perhaps a glass of your favourite Italian white wine.

I'm reliably told that, as a rule, you shouldn't really mix black and white truffle in the same dish, but life would be very boring if we never broke a rule or two – don't you think?

Spaghetti with Roasted 'San Marzano' Tomato Sauce

Serves 2

250g (9oz) pack ripe baby San Marzano tomatoes – on the vine if available (or cherry tomatoes)

2 tbsp extra virgin olive oil

sea salt

freshly ground black pepper

good handful of fresh basil leaves

50ml (¼ cup) tomato passata

200g (7oz) good-quality 'bronze die' spaghetti such as DeCecco

This is another pasta memory from Pisa. It was just supposed to be a quick eat to keep us going through the day as we explored around the city, but it ended up being a long lunch with wine. I very nearly ordered it over again.

All recipes need good ingredients, but the simple ones demand it a little bit more. Nobody should ever dismiss spaghetti and tomato sauce as too basic – it should be a celebration of great tomatoes and well-made pasta, cooked with love and for the love of it. Lunch in Pisa was surrounded by the aromas of Italian food coming out of the rustic little side-street trattoria we chose – where you could eat, drink and inevitably people-watch. The food was hot and fresh and relatively inexpensive...and – frankly – much better than my hunger was already willing to settle for. This is how I remember it. Serve it with warm fresh bread drizzled in your very best extra virgin olive oil.

✿ Preheat the oven to 200°C (400°F). Remove the tomatoes from the vine and halve lengthways. Place facing up on a baking tray and bring them all into the middle. Drizzle with 1 tbsp of olive oil and the sea salt and black pepper. Roughly tear or slice the basil leaves and scatter them over the tomatoes. Place in the oven for 10 minutes, then reduce the heat to 160°C (320°F) for a further 10–15 minutes.

On a medium heat, add the remaining olive oil to a saucepan that will be big enough to take the pasta at the end. Remove the tomatoes from the oven and add to the saucepan along with the passata and stir to combine. Reduce the heat and simmer to reduce and intensify the flavours while you make the pasta – according to packet instructions. Try to keep the pasta al dente to retain a little firmness – it makes for a more authentic finished dish. Once your pasta is cooked, drain and add to the simmering tomato sauce and stir through to combine. Serve in wide pasta bowls with the bread – it should need nothing else!

Lentil and Italian Herb Ragù

with Spaghetti No. 12

Serves 2

200g (1 cup) Umbrian brown lentils

handful of sage leaves

2 sprigs of rosemary

1 garlic clove, peeled

salt and pepper for seasoning

1 carrot, peeled and trimmed, very finely diced

1 celery stick, de-stringed, very finely diced

½ medium red onion, very finely diced

1 tbsp good olive oil

pinch of crushed chilli flakes

1 tsp oregano

1 x 400g (15oz) tin of best-quality chopped tomatoes

small handful of flat-leaf parsley, finely chopped

400g (14oz) 'bronze die' spaghetti – I use DeCecco No. 12

It's a tough call going *testa a testa* with what must be one of the world's most famous dishes, so this is a 'cards on the table' direct alternative for spaghetti bolognese.

I could write a lot about how well it works and how much better I believe it is, but, of course, all that really matters is that you make it and enjoy it and want to make it again. Please make it with care and attention and eat it at its best – but never apologise for cooking it for anyone! It's delicious!

❉ Place the lentils in a pan with the sage leaves, rosemary sprigs and garlic clove. Cover with water and bring to the boil before reducing the heat and simmering for 15–20 minutes, adding a little salt towards the end of the cooking time (not before), until the lentils are only just tender – take care not to overcook them here.

While the lentils are cooking, prepare the trio of vegetables (your 'soffritto') and gently cook in the olive oil for 20–25 minutes until well softened and tender. A little colour on them is no bad thing, but take care not to hard-fry them at all. Once ready, add the chilli flakes, oregano and a grind or two of black pepper and stir through. Add the chopped tomatoes and stir thoroughly. Cook on a medium heat for 10 minutes.

Drain the lentils and remove the sage, rosemary stalks and garlic clove before adding the lentils to the tomato sauce along with the chopped parsley. Stir through to combine everything. It will very likely require a little salt and pepper at this stage.

Now continue to simmer uncovered on a low heat for 10 minutes to allow all the flavours to marry together while you cook the pasta, but keep an eye on it, adding a little water if it's getting too dry and perhaps a drizzle of good olive oil too.

Cook your pasta according to its packet instructions, but keep it al dente.

Check the lentil sauce for seasoning and adjust according to taste. I like a good grind of black pepper to finish.

You might also like to finish the dish with a little Poor Man's 'International' Cheese (page 282).

Bloody Mary Os

(or Anelli Siciliani Alla Vodka)

Serves 2 hungry grown-ups

½ onion, finely chopped

1 tsp olive oil

2 tsp dairy-free butter

1 x 400g (15oz) tin of good-quality chopped tomatoes

150ml (½ cup) water

½ tsp celery salt

few grinds of pepper

couple of dashes of Tabasco (or to taste)

4 tsp good-quality branded vodka

200g (1½ cups) Anelli Siciliani 60A (by La Molisana)

This recipe is part fun and part genuine – although maybe not in equal parts – and it serves to illustrate our loyalty and affection for some foods over and above our basic senses. Childhood memories can play their part too. This is my grown-up spaghetti hoops – very grown-up in fact. It's a marriage of the drink that bears its name and the classic *penne alla vodka*.

Opinion as to the origins of vodka first being used in an Italian tomato sauce is certainly divided. Some claim Bologna and some claim a student of Columbia University, but the story that I like is that it was invented by a chef in New York reaching for the nearest thing to hand in order to thin a tomato sauce he was making – which begs the question, why was it so readily to hand in the first place?

❋ Make the sauce first. It will be an advantage to let it sit a little bit while you are making the pasta.

Gently fry the chopped onion in the olive oil and 1 tsp of dairy-free butter until it softens but only just begins to colour. Add the tinned tomatoes and water. A simple tip here is to use the empty tin to add the water – swilling it around to get all the tomato juice out.

Cook on a medium heat for 15–20 minutes, adding the salt, pepper and Tabasco halfway through, until the sauce is cooked down but still fairly loose when you stir it. Add only 2 tsp vodka here and continue cooking for 5 minutes. Remove from the heat, cover, keep warm and set aside to rest. The sauce must be loose and not paste-like – stir in a little water if you feel it's not thin enough.

Cook the pasta according to packet instructions – the one I use, as with all pasta I use, is 'bronze die' and has a cooking time longer than you might expect for a small pasta – 16–18 minutes. You do want some texture unlike the famous tinned variety. Once cooked, remove from the heat, drain and return to the empty warm pan – add the second tsp of dairy-free butter and remaining 2 tsp of vodka to the pasta and stir through. Warm the tomato

sauce through again and add the pasta to the sauce (not the other way round). Stir through and serve in warmed pasta bowls dressed with a few basil leaves.

Like so many pasta dishes, it's always rewarding to have some warm crusty bread to hand when the pasta is gone but there is still sauce!

Mushroom Sheng Cai Bao

with Asian Pickled Cucumber Relish

Serves 4

1 tsp caster sugar

1 tbsp rice wine vinegar

½ fresh cucumber

1 tbsp chopped coriander, leaves only

200g (½lb) chestnut mushrooms

125g (1 cup) shiitake mushrooms

200g (½lb) cup mushrooms

1 shallot, finely chopped

small tin of water chestnuts, chopped

fresh coriander including stems, finely chopped

1 tsp groundnut oil

2 garlic cloves, very finely chopped

1 small red chilli, deseeded and finely chopped

2–3cm piece of fresh ginger, grated

2 tsp dark soya sauce

1 tsp rice mirin

1 tsp sesame oil

50g (½ cup) cashew nuts, toasted

4 very fresh gem lettuces, base cut off and separated into individual leaves

There are several layers of enjoyment here – the act of building your own wraps, the lightly spiced and deliciously savoury mushroom, the sweet cucumber pickle hit, the textural contrast of cashews...not forgetting the crisp, refreshingly watery crunch of the lettuce. It all becomes greater than the sum of its parts. You could use toasted peanuts instead if you prefer or even take out the pickled cucumber and use the Carrot and Celeriac Pickled Slaw on page 246.

✻ First make the cucumber and coriander pickle. Dissolve the sugar in the rice wine vinegar. Peel half the skin off the cucumber in strips, leaving a striped effect – you don't have to, but it looks a little better in the finished pickle. Dice into small pieces and combine with the rice wine vinegar and chopped coriander leaves. Set aside in the fridge.

Chop the mushrooms into quite fine dice and combine with the shallot, water chestnuts and coriander. Set aside. Heat the groundnut oil and fry the garlic, red chilli and ginger for a few minutes before adding the mushrooms. Stir-fry on a high heat for 5–10 minutes to cook the mushrooms through before adding the soya sauce and rice mirin. Stir through on the heat for a few minutes more, testing the mushrooms for seasoning and flavour. Add the sesame oil.

Serve the mushrooms, pickle and cashews in individual bowls alongside the lettuce leaves so that everyone can build their own wraps. A cold Chinese beer can be a very welcome accompaniment.

Pan-Fried Gnocchi

with Girolles, Sage, Pear and Walnuts

Serves 2

2 handfuls of fresh gnocchi
(page 270)

1 tbsp dairy-free butter

1 tsp olive oil

100g (1 cup) girolle mushrooms
or sliced chestnut mushrooms

1 garlic clove, cut into 4

small handful of sage leaves

1 firm pear, core removed and
finely sliced with the skin on

a few walnuts, roughly chopped

sea salt and ground black
pepper to season

some 'pear' balsamic vinegar or
1 tbsp white balsamic vinegar
mixed with ½ tbsp balsamic

I imagine we all have blind spots or gaps in our experiences. Things we think are obvious once we've seen them, or we wonder how we managed to get this far in life without ever being told about them or eating them. Pan-fried gnocchi is just that for me. It must have passed me by and I never noticed it, and yet it seems so obvious and delicious now. I genuinely had never seen it done until recently and simply had to create a recipe for it, as much for myself as anyone!

This is a dish best made with freshly made gnocchi rather than using some that has been frozen. It just works better.

❀ Cook the gnocchi in a pan of lightly salted boiling water until they rise to the surface. Drain and keep to one side.

Add half the dairy-free butter and half the oil to a frying pan and heat until it froths a little. Add the mushrooms and garlic and sauté for 2–3 minutes (1–2 minutes more if using chestnut mushrooms).

Remove from the pan and set aside on a warm plate, discarding the garlic.

Wipe the pan clean with kitchen paper and add the remaining dairy-free butter and oil, heating until it froths again. Add the sage and the gnocchi and gently fry until the sage is becoming crisp and the gnocchi are becoming caramelised and taking on a golden colour. Try not to move the gnocchi around too much. Reintroduce the mushrooms to the pan and slowly stir around for a minute to reheat them, adding a pinch of sea salt if needed.

Serve in two warmed pasta bowls and garnish with the slices of pear and walnuts and a grind of black pepper.

Finish with a few drops of the pear balsamic dotted around the plate.

Singapore Rice Noodles

with Five-a-Day Mixed Vegetables...

...carrot, red peppers, green peppers, mangetout, baby corn, mushroom, onion, shallot, red onion, broccoli, cabbage, green beans, peas...the list goes on....take your pick

Serves 2 generously

60g (½ cup) cashew nuts

2 tsp walnut oil

30g fresh ginger, finely julienned (approximately ¼ cup)

1 clove garlic, peeled and crushed

4–5 closed-cup mushrooms, sliced

1 tsp mild curry powder

1 tsp turmeric

1 red pepper, deseeded and finely julienned

1 banana shallot, peeled and finely sliced lengthways

1 medium carrot, peeled and finely julienned

handful of mangetout, finely sliced lengthways

1 red chilli, deseeded and finely julienned

1 tsp rice mirin

dash of sesame oil

2 tsp good soya sauce

2 x 150g (5oz) packs of ribbon rice noodles

handful of beansprouts

125g (1 cup) shiitake mushrooms, sliced

1 tsp walnut oil

1 tsp rice mirin

1 tsp soya sauce

3 spring onions, trimmed and finely chopped at an angle

Now that I come to think about it, I don't think I have ever met anyone who doesn't like noodles. They have great texture and are a brilliant foil for other flavours; I love rice dishes, but somehow having noodles always seems to be a treat.

Singapore noodles is another one of those world dishes that is recognisable to all and works effortlessly within plant-based cooking due to its natural heritage. It appears a little similar in principle to many European peasant dishes (Spanish *paella*, for example) in that its cheap main ingredient is affordably supplemented with what is most abundant for the least cost and so making a little go a long way...making this vegetable-based version pretty authentic I think.

✽ Toast the cashews in a dry hot pan for a few minutes until they take on a little colour. Remove and set aside on a cool plate.

Prepare the rice noodles according to the packet instructions and drain.

Heat the walnut oil in a large hot wok and add the ginger, garlic, sliced closed-cup mushrooms, curry powder and turmeric. Stir-fry for 1 min. Add the red pepper, shallot, carrot, mangetout and red chilli, and stir-fry for 4–5 minutes, adding a dash of water as you do.

Next, add the rice mirin, sesame oil, soya sauce, noodles and beansprouts to the wok and stir-fry for 2–3 minutes. Heat a small frying pan and quickly fry off the shiitake mushrooms in the walnut oil, rice mirin and soya sauce at the same time.

Empty the wok into a large warmed serving bowl and immediately top with the shiitake mushrooms, toasted cashew nuts and spring onions. Serve immediately.

Mushroom Caldereta

with Mojo Verde Sauce

Serves 4

Mojo Verde Sauce (page 265)

For the stock

1 clove garlic, crushed

1 small onion, finely chopped

1 small carrot, finely diced

1 celery stick, finely diced

1 tbsp olive oil

50ml (¼ cup) brandy

100ml (½ cup) dry white wine

fresh thyme leaves from a handful of thyme

For the sauce

1 medium onion, chopped

2 garlic gloves, finely sliced

1 romano pepper, deseeded and chopped

2 tbsp olive oil

400g (15oz) tin of chopped tomatoes

1 tsp hot smoked paprika

1 tsp ground tellicherry black peppercorns

sea salt

approximately 16 closed-cup mushrooms, stalks trimmed

Caldereta is a style of stew from the Balearic Islands. It's characterised, not surprisingly, by a rich deep sauce of tomato, red pepper, onion and garlic, and then made, again not surprisingly, with whatever is most plentiful or available.

I've taken the step of adding some hot smoked paprika to further intensify the flavour and the deep red colour of the dish. I can't imagine too many traditionalists objecting, given the provenance.

The colour of food is probably more important than we actually realise – think of your favourite meals and I bet a lot of them are red like this one.

I thought a lot about what to eat with this dish (trying not to be too obvious), but I kept returning to fresh warm or lightly toasted black olive bread – it worked so well that I seriously considered adding black olives to the recipe...which of course you could.

✤ First, make the mojo verde sauce. Set aside.

Create the stock by frying the garlic, onion, carrot and celery in the olive oil for 6–7 minutes until softened and starting to get lightly golden. Add the brandy and cook off a little for 2–3 minutes before repeating with the white wine. Add the thyme leaves and about 1 litre of water. Bring to the boil, then reduce the heat and simmer for 30 minutes. Finally, increase the heat and reduce to approximately 750ml. Turn off the heat and set aside.

Make the caldereta sauce by frying the garlic, onion and pepper in the oil until the onions start to become translucent and the peppers start to soften. Now add the tinned tomatoes, paprika and ground peppercorns followed by a little salt and even a pinch of sugar if you think your tomatoes might be slightly sharper than normal. Bring to the boil, then reduce to simmer for 15–20 minutes. You want to hold some shape in the peppers and tomatoes to create a slightly textured finished sauce for the caldereta.

Meanwhile, place the mushrooms in a bowl, drizzle with a little

olive oil and toss them to coat them with the oil. Place them between two baking trays and apply pressure on them by placing a small ovenproof dish on the top tray to compress the mushrooms a little during the cooking process. An empty dish about 400–500g (1lb) in weight is ideal. Roast in the oven for 15 minutes at 200°C (400°F). This will give the mushrooms a wonderful dense texture and intensify their flavour at the same time. Remove when done and set aside.

Add the stock to the sauce and cook for a further 15–20 minutes on a medium-low heat. Partially blitz the sauce to combine well before adding the mushrooms.

Serve in a large sharing dish with a little mojo verde sauce drizzled over the top and some reserved on the table for those who wish to have more. Serve with lots of bread – perfect for dipping in the sauce when the mushrooms are all gone!

Tandoori-Style Cauliflower

with Tomato and Onion Curry

Serves 4

Tandoori cauliflower

1 large cauliflower, broken or sliced into roughly equal florets

1 tsp My Aromatic Kofta Spice Mix (page 280)

2 tbsp coconut oil

½ tsp Kashmiri chilli powder

Tomato and onion curry

1 tbsp coconut oil

½ tsp black mustard seeds

1 large onion, half roughly chopped, half sliced

1 clove garlic, crushed

1 x 400g (15oz) tin of plum tomatoes

1 tsp sea salt

2 tsp garam masala

1 red chilli, chopped (optional)

2 medium fresh tomatoes, quartered

To finish

small handful of chopped coriander leaves

100g (½ cup) coconut milk yogurt thinned with a squeeze of lemon juice

Cauliflower just has to be one of the most underrated vegetables. When I was young, cauliflower in cheese sauce was all about the sauce covering up this bland but slightly bitter-tasting vegetable, so we parted company for many years. Discovering it could be roasted was a revelation!

❋ Place the cauliflower in a large saucepan of boiling water. Cook for 2 minutes. Transfer to a colander to drain and cool slightly.

Preheat the oven to 200°C (400°F).

Mix the remaining cauliflower ingredients in a large bowl and combine together. Once the florets are cool enough to handle, add them to your spice mix and gently turn them around, coating them well. Be careful not to break up the florets. Spread evenly on a preheated baking tray and roast in the oven for 20 minutes until lightly charred and only just tender in the middle.

Meanwhile, in a good-sized saucepan, heat the oil on a medium heat and add the mustard seeds. Once the seeds start popping, add the onions and garlic and cook for 5 minutes. Roughly chop the tinned tomatoes and add all the contents of the tin to the onions, stirring as you do. (I don't use pre-chopped tinned tomatoes here because I specifically want the larger pieces.)

Cook for 5 minutes, adding a little water if you feel it's drying out – you want to maintain a liquid sauce throughout the dish. Add the salt, garam masala and red chilli (if using). Cook everything through for a further 5 minutes before adding the quartered fresh tomatoes. Continue to cook for 5 minutes again before reducing the heat to low. Add the cauliflower as soon as it's ready and stir through gently. Add a final dash of water again if the sauce needs loosening up a little.

Serve in warm deep white bowls with a scattering of fresh coriander, a drizzle of thinned coconut yogurt zigzagged across the top and an Indian bread of your choice – I think *chapatis* or *rotis* go particularly well. (This is a dish I never serve with rice because I like the sauce to be quite loose – but, of course, you could if you wish to.)

'Sunday Best' Biryani

with Coriander and Mint Relish and Chilli Pickled Red Onions

Serves 4–6

6 carrots

1 medium cauliflower

100g (1 cup) cashew nuts, lightly toasted

100ml (½ cup) rice milk

good pinch of saffron strands

250ml (1 cup) vegetable oil

2 large onions, halved and finely sliced

800g (4 cups) aged basmati rice

100g (½ cup) vegetable ghee

50g (½ cup) pistachio nuts, shelled

3 tsp rose water

1 tsp rapeseed oil

For the cauliflower marinade

250ml (1 cup) coconut milk yogurt

1 tsp lemon juice

1 tbsp water

4 garlic cloves, crushed

40g piece fresh ginger, grated (¼ cup)

1 green chilli, deseeded and finely chopped

1 tsp turmeric

1 tsp Kashmiri chilli powder

1 tsp ground coriander

What a wonderfully liberating experience it was when I matured from the belief that Indian food had to be blazingly hot. What a revelation to be released from that misinformed machismo of my youth and be free to come out and say: it's actually all about the flavour of the spices!

I still love a chilli hot curry sometimes, but I totally adore the intricacies of layered spices and the subtle use of genuine Indian ingredients. You will need a few Indian ingredients for this, and some friends understandably make the point that they don't like buying a whole bag of something just for one recipe…but don't worry, you will make this again and again.

There are many famous rice dishes in the world – paella, risotto and pilaf to name just a few – but biryani must surely be the king of them. If done well and with respect for the ingredients, it will, in the final process, deliver a wonderfully aromatic and luxuriously complex dish. This is, however, no quick week-night dinner – it involves some preparation and some sourcing of ingredients (if you don't already have them in your larder), so plan a little ahead and take the time to prepare – and, above all, enjoy both the making and the sharing of it. It's worth giving a little thought to the dish you will assemble it in, as that will inevitably be your serving dish – and a little table theatre is never a bad idea. That's why I called it 'Sunday Best', but it tastes just as good on a Saturday night too.

❈ First prepare the carrots. Wash and peel and trim the tops and tails off. Cut them diagonally into 2cm pieces and set aside while you prepare the carrot masala. Add all the masala ingredients to a pestle and mortar and crush to combine into a ground powder. In a bowl, combine the carrot pieces with the rapeseed oil and add the masala powder. Coat well. Set aside in the fridge.

Break the cauliflower into medium-sized florets, cutting any large ones in half so they are mostly equal in size. Blanch the florets in boiling water for 2 minutes, then put into cold water to

For the carrot biryani masala

5cm (2 inch) cinnamon stick

1 tsp black peppercorns

½ tsp cardamom seeds

1 dried red chilli

4 cloves

1 tsp caraway seeds

½ tsp ground mace

For the biryani masala sauce

1 tbsp vegetable ghee

½ tsp cloves

4 green cardamom pods

1 piece cinnamon stick

1 tsp black cumin seeds

small handful of curry leaves

2 chopped tomatoes

1 tsp sea salt

For the coriander and mint relish

large handful of fresh coriander including stems, chopped

large handful of fresh mint leaves, chopped

1 shallot, roughly chopped

1 tsp black cumin seeds

juice of 1 lime

1 tsp palm sugar

½ tsp sea salt

For the chilli pickled red onions

2 medium red onions

1 green chilli, deseeded and finely chopped

2 tbsp chopped coriander

1 tsp black cumin seeds

3 tbsp cane vinegar

1 tsp sea salt

stop them cooking further. Drain and set aside in a clean bowl while you make the cauliflower marinade.

Combine the coconut milk yogurt with the lemon juice and, if required, a little water, to further loosen the yogurt. Add the remaining marinade ingredients and mix thoroughly to combine before adding to the cauliflower, gently turning over to coat the florets. Set aside to marinade in the fridge.

In a dry frying pan, toast the whole cashew nuts until they have a good colouring without burning. Set aside to cool.

Warm the rice milk and add the saffron strands. Set aside to cool and combine.

In a deep frying pan, heat the vegetable oil and fry the sliced onions for 10–15 minutes until golden brown and crisp. Remove with a metal slotted spoon and drain on kitchen paper. Set aside to cool.

Preheat the oven to 200°C (400°F).

Place the carrots and cauliflower in separate ovenproof dishes ready to roast. Place the carrots in for 20–25 minutes and the cauliflower in 10 minutes later so they finish at the same time. You want them to only just give when you pierce them with a knife. They will cook a little further in the final dish.

To create the masala sauce, heat the ghee in a saucepan and fry the cloves, cardamom pods, cinnamon stick, cumin seeds and curry leaves for 1–2 minutes. Add the tomatoes and salt and stir through, continuing to cook on a medium heat for 10 minutes to allow the tomatoes to break up and cook down into the spices. Remove from the heat and keep warm.

Cook the rice in boiling salted water according to the rice packet instructions but only for 6–7 minutes. You want the rice to be just a little firm as it will also cook on a little further in the final dish. Don't overcook the rice – it will make for a soft biryani, and nobody likes soft rice unless you're eating pudding! It will depend on your rice a little, so use a brand you have used before and know. I use a 'superior aged' basmati which I cook for 6–7 minutes only.

Once the vegetables are ready you can layer up the biryani – melt some ghee and drizzle a little in the bottom of your serving dish with a dash of water (the water will help steam the flavours through).

Lay just under a third of the rice on the bottom followed by half the vegetables, half the masala sauce, half the toasted cashews, a third of the crispy onions, a third of the saffron milk, a third of the pistachios and a third of the rose water.

Lay a second third of the rice on top and repeat the process. Finally top with the last third of rice, saffron milk, pistachios, rose water and crispy onions. Drizzle a little more melted ghee around the inside of the dish walls – it will help prevent sticking and add flavour too.

Seal the top with a well-fitting lid or tightly with tinfoil so steam won't escape. Place in the oven for 30 minutes at 180°C (350°F). Once ready, open at the table so everyone gets the aromas and visual effect.

Serve with Indian breads such as chapati and parathas, or a favourite naan bread.

To make the coriander and mint relish
Combine all the ingredients in a blender to form the relish. Adjust seasoning to taste.

To make the chilli pickled red onions
Peel, halve and finely slice the onions. Mix with the remaining ingredients and set aside to marinate together. They should be sharp and just slightly sweet with a touch of chilli heat.

Kachin Cashew Nut and Green Bean Curry

with Coconut Yogurt

Serves 2 generously

250g (1½ cups) cashew nuts, unsalted

2 garlic cloves, crushed

2 or 3 dried bird's eye chillies

1 tbsp grated fresh ginger

1 level tsp powdered turmeric

1 tsp ground coriander

1 tsp sea salt

100g green beans, trimmed (1 cup chopped)

125g (½ cup) basmati rice

1 tbsp vegetable ghee

100g (½ cup) coconut milk yogurt

handful of fresh coriander

Kachin is the northernmost state of Myanmar (Burma), sharing borders with China and India. I have never been there and possibly never will, but when I first came across this dish, I simply adored the power of its simple ingredients and resultant fragrant flavour. I've adapted it here to use cashews, which work particularly well in curried dishes, and also some coconut yogurt to enrich the sauce a little, which is without doubt not so in keeping with authentic Kachin cuisine, but it completes the balance here. It's a recipe I make over and over again because it's so simple and yet delivers such a wonderful finished dish. Earthy turmeric and pungent garlic combined with fiery chilli and warming ground coriander, all harmonising perfectly with creamy cashew nuts and emerald green beans. I particularly insist on plain boiled long-grain basmati rice here as it really takes up the sauce and becomes an integral part of the dish, as it should be, and not just the accompaniment. I use XXL Basmati here, but get the best-quality basmati you can find – it is genuinely worth it and it comes in such wonderful packaging!

❀ Place 200g (7oz) of the cashews in hot water (not boiling) and leave to soak for 30 minutes. This softens them a little and brings them closer to the texture of fresh ones. Gently toast the remaining cashews in a dry frying pan until they begin to colour up. Set aside to cool.

Pound the garlic, chillies, grated ginger, turmeric and ground coriander in a pestle and mortar with a little salt to form a paste. Add a tbsp or two of water to loosen the mixture and combine well. Set aside until the cashews have finished soaking.

Add the drained nuts to the paste and leave to stand for another 30 minutes.

Place the beans in a pan of lightly salted boiling water and cook for 5–6 minutes until tender but still maintaining a bite. Drain and chop into cashew-nut-sized pieces. Set aside and keep warm.

Cook the rice you are using accordingly. I like to fractionally

under-cook my rice and let it sit steaming under a clean tea towel for 5 minutes before fluffing up and serving.

While the rice is cooking, heat the ghee in a saucepan on a medium heat and add the nuts. Continue to cook slowly, covered, for 15 minutes. You are basically cooking the sauce out as the nuts don't require any cooking, of course.

Add half the coconut yogurt and continue cooking, uncovered, for a further 5 minutes, stirring occasionally to prevent the curry catching on the pan. Some nuts may start to colour but I like that. Add the cooked beans, and stir through the curry for a minute or two. Remove from the heat.

Check for seasoning and heat, adding a little extra sea salt if required and/or a little more coconut yogurt if wanting to soften the tone a little more.

Serve in wide bowls with the remaining coconut milk yogurt drizzled over, a little fresh chopped coriander and the toasted cashews scattered over each serving for colour and contrast.

Cashew nuts are quite substantial and filling, but I'm sure some people will appreciate a wholemeal chapati to accompany.

Stir-Fry of Broccoli and Black Bean Sauce

with Sweet Pepper, Elephant Garlic and Szechuan Chilli Oil

Serves 2

200g (7oz) tenderstem broccoli, ends trimmed

1 tsp groundnut oil

1 red chilli, sliced at an angle and deseeded

1 clove of elephant garlic, sliced

1 small sweet orange pepper, deseeded and sliced into rings

2 tbsp black bean paste

100ml (½ cup) water

small handful of toasted pine nuts

3 spring onions, white stems sliced at an angle

1 tbsp Szechuan chilli oil

1 tsp maple syrup or agave nectar

pinch of Chinese five-spice

This is strange, I know, but I first learned to stir-fry in Dublin airport. It's not a joke – I really did. I was in the waiting lounge returning from a long weekend and there was a Chinese chef doing a demonstration of stir-frying. I had hours to wait for my flight back to Edinburgh, so I sat and watched him while he went through his routine over and over again.

Black bean will be familiar to many as a delicious Chinese sauce that works effortlessly with vegetables. I've created a balanced heat to accompany the sauce by using Szechuan chilli oil and deseeding the chillies in order to create a warmth rather than a spike of chilli heat. The elephant garlic is less easy to come by than ordinary garlic, but it is available. It's very mild, so it adds a subtle garlic note while acting almost like another vegetable. I don't actually stir-fry the broccoli here because I want a clean-looking dish, and that means dressing the broccoli with the stir-fry sauce, before adding final layers of texture, sweetness and aromatics.

❊ Warm two deep serving bowls.

Shred each broccoli stem into 2 or 3 longer stems. Cook in lightly salted boiling water for 4 minutes.

Meanwhile, heat the groundnut oil in a wok or deep-sided frying pan and add the chilli, garlic and sliced peppers. Stir-fry for 1 minute, then add the black bean paste and the water. Bring to the boil and stir-fry for a final 2 minutes.

Drain the broccoli and divide it equally between the two warmed bowls. Dress it with the black bean sauce and scatter over the pine nuts and sliced spring onion.

Drizzle over the Szechuan oil and maple syrup, and finish with a light pinch of Chinese five-spice. Serve hot with or without boiled rice as you prefer.

Vietnamese
Sticky Carrots

with Rice Noodles

Serves 4

100g (1 cup) cashew nuts

½ cucumber

4–5 large good-quality carrots, peeled

300g (12oz) 5mm rice noodles

1 tbsp groundnut oil

1 red onion, finely sliced

1 red chilli, sliced into diagonal discs

2 fat garlic cloves, finely sliced

2 tbsp agave syrup or maple syrup

2 tbsp soya sauce

freshly squeezed juice of 1 lime

1 tsp sesame oil

handful of fresh coriander, leaves roughly chopped

1 tbsp toasted sesame seeds

Carrots really work superbly here, being no stranger to Asian dishes due to their natural texture, sweetness and colour. If you cut the carrots into good-sized, attractively angled pieces and don't overcook them, you will see what I mean. The whole thing marries as a great dish. The kick of spicy chilli, the sour lime and the salty soya sauce against the substantial sweet firm carrots and the moreish noodles – it all delivers one of those meals you feel is already doing you good as you're eating it.

❊ Toast the cashew nuts in a dry frying pan – set aside to cool. Peel the cucumber at intervals to produce a striped effect on the skin, cut in half lengthways and slice at 45° angles into 5mm slices. Set aside.

Cut your prepared carrots in half lengthways and then into large 2–3cm long pieces at 'jaunty angles' (45° in plain speak) and cook in lightly salted boiling water for 8–10 minutes or until only just becoming tender – you want to keep some bite and firmness. Drain, set aside and keep warm.

Meanwhile, prepare the rice noodles according to the manufacturer's instructions and set aside to keep warm. Mix through a little drizzle of groundnut oil to prevent them sticking together. Set a clean pan of boiling water to simmer.

Heat a wok or high-sided frying pan on a high heat, add the oil in a circular motion and stir-fry the onions, chilli and garlic for 3–4 minutes. Add the carrots, agave or maple syrup and soya sauce, and stir-fry for a further 2–3 minutes before adding the lime juice. Remove the wok from the heat. Plunge the noodles in the pan of hot simmering water for 1 minute to reheat and then fully drain. Drizzle with a little sesame oil this time.

Assemble in four warmed bowls – hot carrots on warm noodles, topped with cold cucumber slices. Sprinkle each bowl with some coriander leaves, toasted sesame seeds and the toasted cashew nuts before serving.

Butternut Squash and Spinach Curry

with Coriander and Lime Pickle Rice

Serves 4

For the curry paste

3 Indonesian long peppercorns

20g (¼ cup) macadamia nuts

½ medium onion, roughly chopped

3 tbsp fresh grated ginger

1½ tsp turmeric powder

2 lemongrass stalks, base trimmed and outer leaves removed, core finely chopped

2 fat cloves of garlic, chopped

juice of 1 small lime

2 red chillies, chopped

1 tsp soya sauce

1 tbsp palm sugar

1 tbsp tamarind water

2 tbsp rapeseed oil

For the fried onions

1 small onion, finely sliced for frying

125ml (½ cup) vegetable oil

For the curry

1 medium butternut squash, peeled, deseeded and diced equally

1 tsp salt

4 kaffir lime leaves

1 stick of cinnamon

300ml (1¼ cups) coconut milk

100ml (½ cup) vegetable stock

120g (5 cups) baby spinach

Southern Asian curries simply excel at being vegetable-friendly. I feel they have the advantage over many other curries simply due to the fact that the sauce is really the star of the dish because of the stunning marriage of aromatic flavours it can boast. The sauce combines to create the perfect vehicle from which to eat any vegetable you care to add. You could use okra and new potatoes, carrots and broccoli, or green beans and aubergine, for example. Just look for a contrast in colour and texture to help give the dish a visual bite too.

There are a few less common ingredients to source, depending, of course, on your shopping style, but that's what drives the originality of the flavours and delivers the unique aromatics within the curry. The lemongrass, lime leaves and Indonesian long peppercorns are particularly essential.

❋ To make the curry paste

Grind the Indonesian long peppercorns in a pestle and mortar to a coarse powder. Add the nuts and crush them down in the pepper before combining the remaining ingredients and blending into a smooth paste with a hand blender. Set aside for an hour if you can.

To make the fried onions

Fry the sliced onions in vegetable oil until turning gold and crisp. Remove and drain on kitchen paper before setting aside.

To make the curry

Heat a little oil in a saucepan and fry the paste for a minute or two. Add the diced squash, salt, lime leaves, cinnamon stick, coconut milk and stock. Stir through on the heat, then cover and cook on a gentle simmer for 15 minutes until the squash is just becoming tender.

Make the rice while the squash is cooking.

Once the squash is just tender, add the spinach and cover again. Continue to cook for a further 5 minutes to allow all the spinach to wilt. Stir through and serve.

For the rice

250g (1 cup) basmati rice

small handful of coriander leaves, finely chopped

1 tsp lime pickle, loosened with 1 tsp water and lime pieces removed

To make the rice

Cook the rice according to the instructions on the packet. Once ready, mix the finely chopped coriander and lime pickle through thoroughly to coat all the grains. You can leave the lime pickle out if you're not a fan – not everybody is.

Serve each portion of curry topped with the fried onions.

Falafel Koftas

with Yogurt and Tomato Sauce

*Serves 2 hungry, 3 sharing or
4 very polite people*

8 torpedo falafels (page 272)

1 small onion, chopped

2 tbsp extra virgin rapeseed oil

1 clove of garlic, finely sliced

1 tsp chilli flakes (or more if you
prefer)

400g (15oz) tin of chopped
tomatoes

1 tsp sea salt

pinch of sugar

pinch of saffron

500ml (2 cups) vegetable oil for
frying

4 small pitta breads

2 tsp sumac

300g (1 cup) coconut milk
yogurt

handful of toasted pine nuts

handful of chopped coriander

I just love this dish. I could eat it every week and I probably do
eat it too often, but there you go! It's just got so much contrast of
flavour and texture – my favourite things. Crunchy toasted pitta
pieces, saffron and chilli-infused tomato sauce, cooling yogurt,
tangy sumac...and we haven't discussed the pine nuts, coriander
and falafels yet!

❈ Pre-make the falafels and keep chilled in the fridge until 10–15
minutes before you're ready to fry.

Make the tomato sauce. Fry the onion in the oil until soft
and translucent. Add the finely sliced garlic and chilli flakes.
Stir through for a minute on a medium heat before adding the
tomatoes, sea salt and sugar. At this stage add a little water (about
a quarter of the tomato tin – swirled around so you get all the juice
out) and add the pinch of saffron. Cook for 10–15 minutes on a
medium heat, stirring occasionally, until the tomatoes have broken
down and formed a rich sauce with a slight golden hew around
the edges from the saffron. Turn the heat right down and begin
assembling the dish – keeping an eye on the sauce.

Heat the oil in a wok or shallow fryer to approximately 170°C
(340°F) or until a piece of bread dropped in sizzles on the top.
Carefully fry the falafel in batches of two for 2–3 minutes each –
placing them on kitchen paper to dry when done. Keep in a warm
oven while you fry the remaining batches.

Assemble the dish – toast the pittas and cut them through so
each pitta forms two thin pittas. Toast on a low heat if they are
still soft – you want them crisp. Break them up and layer them
on a sharing plate and sprinkle with 1 tsp of sumac. Pour the hot
tomato sauce over them and then evenly drizzle over two-thirds of
the yogurt. Place the hot falafel koftas on top like spokes in a wheel
and drizzle the remaining yogurt over the dish. Sprinkle another
tsp of sumac followed by the pine nuts and a little coriander. Serve
immediately – it needs no accompaniment other than perhaps a
cold beer.

'Long Pepper' Pineapple Koftas

with Carrot and Celeriac Pickled Slaw (and Mild Jalapeño Yogurt Dressing)

Serves 2

For the pickled slaw (make this a few hours in advance)

1 large carrot, peeled and shredded on a mandolin

½ celeriac, peeled and shredded on a mandolin

1 tsp sea salt

150ml (½ cup) rice wine

150ml (½ cup) water

4 tbsp caster sugar

juice of 2 limes

For the mild jalapeño yogurt dressing

2 tbsp coconut milk yogurt

½ tsp Tabasco mild jalapeño chilli sauce (more if you prefer)

½ medium-size ripe pineapple

2 Indonesian long peppercorns

2 x quantity flatbread (page 274)

handful of fresh coriander leaves

I'm tempted to say there is something for everyone here – sweet, sour, spicy, creamy, crunchy, peppery...I could go on...but the real point is that there is so much flavour here – so much satisfaction for the senses. On top of all that, your senses are already being challenged by the hot griddled pineapple in the first place. If you're a little chilli-heat-sensitive, you could simply use plain coconut milk yogurt (although the yogurt dressing is really quite mild) – the Indonesian long peppercorns will still do their wonderfully aromatic thing. I just prefer a little secondary heat from the mild jalapeño chilli.

❋ First, make the pickled slaw. Place the shredded carrots and celeriac in a colander and sprinkle with the salt. Toss them around a little and leave to drain over a bowl for 20–30 minutes. Combine the rice wine, water and sugar in a small pan and heat through to dissolve the sugar. Once cooled, add the lime juice.

When ready, rinse well and drain the carrots and celeriac before drying on a clean tea towel. Then add to the pickling liquid and set aside to chill until required.

Add the chilli sauce to the yogurt and combine well to make the chilli yogurt dressing.

Cut the top and bottom off the pineapple and cut away the outer skin, then halve the pineapple, keeping one half and storing the other for another use. Quarter the retained half to achieve four pieces. Cut the inner core away on each piece so you have tender segments remaining – it's a good idea at this point to trim them a little so each has a fairly flat back and front. Crush the peppercorns in a pestle and mortar and grind into a fine powder – the aroma with be wonderful. Place the pineapple segments on a plate and sprinkle front and back evenly with the ground pepper and set aside.

Preheat the oven for the flatbreads and roll out the individual doughs ready to use – cooking them according to the recipe on page 274, setting aside to keep warm.

Lift about half the slaw out of the pickling liquid and dry it off a little, ready to use.

Heat the griddle pan on high. Sear the pineapple pieces diagonally against the grill lines to achieve good chargrill marks – about 2–3 minutes each side. This will caramelise the sugars in the pineapple and give a smoky edge to the flavour.

Assemble... Hot flatbread spooned over with yogurt sauce, layer with some slaw and plenty of coriander leaves, add the griddled pineapple pieces – wrap and enjoy!

You could also add some dry-toasted cashew nuts for extra texture if you like, or toasted peanuts.

Briam

with Roasted Red Pepper Sauce and
Garlic Cashew Nut Cream

Serves 4–6

**For the garlic cashew
nut cream**

120g (1¼ cups) cashew nuts

185ml (¾ cup) water

2 cloves of garlic

sea salt

juice of 1 small lemon

**For the roasted red
pepper sauce**

2 or 3 roasted red peppers from
a jar

1 fresh tomato and 2 small
skinned tomatoes (from the
tinned tomatoes, below)

1 tsp pul biber – Turkish pepper
flakes (optional)

1 tbsp olive oil

pinch of sugar

salt and pepper to season

For the briam

500g (1lb) Charlotte potatoes,
peeled and halved lengthways,
larger ones in thirds

2 medium red onions, peeled,
halved and thickly sliced

I thought twice about including this recipe. Largely because it could
be seen as too obvious or too simple – it is, after all, really just a roasted
stew of vegetables the Greek way. That said – *briam* is a traditional Greek
classic, ever-present as a plant-based recipe...and it is truly delicious!

Bringing the red pepper out to create a sweet accompanying
sauce ensures an extra boost of flavour, and the rich garlicky cream
adds a little further depth. It's a perfect dish for sharing with some
bread, particularly when you have a few too many vegetables all
ready at the same time in the garden.

Don't be put off by the list of ingredients – make the cream and
sauce in advance and the *briam* is really just chopping followed by
a little construction...the oven does all the hard work!

✿ To make the cream
Soak the cashews in water for 2 hours before draining and
combining with 185ml fresh water and the garlic. Blend to a very
smooth paste, adding a little more water to get the consistency
you want – I prefer it like single cream. Add the salt and half the
lemon juice. Taste and add the remaining lemon juice to season
further – if required.

To make the sauce
Chop the peppers and tomatoes together and cook on a medium heat
in the olive oil for 5–10 minutes. Remove to a bowl and once cooled
add the remaining ingredients and blend to a semi-smooth sauce.

Add a little water if it thickens too much. You want the consistency
of yogurt so that it will hold the garlic cream and coat the briam as
you eat. Allow to cool completely. You can serve the sauce warm or
hot if you wish, but I prefer the contrast of temperature.

To make the briam
Layer the vegetables in a good-sized roasting tin or large ovenproof
dish, seasoning lightly with each layer (this is important) – potatoes

2 courgettes, ends trimmed and thickly sliced at an angle

1 orange pepper, deseeded and sliced into rings

1 green pepper, deseeded and sliced into rings

1 medium aubergine, cubed in large pieces

sea salt

crushed black peppercorns

2 x 400g (15oz) tin of plum tomatoes

2 tbsp good-quality dried oregano

large handful of fresh dill, chopped (including stalks)

200ml (¾ cup) water

1 tsp tomato purée

150ml (½ cup) extra virgin olive oil

first, cut sides facing up, then onions, courgettes, peppers and aubergine. Try to find snug little spaces for the aubergine pieces and keep the layers as low as possible. Next, lift the whole tomatoes out of the tins, leaving the juice behind for now, and crush them a little in your hand as you spread them over the vegetables, pushing them down into spaces as you go. Sprinkle over the oregano and chopped dill. Add the water to the tomato tins and swirl around to catch all the tomato juice before combining the contents of both in one tin – add the tomato purée to the tomato water and whisk in to combine before pouring over the vegetables. Drizzle liberally with extra virgin olive oil and a last seasoning of sea salt and pepper.

Cover loosely with foil and roast at 200°C (400°F) for 1½ hours. Remove from the oven and carefully turn everything around a little in the dish. Check the seasoning at this point. Reduce the heat to 180°C (350°F) and roast for a further 30 minutes uncovered. The vegetables should be slightiy charred and coloured on top, but not burnt, and with a lot of the moisture now driven off. Check the potatoes are tender – if need be, roast a little longer.

To assemble... Spoon the red pepper sauce on to each serving plate and swirl with the back of a spoon or ladle to cover the centre of the plate. Using a slotted spoon, place servings of the briam piled in the centre and drizzle generously with the garlic cashew cream.

A few toasted pitta breads go well on the side.

Seeking Solace in the Kitchen

I have to give credit where it's due here. This chapter was all Jen's idea, but I wish it had been mine. In my world, the kitchen is the beating heart of a house and the soul of a home. It's the place where most discussion happens, where plans are made over good wine and where food is served and eaten most often. A long time ago we dispensed with any kind of dining room and opted for a large kitchen/dining space instead, and we never looked back. I prefer a relaxed casual space over a formal setting every time.

The kitchen works equally well as a private space too. Quiet preparation bordering on meditation or cooking to whatever the iPod throws out on shuffle – it's all 'me' time and I believe we all need some of that. I remember chef friends in my early hotel days, bemoaning the day shifts for being full of food prep – hours upon hours of preparing vegetables, while an emotionally unstable head chef stared out at them from his window-paned office like a bad-tempered praying mantis in a greenhouse. Trust me, it's no exaggeration to say head chefs used to throw pots and pans (and other sharper objects) across kitchens in temper, and yet here I am extolling the virtues of spending hours ensconced in recipe preparation or creation. How things change as we mature? (Sorry, Chris...sorry, Stuart...)

But there's the truth of it. When I actually stop to think about it, I am rarely happier than when I'm in the kitchen cooking for friends and family or just making things, and that includes the hours of preparational solitude it can often require. Time spent grinding spices, making sauces and pickles or simply making bread can be so rewarding *if* you can set that time aside. It will afford choice and variation in simple ways later on and can add an extra dimension to meals with friends or family, particularly when things happen at late notice – which are often the best lunches or evenings.

These recipes are for the longer preparation and/or making of...so turn your iPod to shuffle – turn the volume up or down, whatever suits your mood – and spend some quality 'me' time here.

Dressings

Sometimes you want to eat something really tasty but you just don't want to spend hours preparing it. I love 'prep' as chefs call it, but I remember from my hotel days that chef friends hated long afternoon shifts preparing vegetables. Dressings are a great way to add wonderfully fresh and lively flavour to things quickly. There are, of course, many, many dressing variations, so please adapt and improvise, but always use the best oil you can, the best-quality sea salt and pepper you can, the best lemons you can get, the freshest herbs...it really matters.

200ml (¾ cup) best-quality extra virgin olive oil

2 tbsp fresh mint, chopped

1 fat garlic clove, crushed

small sprinkle of caster sugar

1 tbsp chardonnay wine vinegar

sea salt

freshly ground peppercorns

Garlic and Fresh Mint Dressing

✤ Combine together with a whisk and season to taste with the salt and pepper.

Perfect over a small bowl of freshly boiled waxy salad potatoes.

5 tbsp best-quality extra virgin olive oil

juice of 1 lemon

grated zest of 1 lemon

1 tsp good white wine vinegar

½ preserved lemon

sea salt

freshly ground peppercorns

Preserved Lemon Dressing

✤ Combine the oil, lemon juice and zest and white wine vinegar with a whisk. Cut away all the flesh of the preserved lemon and julienne (cut into fine matchsticks) the skin. Mix with your dressing and add sea salt and pepper to taste.

(Delicious poured over some steamed tenderstem broccoli.)

Apple Pesto

1 clove garlic, peeled and
roughly chopped

large handful of good fresh basil
leaves

1 fresh green apple, cored,
peeled and roughly chopped

40g (¼ cup) toasted pine nuts

80ml (⅓ cup) extra virgin olive
oil, the best you have

squeeze of lemon juice

sea salt

freshly ground black pepper

We all know pesto so well now. I guess there was a time when
it was a rare commodity in the UK, like good olive oil or real
spaghetti, but now we use it almost too easily. It's manufactured
and packed on to our supermarket shelves like any other sauce
or dressing – and is much the worse for it in my opinion. I first
experienced the real thing while on honeymoon in Tuscany many
years ago. The owner of the villa we were staying in had left a
welcome pack of food – as the villa was situated way up in the
mountains, some way from any local shop (which incidentally was
packed high with pasta flour but not a packet of pasta in sight…
tells you something, eh?) – and it included beautiful fresh pesto
and fresh bread, as well as some of his own sparkling wine. Maybe
I was starry-eyed in love or maybe hungry from my wedding
hangover but…that was pesto! It was nothing like the stuff sold
in jars here. It's so much more worthwhile making some than
buying some – it just tastes so much better and inevitably less
'manufactured'.

❈ Combine all the ingredients, except the lemon juice, in a food
processor or large pestle and mortar if you have one, and blend to
create the pesto. Add the lemon juice and stir through. Taste and
adjust for seasoning with a little salt and pepper if you think it's
required. It will be subtly sweeter than you're used to, although it
shouldn't be over-sweet. Just delicious!

My 'Isle of Skye' Porridge Bread

a little flour or polenta for dusting

250g (1 cup) plain white flour

250g (1 cup) wholemeal flour

60g (½ cup) Scottish porridge oats, plus some to scatter

1 tsp bicarbonate of soda

½ tsp sea salt

2 tbsp golden syrup

400ml (1½ cups) almond milk

Every time we travel to the Isle of Skye, we stop off at the same place to buy a delicious bread made with Scottish oats to take with us – well, two actually. It's a wonderful bread for toasting at breakfast because it tastes like slices of hot crunchy porridge. It doesn't work quite so well at any other time of the day – mindset, I suppose, or childhood conditioning... It is 'porridge' bread after all.

It could be, of course, that I'm romanticising about this bread while I'm gazing over at the stunning sea cliffs in the far north of Skye. But, then, why not? Whether it's eating olives in the hot sun by the Mediterranean or delicious hot oaty toast on a bracing early-winter morning in Skye, we are all entitled to our special foodie moments.

Here's my homemade version to take with you on your travels.

❉ Prepare a baking tray with a light dusting of flour or polenta. Preheat the oven to 200°C (400°F).

Combine the two flours with the porridge oats, bicarbonate of soda and salt in a clean bowl. Warm the golden syrup enough to make it more liquid, but don't allow it to get too hot or boil. Add the syrup to the almond milk and stir through.

Make a well in the middle of the flour and add the milk, stirring well to combine everything into a sticky dough. Tip the dough on to a clean well-floured surface and shape with your hands to form a rounded dome.

Place the shaped dough on the baking tray and use a sharp knife to score a cross on the top the width of the bread, before topping with some extra oats and dusting with a little more flour. Bake in the oven for 35–40 minutes and then allow to cool on a wire rack before eating. You can check it's done by knocking on the base and listening for a hollow sound.

I think it's particularly satisfying toasted once cooled.

See you in Skye!

Oven-Roasted Tinned Tomatoes

with Orange Pepper Seasoning in Garlic-Flavoured Oil

2 x 400g (15oz) tins of plum tomatoes

sea salt

olive oil to drizzle

orange pepper seasoning

2 garlic cloves, very finely sliced

approximately 300ml (1¼ cups) good-quality extra virgin olive oil to store in

This is simple to do and it works really well. I'm not sure I can say a lot more than that, other than to add they are delicious, cheap to make and obviously as versatile as any of the more expensive bought ones. If you can't get orange pepper seasoning, then good-quality freshly ground peppercorns like tellicherry will work well too.

❋ Preheat the oven to 180°C (350°F).

Separate the whole tomatoes from all their juice using a sieve. Reserve the juice to use in another recipe. It's very useful for soup.

Carefully spread the tomatoes out on an oven tray lined with baking paper, cutting all but the small or broken ones in half, from top to bottom. Sprinkle with a pinch of sea salt, a drizzle of olive oil and a shake of orange pepper. Place in the oven for 10 minutes before reducing the heat to 100°C (200°F) and gently roasting for a further 40 minutes – turning halfway through. Remove from the oven and allow to cool. Place them in a sterilised jar with the garlic slices and a further good pinch of orange pepper and cover with the olive oil. Store in the fridge and use within a couple of weeks.

They are particularly good spread on hot toast as a simple bruschetta or used as part of the Peperonata recipe on page 276.

Some brands are better than others, and actually some of the cheaper brands can work better for this recipe as they have a less concentrated juice which I find more suited for this process. Plus you would need to slow-roast fresh ones for much longer.

Harissa

2 tsp caraway seeds

2 tsp coriander seeds

1 tsp cumin seeds

1 tsp black cumin seeds

4 fresh red long chillies, halved and deseeded

2 roasted red peppers, roughly chopped (from a jar is fine)

4 garlic cloves, peeled and roughly chopped

1 tsp Turkish red pepper flakes

juice of ½ lemon

pinch sea salt

80ml (⅓ cup) olive oil, and extra to top in the jar

1 tsp coriander leaves, very finely chopped

I have looked at, played with, tasted and re-tasted, read and re-read, made and, yes, re-made harissa till my heart is more than content. There are so many recipes, and several of them are frustratingly too bitter or just too hot, so I felt it was worth making this a stand-alone recipe rather than a footnote. I want to be able to use it often enough to make it worthwhile making, and I want it to be versatile while still retaining its wonderfully unique flavour and fiery heat. I think the black cumin and Turkish flakes are the secret...of course, they're not a secret now!

❋ Carefully toast the seeds in a dry frying pan for a few minutes until they start to release their aromas. Be very careful not to burn them – it will be really obvious in your harissa. Once cooled a little, crush to a powder in a pestle and mortar.

Combine the ground powder and the remaining ingredients (except the olive oil and coriander) and pulse with a hand blender to form a coarse paste. Add in the oil and chopped coriander and stir through to combine. Place in a sealable jar and top with extra olive oil to help keep it for longer. It will keep refrigerated for a good couple of months if you keep it under oil.

'Sunshine' Tomato Sauce

3 tbsp olive oil

1 large clove of garlic, crushed

1 x 400g (15oz) tin of good-quality chopped tomatoes or 350g (1½ cups) good-quality passata, crushed or sieved

120ml (½ cup) water

good pinch of saffron

a little freshly ground black pepper

pinch of sea salt

pinch of sugar, if required

It's a slightly sad fact that many people still rely on heavily 'branded' processed tomato sauces. Time constraints and conflicting commitments are ever-present, but a good tomato sauce is pretty simple, rewarding and keeps well as it's easily frozen.

I unashamedly call this 'sunshine' tomato sauce because of my use of saffron. It's a spice that screams hot sun and holidays to me every time I sense its aroma and taste its heady Mediterranean flavour.

You can, of course, make this sauce without the saffron, if just a good basic tomato sauce is required, or substitute a herb such as thyme, oregano or shredded basil leaves – but saffron does a wonderful thing all of its own here. I do occasionally add salted capers to this version too (add 2 tbsp at the same time as the saffron if you want to vary it).

Either way, if you don't already do so, please make your own whenever and wherever possible. It's so much better for you.

Whether you use chopped, crushed or sieved tomatoes is entirely your choice as to the texture of sauce you prefer. More often than not, I decide just before I start making it.

✽ Heat 2 tbsp of the olive oil on a medium heat in a frying pan with the crushed garlic and gently fry for 1 minute. Stir the garlic through the oil and add the tomatoes before it starts to colour. Add the water – whatever container the tomatoes came in, a third full is an ideal measure – swirl it around a little first.

Add the saffron and stir it through the tomatoes. Add the black pepper and salt and cook the sauce on a low simmer for 20 minutes so it's just bubbling away, stirring occasionally.

Two or three minutes from the end, add the final tbsp of olive oil and stir through again.

Check for seasoning and adjust to your taste, including a pinch of sugar if the tomatoes are a little sharp.

Spiced Tomato and Mint Chutney

2 x 400g (15oz) tins of chopped tomatoes

1 dried bird's eye chilli

1 tsp onion seeds

1 tsp fennel seeds

½ tsp black cumin seeds and ½ tsp cumin seeds (or 1 tsp cumin seeds)

1 tsp black mustard seeds

2 tbsp rapeseed oil

150ml (½ cup) cane vinegar (or white wine vinegar)

30g (¼ cup) palm sugar

handful of fresh mint leaves, chopped

1 tsp sea salt

1 tsp dried mint

I created this quick chutney specifically to accompany the Indian-Inspired Kale and Kasuri Methi Potato Cakes, but I already use it with many more dishes because I find it so irresistible. I suppose in the true old-fashioned tradition it's the job of any chutney to enliven whatever it's paired with, so no surprise that it's versatile – but the marriage of the spices and the authentic sweet and sour 'tangy' combination of the palm sugar and cane vinegar really work beautifully here – particularly with the added level of mint.

✿ Sieve the tinned tomatoes to drain off the juice, shaking gently to help get as much of the juice separated as you can. (Reserve the drained juice to make soup...)

Crush the dried chilli with the spices and gently fry all the spices in the rapeseed oil for 1–2 minutes on a medium heat until they start to sizzle. Take care not to burn them! Take the pan off the heat and very carefully add the cane vinegar and then the palm sugar. Place back on the heat and stir until the sugar has dissolved. Now add the strained tomatoes, fresh mint and the salt, and stir through to combine everything. Bring the heat up until you get the tomatoes bubbling and then lower the heat to simmer gently for 15–20 minutes, adding the dried mint about halfway through. Allow everything to reduce and intensify, checking and stirring through occasionally. If you feel it's all getting a little dry too soon, then add a dash of water to loosen the chutney, but remember you are aiming for a chutney, not a sauce.

Mojo Verde Sauce

2 tsp cumin seeds

1 tsp sea salt

1 garlic clove, crushed

small handful of fresh flat-leaf parsley, chopped

large handful of chopped fresh coriander leaves, including stalks

1 bird's eye chilli, crushed

juice of ½ lemon

150ml (½ cup) extra virgin rapeseed oil

Mojo verde is a classic Spanish green sauce that can accompany many things. It's probably most commonly seen accompanying Canarian potatoes alongside a similar red sauce, but its uses are varied due to its wonderful combination of fresh flavours. It's a great plant-based sauce which I haven't added to or subtracted from – I've simply tinkered with the levels to suit my use.

�֍ Toast the cumin seeds in a dry pan on a medium heat until aromatic (about 1–2 minutes at most) and then grind in a pestle and mortar to a fine powder. (Toasting the cumin is very important to getting the right flavour here.)

Combine the ground cumin and remaining ingredients in a bowl and pulse with a hand blender to combine everything. Check for seasoning and adjust if necessary.

White Grape and Pistachio Focaccia

500g (2 cups) strong white bread flour

1 tsp fine salt

15g (1 tbsp) dried yeast, prepared according to packet instructions with 150ml (½ cup) warm water

2 tbsp extra virgin olive oil

a further 200ml (1 cup) warm water

approximately 20 seedless white grapes

100g (½ cup) pistachio nuts, shelled

a little more extra virgin olive oil and sea salt for the top

There is something very special about the combination of bread and fruit like this. Apart from the wonderful 'table theatre' attributes, it just tastes so delicious. It's the sweet and savoury flavour, I guess – the way the grapes burst and sweeten the bread and the texture the savoury pistachios contribute.

The only down side I can think of to making your own bread is the ten minutes or so of arm-tiring kneading that's required...so here's my tip to make that bit enjoyable too.

Choose a ten-minute-plus song or piece of music specifically as your kneading song* and time yourself to that. It makes kneading a pleasure!

✿ Make the dough by combining the flour, salt, yeast, olive oil and 200ml (1 cup) warm water. Knead on an oiled surface for 10 minutes (or until the song ends) before allowing the dough to rise in a clean, covered bowl to double its size – approximately 1 hour, but more if necessary.

Knock back the dough and knead the pistachios in for 2–3 minutes. Place the dough in a well-oiled, high-sided baking tray and gently push it out to fill the rectangle shape. Make regular indentations on the top of the dough with your fingers and place a grape in each before drizzling over with a little more olive oil. Cover loosely with oiled clingfilm and leave to rise for a further 30–40 minutes in a warm place – ideally somewhere close to the oven as you preheat it to 200°C (400°F).

Once the dough has risen again (it should rise enough to partially encase the grapes), sprinkle with good sea salt and bake in the preheated oven for 20–25 minutes until crisp and coloured on top. Serve cut into small squares, each with a grape if possible.

Mine is 'Hear My Train a Comin' by Jimi Hendrix from the album Rainbow Bridge – 11.14 minutes.

Saffron and Rosemary Focaccia

good pinch of saffron strands

200ml (¾ cup) hot water

500g (2 cups) strong white bread flour

1 tsp fine salt

15g (1 tbsp) dried yeast, prepared according to packet instructions with 150ml (½ cup) warm water

2 tbsp extra virgin olive oil

3–4 long stalks of fresh rosemary, broken into smaller sprigs

a little more extra virgin olive oil and sea salt for the top

The aroma of saffron, as I've said already, sings out sunshine, holiday food to me. There isn't another smell like it that I can think of – nothing to confuse it with.

However, be warned – use a little too much and that alluring aroma of saffron can go from Mediterranean to medicinal quite easily.

I love the Greek legend about saffron. Food deserves its historical story, and it's even better when it's embellished by a Greek legend.

✿ Steep the saffron in 200ml (¾ cup) hot water for 20–30 minutes.

Make the dough by combining the flour, salt, yeast, olive oil and 200ml of saffron water. Knead on an oiled surface for at least 10 minutes (or until the song ends) before allowing to rise in a clean covered bowl to double in size – approximately 1 hour but more if necessary.

Knock back the dough before placing it in a well-oiled high-sided baking tray. Gently push it out to fill the rectangle shape. Make regular indentations on the top of the dough with your fingers and stand a small sprig of rosemary in each before drizzling over with a little more olive oil. Cover loosely with oiled clingfilm and leave to rise for a further 30–40 minutes in a warm place – ideally somewhere close to the oven as you preheat it to 200°C (400°F).

Once the dough has risen again (it should rise enough to partially encase the rosemary sprigs), sprinkle with good sea salt and bake in the preheated oven for 20–25 minutes until crisp and coloured on top. Serve cut into small squares, each with a rosemary sprig if possible.

Alternative kneading song – 'Thinking of a Place' by The War on Drugs from the album A Deeper Understanding – 11.11 minutes.

The legend of Crocus and Smilax

In Ancient Greece, spices such as saffron were highly valued, and sailors often undertook arduous and perilous voyages in search of these aromatic treasures. Crocus was a handsome young Athenian who became obsessed with a beautiful wood nymph named Smilax. Smilax was flattered by the attention, but all too soon became tired of his attentions, toying with his affections without mercy

– much to the consternation of the gods. However, Crocus was driven by his passion and was unwilling to give up easily. Some legends tell that Smilax bewitched Crocus and turned him into the flower that now bears his name...but Ovid's account suggests that he pined away, and the gods transformed him into the flower, whose vibrant orange-red stigmas symbolise the glow of his unrequited passion.

Homemade Gnocchi

Makes enough for 4

6 large waxy-textured baking potatoes (approximately 1kg or 2lb)

olive oil

100g (½ cup) '00' pasta flour, plus a little for dusting

Gnocchi is one of those recipes people often avoid, believing it to be messy, time-consuming and difficult to get right. I know because I was one of them. I would liken it to making bread, in that you might get it wrong first time (who doesn't?) and you do need to take care and follow some rules, but it needn't engulf your kitchen in flour and it's not so challenging as not to be worthwhile.

I'm not actually against packet gnocchi – it's a useful store cupboard fallback, if a little dense in texture, but, then, if you like the texture, as I do, it's a comfortable vehicle for a well-made sauce. Homemade gnocchi represents another level as it really reflects the flavour of the potato you use and contributes a soft pillowy comforting texture to the meal which elevates a sauce.

❋ Prick each potato once or twice with the tip of a sharp knife. In your hands, coat each potato in a light film of olive oil and lay them out on a baking tray. Bake for 50 minutes at 220°C (425°F) or until tender in the middle.

As soon as you can after removing them from the oven, cut a deep cross on the top and push them open to release the steam. Leave to cool slightly like this for 4–5 minutes. It's this process that will help drive off some excess moisture. Carefully scrape the potato flesh out of the skins into a wide shallow dish, taking great care to avoid including any skin or flecks of skin. You don't want speckled gnocchi!

Pass the potato through a potato ricer back into a shallow dish or mash with a potato masher – if using a masher, do so as minimally as possible to avoid overworking the potato.

Dust the flour over the potato using a sieve and gently begin to combine by cutting the flour in with a scraper or spatula. Don't knead like bread – it will overwork the potato. Once it's mostly incorporated, bring the mixture out of the shallow dish and on to a lightly floured surface, and press down to form a rough rectangle. Now fold over on itself and press down again, repeating the

It is worth mentioning that while flour incorporated into the dough will have an effect on the density of the gnocchi, as already stated, within reason any flour dusted on after to keep them dry and separate will have a limited effect and wash off in the cooking...and you really don't want them sticking together!

process for a minute or two until you are happy that the two ingredients are well combined. If the mixture become a little sticky during the process, dust a little more '00' flour on the surface, but remember the more flour you add, the heavier the gnocchi. Once it's done, split the dough in half. Roll out one half with your hands to form a long, slim 'snake' of dough about 2cm thick; then with a sharp knife, cut it into pillow shapes just a little bit longer than they are wide, placing the gnocchi pieces on a floured plate and dusting them lightly with flour to prevent them sticking together. Repeat with the second half of dough. Feel free to lightly indent each gnocchi on one side with a fork to create a ridge effect, but I prefer to leave well alone.

If using straight away, then cover with clingfilm and keep chilled in the fridge until you're ready to cook them.

Otherwise, ensuring they have a gentle dusting of flour all over, place on a plate in the freezer for 30–45 minutes until they are becoming a little rigid (this will ensure they don't all stick in one clump) before placing in a freezer bag and freezing for future use. When you come to use the frozen ones, simply cook as normal in their frozen state and they will still float to the top when ready... they'll just take a little longer, of course.

My Falafels

Makes approximately 8 falafels

125g (½ cup) dried chickpeas, soaked in cold water overnight

1 small onion, peeled and roughly chopped

1 green chilli, deseeded or not and roughly chopped

1 garlic clove, peeled and chopped

handful of fresh coriander leaves

½ tsp ground black cumin seeds

½ tsp ground cumin seeds

½ tsp sea salt

2 tbsp sesame seeds

2 tbsp gram flour

1 tsp baking powder

½ tsp ground cardamom seeds from about 12–15 pods

Fresh homemade falafels are unbeatable...and they're not difficult and they're a big reward. Wonderful with a simple dip as a snack or made into a sharing dish like this – they deliver on all the senses. If you all too often revert to tinned chickpeas, then please make the effort this time to use the dried ones here. It makes such a difference and, really, how much work is soaking?

✼ Drain the chickpeas. Pulse the onion, green chilli, garlic and coriander leaves to a rough mixture in a blender before adding the chickpeas. Pulse to a finer mixture to achieve something closer to a rough paste. Remove the paste to a clean bowl and add the remaining ingredients and mix together thoroughly by hand.

Form torpedo-shaped falafels by shaping a ball of the mixture inside your palm, closing your fingers around it to gently shape it accordingly.

Place on a plate, cover and refrigerate for an hour or more before using to help them firm up and keep their shape. Remove from the refrigerator 10 minutes before cooking.

Heat the oil in a wok or shallow fryer to approximately 170°C (340°F) or until a piece of bread dropped in sizzles on the top. Carefully fry the falafel in batches of two for 2–3 minutes each – placing them on kitchen paper to dry when done. Keep in a warm oven while you fry the remaining batches.

Flatbreads

Flavoured or Not...

1 tsp sugar

270ml (1 cup) warm water

15g (1 tbsp) dried yeast

1 tsp salt

500g (2 cups) strong white flour

60ml (¼ cup) olive oil

I make these with monotonous regularity. They taste so much better freshly baked out of the oven and you can add extra flavours (sparingly) into the dough, such as onion seeds, garlic, chilli flakes or even some dried fenugreek leaves. I often use a dash of infused rapeseed oil to add flavour without further texture or colour – it just depends what I'm doing with them, or what mood I'm in.

❁ Activate the yeast by dissolving the sugar in 150ml (½ cup) of the warm water and then adding the yeast. Whisk briefly and set aside for 15 minutes. Meanwhile, add salt to the flour in a large bowl and measure out your oil and remaining 120ml (½ cup) warm water. Once the yeast is ready, combine all ingredients (including any flavourings) to form a dough and knead for 10 minutes on a lightly floured surface to the song of your choice – see the focaccia recipes earlier for suggestions. Place in an oiled bowl, cover with a damp tea towel and leave to rise at room temperature for at least an hour or until doubled in size.

Once the dough is proved/risen, knock it back and divide into eight roughly equal pieces. Individually wrap any you are not going to use straight away in clingfilm and freeze for another time. When you want to use them, simply defrost thoroughly.

Preheat the oven to 220°C (425°F). On a lightly floured surface, roll each piece out into a very rough thin round and bake on a lightly oiled preheated baking tray for 5–6 minutes. They should blister up a little in the cooking process and turn a pale golden colour. Keep them warm in a dry tea towel until you need them. They should be just pliant when served.

Peperonata

with Capers, Garlic and Olives

1 long red pepper and 1 long
yellow pepper

olive oil

3 small garlic cloves, finely
sliced

1 tbsp of salted capers (the
larger the better), briefly rinsed

½ quantity Oven-Roasted
Tinned Tomatoes (page 258)
(including the olive oil)

5 or 6 small pitted green or
black olives

½ tsp sweet smoked paprika
(dulce)

1 tsp red wine vinegar

1 tsp dried rosemary or oregano

Over the years I've seen many recipes for peperonata, and many variations. Some complicated – some not. Some traditional – some not. Many of them delicious – and some most definitely not! This is one of my favourite ways to make it when I plan to use it cold. It's very versatile as it's delicious on hot griddled bread or mixed through many styles of pasta, both long and short, and, of course, it works very well as part of the Warm Mediterranean Potato Salad.

It will keep for several weeks in the fridge once made, but I truly doubt you will keep it that long without finishing it and making it again.

I much prefer to use long peppers here as they are a little sweeter, but the more common bell ones will work well.

❋ Preheat the oven to 180°C (350°F).

Slice the peppers in half lengthways and remove the seeds. Coat all over with a little olive oil and place in an ovenproof dish. Scatter the sliced garlic equally inside the hollow peppers and mix around to get them coated in olive oil. Roast for approximately 15 minutes until the peppers are soft and slightly charred.

Remove from the oven and, once cool enough, slice widthways into 1cm-wide slices. Return them to the roasting dish with any residual oil and garlic slices. Add the capers, tomatoes in oil, olives, sweet smoked paprika, vinegar and dried rosemary to the peppers and gently mix through to combine everything well. Allow to cool before pouring into a sterilised glass jar and topping up with olive oil, ensuring everything is covered. I don't add salt as the salted capers should contribute enough, but check for flavour and adjust the seasoning if you prefer. Leave for a day or more before using if you can, and remember they are best brought out of the fridge half an hour or so before using.

Caponata Revisited

(Sicilian Sweet and Sour Loose Chutney with Aubergine, Celery and Fennel)

- 1 medium-large aubergine, diced into 1.5cm (½ inch) pieces
- 2 tbsp olive oil
- 3 celery sticks, trimmed, de-stringed and chopped into 1cm pieces
- 1 medium onion, one half chopped a little larger than the other
- 1 small fennel bulb, trimmed and finely chopped
- 3 tbsp red wine vinegar
- 200g (¾ cup) chopped tinned tomatoes
- 1 tsp caster sugar
- 1 tbsp salted capers, rinsed
- sea salt and pepper
- handful of toasted pine nuts
- handful of basil leaves, torn at the last minute

Most of us are pretty familiar with caponata, I would have thought – the famous Sicilian dish that bears more than a passing resemblance to France's ratatouille or, not wishing to offend anyone, vice versa. When it's made well, it is utterly delicious and quite often better the following day, when its flavours have been allowed to develop (if you make enough, that is). However, I can't help thinking it's a little forgotten now. The problem is that, when people don't have a lot of time to create a dish like caponata from scratch, they revert to the bought version and then, inevitably, stop buying because bought can taste like bland stewed vegetables. We often forget how great some simple classic dishes are, so I really think you'll be delighted to rediscover good caponata again.

I know it may seem obvious to say, but the greatest attention to seasoning will deliver the very best caponata – otherwise it *will be* just stewed vegetables – and seasoning includes the quality of the red wine vinegar and capers. Caponata is a vibrant loose chutney style of dish with a sweet and sour combination that should never be bland! It's also a perfect example of traditional plant-based food.

It's common to have raisins in caponata, but they are excluded here because I'm really not a fan of the texture of cooked raisins (we all have our foodie blind spots), but feel free to add some in if you are – just leave out the sugar. Furthermore, I have eaten several variations where toasted flaked almonds and mint are used to finish the dish, and they do work wonderfully well, but I just prefer the more familiar toasted pine nuts and basil.

❊ Soak the diced aubergine in cold water for 10 minutes, then drain and dry on kitchen paper.

Fry the aubergine in olive oil for 5 minutes, then remove and set aside. Fry the chopped celery and onion for 5 minutes, then remove and set aside. Fry the chopped fennel for 5 minutes before adding the celery and onion back in. Add the vinegar and allow to reduce a little for 30 seconds before adding the tomatoes, sugar

and capers. Stir through, cover and continue to cook for 6 minutes.

Add the aubergine back in and fold through. Reduce the heat and continue to cook, covered, for a further 10–12 minutes to allow the vegetables to stew together and soften a little more (if you feel you need to, add a little dash of water to help process). You don't want to break the aubergine down too much, so be gentle when combining everything. Check for seasoning and adjust with sea salt and pepper as required. The aubergine should be soft but still highly visible and the celery should be yielding but still with a little firmness that contributes to the enjoyment of the dish. The balance should be clean and sharp from the red wine vinegar and mellowed a little by the note of sweetness.

Remove from the heat and fold through the pine nuts and torn basil leaves. Allow to cool, covered.

Serve at room temperature or chilled on hot toast as a starter or lunch. Alternatively, include as a small plate, picnic dish, evening meal side dish or just steal from the fridge with a little bread when you just can't stop yourself!

Larder Recipes

If you can catch yourself in the frame of mind to make things not in advance but for later use, then you will have a lot of very nice things to add to and supplement dishes with – and you will be rewarded with a lot of pleasure.

Time spent making some store cupboard or larder items will add variety to future dishes and you will be so thankful that you put the time aside in the first place.

2 tsp coriander seeds

½ tsp cardamom pod seeds

½ tsp black cumin seeds

½ tsp black mustard seeds

3 cloves

½ tsp dried fenugreek leaves

½ tsp ground ginger

½ tsp turmeric

¼ tsp Kashmiri chilli powder

Mild Curry Powder Mix

✤ In a dry frying pan, gently toast the seeds and cloves until they start to become aromatic. Take care not to burn them. Allow to cool and combine with the remaining ingredients in a pestle and mortar and grind to a fine powder. Keep in a sealed jar.

3 cloves

2 tsp coriander seeds

1 tsp cardamom seeds

1 tsp black cumin seeds

1 tsp black peppercorns

1 tsp crushed red chillis

1 tsp ground cinnamon

1 tsp ground ginger

3 tsp amchur powder

1½ tsp dried fenugreek leaves

1 tsp sweet paprika

My Aromatic Kofta Spice Mix

✤ Toast the seeds and peppercorns for 1–2 minutes in a dry frying pan to release the oils and heighten their aroma. Take great care not to burn them. Cool slightly and grind together in a pestle and mortar or spice grinder before adding the remaining spices. Mix well to combine. Store in a sealed jar.

Poor Man's 'International' Cheese

Versatile Flavoured Breadcrumbs for General Use

Use these as directed in several recipes within the book, or even as delicious textural additions to salads.

❋ Cut about a quarter off a ciabatta loaf and roughly dice it – pulse it in a blender to form rough crumbs and spread these on a baking tray. Toast in a hot oven (about 200°C/400°F) for 5 minutes until they are golden and dry.

Combine about 4 tbsp with your chosen ingredients accordingly.

Greek

1 tsp dried oregano

1 tbsp finely chopped pistachios

Swedish

1 tbsp chopped dill

1 tsp ground black pepper

French

1 clove garlic, finely chopped and baked with the crumbs in the oven

1 tsp herbes de Provence

Italian (or Pangrattato)

1 tsp lemon zest

2 tsp flat-leaf parsley

pinch of chilli

Spanish (or Migas de Pan)

1 tbsp chopped toasted almonds

1 tbsp chopped flat-leaf parsley

1 tsp sweet paprika

Pickled Carrots

These are wonderful simply included in a salad or a sandwich.

❋ Peel and trim the carrots. Halve them and cut them into long matchsticks (juliennes) and place them in the sterilised container you intend to keep them in. In a pan, combine the other ingredients and bring to the boil. Once it reaches the boil, turn the heat off and pour the liquid over the carrots. Ensure all the carrots are submerged and leave to cool before closing and storing in the fridge. Keep for a day or two in order to infuse the flavours well and then use within 2–3 weeks.

1 large sealable glass jar, sterilised

4 carrots

150ml (½ cup) cider vinegar (white wine vinegar is fine)

100ml (⅓ cup) water

3 tbsp sugar

½ tsp sea salt

1 tbsp coriander seeds

1 tsp caraway seeds

1 bay leaf

Preserved Lemons

1 large sealable glass jar, sterilised

unwaxed lemons – the best you can get but not too large (enough to fill your chosen jar)

sea salt

2 tsp whole coriander seeds

1 tsp whole black peppercorns

filtered water

olive oil

These are easy to make, wonderful to use and look impressive on your shelf. When you need to use them, it's usually only one or two quarters at a time, so they last for a good while.

✻ Quarter each lemon from top to bottom to within an inch of its base but not completely through. Stuff the exposed flesh with sea salt, squeeze closed and place inside a large sealable, sterilised jar. Pack them in as close and tight as you can, wedging them together so they don't rise up when you add the water. Add the coriander seeds and peppercorns and cover everything with the water.

I use freshly squeezed lemon juice instead of water when I can as it's even better, but water works well and is cheaper.

Ensure the lemons are submerged and not breaking through the water at any time. Pour some olive oil on the top, seal closed and store for at least a month before using. Once you start using them, make sure the lemons always remain under the liquid.

Easy Pickled Cucumbers

1 x 500ml (16fl oz) sealable jar, sterilised

200ml (3/4 cup) cider vinegar

juice of 1 small lemon

100g (1/2 cup) granulated sugar

1 tsp sea salt

1 tsp whole tellicherry black peppercorns

2 tsp fennel seeds

1 cucumber

handful of fresh dill, roughly chopped

I love these pickled cucumbers. It's the dill and fennel that do it. I have to confess to these being a bit of a 'fridge-raider' food.

✻ Bring all the ingredients, except the cucumber and dill, to the boil in a pan and simmer long enough to fully dissolve the sugar.

Using a peeler, take strips off the cucumber lengthways, leaving a stripped effect on the skin. It's not utterly necessary, but it does give the pickles a more interesting appearance.

Using a mandolin or sharp knife, slice the cucumber widthways at a 45° angle into slices.

Add all the cucumber slices and dill into your sterilised jar and pour over the hot pickling liquid – mix around a little and cover. Once cool, stir through again to mix everything up well. Ensure all the cucumber slices are submerged, seal and store for a day or two before using. Keep in the fridge once and use within 2–3 weeks.

Easy Pickled Beetroot

1 x 500ml (16fl oz) sealable jar, sterilised

3 large pre-cooked beetroots

200ml (¾ cup) cider vinegar

juice of 1 small lemon

100g (½ cup) granulated sugar

1 tsp sea salt

1 tsp whole tellicherry black peppercorns

2 tsp fennel seeds

pinch of chilli flakes

handful of fresh dill, roughly chopped

This is similar to the recipe for my pickled cucumbers – for which I make no apologies on two counts: it simply works extremely well with either, and either is extremely simple to make. I still can't make up my mind which is my favourite, although given that beetroot does stain fingers, it's slightly less incriminating to raid the fridge for the cucumbers!

❋ Using a mandolin or sharp knife, slice the beetroot widthways into thin slices. Bring all the ingredients, except the beetroot and dill, to the boil in a pan and simmer long enough to fully dissolve the sugar.

Add all the beetroot slices and dill into your sterilised jar and cover with the hot pickling liquid. Stir through once to mix everything up well. Ensure all the beetroot is submerged, seal and allow to cool fully. Ideally store for a day before using. Keep in the fridge and use within 2–3 weeks.

Chermoula

2 garlic cloves

1 tsp mild paprika

1 red chilli, deseeded and roughly chopped

1 tsp ground cumin seeds

pinch of saffron strands

1 tsp chopped preserved lemon skin

handful of fresh coriander leaves

handful of fresh mint leaves

1 tsp sea salt

5 tbsp extra virgin olive oil

I think everyone's *chermoula* is, and possibly should be, a little different. It seems to me it's like *garam masala* – every house has its own blend according to taste. In that respect, use this as a template and by all means adjust to suit your taste.

❋ Combine all the ingredients and blend with a hand blender. Store in an airtight jar, topped with some more olive oil. It will keep well for quite a few days.

Dill Oil

large handful of fresh dill

small handful of spinach leaves (optional)

160ml (⅔ cup) extra virgin cold-pressed rapeseed oil

I always think of dill as an underused herb, probably because I have come to like it very much over the years and I don't see it used that often when I eat out, although to be fair that's hardly conclusive evidence. This dill oil can be used for many things including soups and salads and wouldn't be out of place drizzled on the Briam dish (page 248), but it stands out particularly well in the Fennel Vichyssoise recipe for which it's included here.

❋ Blanch the dill (and spinach if using) in lightly salted boiling water for 15 seconds. Remove and refresh in ice-cold water. Drain and squeeze out the excess water from the dill.

Using a hand blender, blend the oil and dill (and spinach leaves if using) together until well combined. Strain the blended oil through a muslin cloth into a clean jar and keep for a week or so at room temperature.

The spinach leaves will impart an even deeper vibrant green colour but are by no means essential – you could call it a wee chefy trick.

Simple Pizza Sauce

2 tbsp olive oil

350ml (1½ cups) crushed tomato passata

1 tsp dried oregano

1 tsp sea salt

½ tsp sugar

2 or 3 fresh rosemary sprigs

There are endless pizza sauce recipes in the world. Here's how I make mine, and I think it tastes pretty good – but each to their own!

❋ Heat the olive oil in a frying pan on a medium setting and add the passata followed by 100ml of water that's been swirled around in the empty passata bottle. Add the oregano, salt and sugar and stir through. Lay in the sprigs of rosemary and stir through again. Leave to simmer on a gentle heat for 5 minutes, stirring occasionally. Remove from the heat and allow to cool to room temperature while the herbs continue to infuse before removing the rosemary and storing the sauce in the fridge until required. It will keep for 2–3 days or freeze for a month.

Desserts

Sweet tooth or not sweet tooth...that really is the question. Whether one abstains or indulges.

The beauty of plant food, of course, is that inevitably you're starting from a position of advantage. Yes, there is sweetness that can come from sugar or the sugars present in fruit, but for the reasons I've prioritised here, fruit is still a wonderfully natural thing to be enjoyed and heralded wherever possible, and nowhere is it easier to do so than within desserts!

I have made a purposeful effort to avoid overtly clever or complicated recipes. Not out of disdain for any such desserts, but more out of a will to create great-tasting, attractive desserts that make the most of different fruits.

There are some wonderful creations out there, but I think we occasionally lose sight of our rich fruit heritage in a bid to chase down clever choices when often the best option is on our doorstep or in our market. Since we first cared about food, we have been tweaking, twisting and seeking ever more complicated and inspired ways of eating it, often none more so than sweet dishes. There is a simple beauty to all fruit, be it homegrown or from warmer shores, and an abundance of choice. It's plant-based food's natural sweet larder.

Rhubarb and Indonesian Long Pepper Crumble

Serves about 6 (individual or otherwise)

Rhubarb

900g (2lb) prepared and chopped rhubarb, roughly 3cm (1 inch) pieces

80g (⅓ cup) golden sugar

1 tbsp fresh ginger, grated

3 tbsp port (optional)

Crumble topping

180g (1¼ cups) self-raising flour

100g (¼lb) dairy-free butter, chilled

110g (½ cup) demerara sugar

100g (½ cup) pistachios, shelled and chopped

handful of flaked almonds

1 level tsp ground cinnamon

6 Indonesian long peppercorns, ground in pestle and mortar

I know it's not necessarily the done thing to praise your own food, but this is fantastic! I'll be honest: I'm more of a slave to a savoury tongue than any sweet tooth, which is probably why I like this so much. All the natural sweetness you would associate with such a crumble is still here, but just given another dimension by the inclusion of the Indonesian pepper. In much the same way that balsamic vinegar suits strawberries, the Indonesian long peppercorns' distinctive flavour works wonderfully well to complement the rhubarb.

It's another combination that at first messes with your senses a little, but I wouldn't call it radical – just pushing a few natural boundaries.

And anyway – who doesn't want their very own individual crumble?!

❋ Combine the rhubarb with the sugar and ginger and simmer on a low heat in a covered saucepan for about 15 minutes until soft but still holding its shape. While the rhubarb is cooking, make the topping by combining the flour and dairy-free butter by hand to form a crumbly mixture. Add the sugar, nuts, ground cinnamon and half of the ground peppercorns and combine well.

Preheat the oven to 200°C (400°F).

Either fill individual pans with the cooked rhubarb as I have or use a single baking dish if you prefer, leaving some room to add the topping. Add the crumb topping to the dishes and sprinkle with the remaining ground peppercorns.

Bake for 30 minutes or until golden brown on top.

Serve with quenelles (oval scoops shaped between two dessert spoons) of vanilla coconut yogurt or dairy-free ice cream placed on top of the hot crumble.

Apple and Calvados Cranachan

Serves 4

4–5 apples, peeled and cored, cooking apples or even your own

1 tbsp caster sugar

3 tbsp agave syrup plus a little to finish

35g (¼ cup) rolled oats

250g (1 cup) coconut milk yogurt

2 tbsp calvados plus a little to finish

Ooh, I could get into quite a lot of trouble with this! A good Highland lad tampering with a classic Scottish recipe like Cranachan.

Well, my reason is that we have a small orchard and a large quantity of apples, so the mind engages. It's actually a delicious alternative, and I get such satisfaction out of using any of our garden produce when it's at its best.

❈ Dice the apples and place in a pan with 150ml water and the caster sugar. Bring to the boil, then reduce to a simmer, cooking the apples gently for 15–20 minutes or until broken down and soft. Keep checking they don't dry out. Stir in 1 tbsp of the agave syrup and set aside to cool completely.

Toast the oats in a dry frying pan on a medium heat until they start to colour. Remove immediately and transfer to a plate to cool. Once cooled, drizzle with 1 tbsp of agave syrup and stir through to coat all the oats.

Whisk the coconut yogurt in a bowl for a couple of minutes to get air in and lighten the yogurt. Add the last tbsp of the agave syrup and 2 tbsp of calvados and whisk together again to combine well.

Layer the dessert in four individual glass tumblers: apple, yogurt, apple, yogurt, toasted oats...and finish with a final drizzle of agave syrup and a drizzle of calvados on the top of each serving. Leave in the fridge until ready to serve.

Very Berry Delight

with Elderflower

Serves 4

1 tbsp elderflower cordial plus 1 tsp extra

500g (2 cups) vanilla coconut milk yogurt

125g (1 cup) blueberries

125g (1 cup) raspberries

125g (1 cup) blackberries

125g (1 cup) strawberries, hulled

1 tbsp caster sugar

fresh mint leaves to garnish (optional)

You could also orchestrate a little twist using a dash of artisan gin when you add the cordial if you think all your guests are gin-friendly – it's enjoying a well-deserved revival now, and elderflower is one of many botanicals used in gin distilling.

This is an old favourite reworked. I make no apologies for adjusting this classic recipe, mostly because I prefer it this way anyway – I think the coconut yogurt here is a perfect example of a complementary addition rather than an alternative substitute. It's also quite remarkable how much elderflower cordial transforms both the dish and itself in this dessert. I'm not overly fond of elderflower as a flavour in general as I find it too overpowering and floral for my taste, but I find myself craving it in this recipe.

Add the extra tsp of elderflower cordial to the yogurt and whisk together to fully combine. Divide equally between four glasses, leaving plenty of room to add the fruit. Don't try to make the yogurt too perfect as you want some of the fruit juices to fall down the sides inside – it adds to the visual effect of the dessert (assuming you're using clear glasses, of course!).

Chill in the fridge while you prepare the fruit.

Halve or quarter the strawberries depending on their size. Place all the fruit in a bowl and add the sugar and 1 tbsp elderflower cordial. Gently combine to coat all the fruit in the cordial and leave to chill and macerate for an hour in the fridge before topping the yogurt with equal portions.

Keep in the fridge for another hour before serving to allow the fruit juices to sink down the sides of your glasses...and garnish with fresh mint leaves if you wish.

Mango and Coconut Frozen Yogurt

with Cardamom-Coated Sweet Macadamias

juice of 1 lime

250g (1 cup) natural coconut milk yogurt

250g (1 cup) good-quality mango pulp

2 tbsp agave syrup

2 tbsp caster sugar

½ tsp crushed cardamom seeds from about 12 green cardamom pods

1 tbsp dairy-free butter

2 tbsp maple syrup

50g (½ cup) macadamia nuts

Alphonso mangoes, named after Alfonso de Albuquerque, a nobleman and military expert who helped establish the Portuguese colony in India, are in season in India between April and June. You can buy Alphonso mangoes here in the UK from Asian supermarkets and some online retailers...and I urge you to do so.

There are some commercial dairy-free frozen yogurts on the market now but inevitably, due to the current lower consumer demand, there is minimal choice of flavour. We all like choice because we all have favourites – one of mine is mango, and it goes particularly well with the coconut and cardamom in this recipe. In fact maybe mango is my favourite now!

I lost a bet once over the sweetness of a mango. An Indian restaurateur friend of mine once served me some mango slices after a meal, and I claimed they were so sweet and buttery that he had either marinated them or injected them with something. He had done neither – they were my first experience of Indian 'Alphonso' mangoes. He is still chasing me to this day to make good the wager, but neither of us can remember exactly what the bet was.

✻ Add the lime juice to the coconut yogurt and mix thoroughly to loosen the yogurt a little. Add the mango pulp and agave syrup and mix thoroughly again. Chill the mixture in the fridge for at least an hour. Freeze the mixture in an ice cream machine according to the manufacturer's instructions – but remember the longer you churn, the greater the chance of air getting into the mixture and causing ice crystals. If you're not using an ice cream machine, freeze the mixture in a sealable container, churning manually two or three times during the first few hours of freezing.

To make the nuts, combine the caster sugar and crushed cardamom seeds and set aside in a bowl.

Melt the dairy-free butter and maple syrup in a frying pan and stir in the nuts. Cook on a medium heat for 5–6 minutes, stirring often, until the nuts are coloured and caramelised.

Remove the nuts with a metal slotted spoon and stir them into the sugar coating. Spread them out on a sheet of baking paper to cool completely. Store in an airtight container.

Cherry Chocolate Cake

with Cherry Sauce

240g (1½ cups) plain flour

70g (⅓ cup) cocoa powder

1½ tsp espresso coffee powder

1½ tsp bicarbonate of soda

½ tsp salt

250g (1 cup) soft dark sugar

225g (1 cup) cherries in kirsch, drained weight

350ml (1⅓ cups) hot water (let a boiled kettle stand for 5 minutes)

70g (⅓ cup) coconut oil

1½ tsp apple vinegar or cider vinegar

Icing sugar for dusting

For the cherry sauce

250g (2 cups) cherries, pitted and halved

60ml (¼ cup) water

2 tbsp caster sugar

2 tsp lemon juice

50ml (¼ cup) port (optional)

As a child, I loved Black Forest Gateau, as did my father. Back then everyone thought it was the most extravagant dessert and it was something of a rare dinner table treat for us. It wasn't the layers of cream that enticed me…it was the moist cake strewn with soft black cherries that got me hooked. To this day, I still think of my late father when I see it.

This, however, is by no means an 'alternative' gateau – it's simply a delicious chocolate cake with some very favourite things in it and some very dairy things left out. Dark, rich and laden with soft sweet dark cherries, it's also wonderful on its own with a strong, freshly brewed black coffee at break time.

✤ Prepare a 20cm (8 inch) springform or loose-base cake tin by lining the base with baking parchment.

Preheat the oven to 180°C (350°F).

Combine the dry ingredients in a bowl, mixing through thoroughly.

Combine the wet ingredients in a separate bowl and again combine thoroughly.

Pour the wet ingredients into the dry mix bowl and stir well together before pouring the mix into the prepared cake tin. Bake for 35–40 minutes or until an inserted skewer comes out clean.

Transfer to a wire cake rack and allow to cool completely, remembering to remove the parchment paper from the base.

Make your cherry sauce. Place the cherries in a pan with the other ingredients and bring to the boil before reducing the heat and cooking for about 5 minutes. Blend the mixture with a hand blender and then strain through a fine sieve into a clean bowl. Check for sweetness and add a little extra sugar if you feel it's too sharp. Set aside to cool in the fridge.

Once the cake is fully cooled, dust with a little icing sugar to finish and serve each slice with a drizzle of cherry sauce on the plate.

Pears Poached in Craft Cider

Serves 2

2 pears – Comice or Williams are ideal

1 vanilla pod

500ml (2 cups) 'Donhead' Cider or other craft cider

60g (¼ cup) granulated sugar

1 tbsp maple syrup

1 cinnamon stick

juice of ½ small lemon

1 tsp peppercorns

We have friends who own a craft cider making business in Dorset, so it seemed only natural to think of using their cider in this dish. Being a craft cider, it has good balanced strength but they somehow manage to incorporate a wonderfully delicate flavour into it as well. Perfect for this dish.

Poached pears are thought to be a little out of fashion these days, and yet I think of pears as a particularly delicious fruit. Perhaps that's it: we are all thinking of them fondly but not eating them. I won't deny you have to keep one eye on a pear to catch it just ripe and perfect to eat.

Poaching pears this way, however, takes less patience than that and the result is equally rewarding.

❋ Preheat the oven to 190°C (375°F).

Peel, halve and core the pears. Place them in an ovenproof dish that will comfortably take the liquid when poured in.

Halve the vanilla pod lengthways and scrape out all the seeds. Combine the pod and seeds with the remaining ingredients in a saucepan and bring briefly to the boil, stirring to fully dissolve the sugar. Remove from the heat and pour over the pears. Cover and bake in the oven for 50–60 minutes. Cooking time will depend on the pears, so check to see when they are tender by inserting a skewer. Try not to overcook them as you really want them tender, but not falling apart.

Remove with a slotted spoon and set aside to cool.

Strain the poaching liquid into its original saucepan, remove the vanilla pod (retain it) and reduce on the heat until you have a rich syrupy liquor at the bottom – approximately 150ml.

Arrange the pears on your serving plates and pour over enough liquor to surround the pears. Cover and refrigerate for about an hour until fully chilled.

Dress the pears with half a vanilla pod placed across them for visual contrast – but not, of course, to eat.

Limoncello and Lime Baked Rice Pudding

Serves 4

a little dairy-free butter

750ml (3 cups) rice milk

110g (½ cup) caster sugar

150g (⅔ cup) arborio rice

zest of ½ lemon

zest of ½ lime

2 tsp Limoncello

1 tbsp dairy-free butter

a little lemon and lime
marmalade (optional)

I know now I was very fortunate as a child. My brothers and I had a very good upbringing and my mother was a very good cook. Getting older has taught me to be very grateful for both of those things.

I have no childhood mealtime horror stories, just a few obligatory dislikes that every child has, most of which have now been conquered.

This is a variation on a favourite childhood pudding, made so, like many other dishes put before us at the dinner table, because my mother really could cook.

❁ Preheat the oven to 140°C (275°F). Coat a suitable baking dish lightly with some dairy-free butter.

Combine the milk, sugar, rice and two zests in a pan and heat through until the mixture begins to simmer, stirring occasionally. Remove from the heat and pour the contents into the prepared ovenproof dish. Stir around a little and then place a knob of dairy-free butter on top before baking in the oven for 1½ to 2 hours, stirring the pudding again halfway through.

It's ready when it is lightly golden and the rice is set, but still yielding in texture. You can finish under the grill if you like a darker skin to your pudding.

Serve warm but not piping hot in order to allow the flavours to stand out and with a teaspoon or two of lemon and lime marmalade on top if you like. There are several good options on the market and one quite famous one.

Spiced Nectarine Tarte Tatin

Serves 6...although maybe fewer around Christmas time

100ml (⅓ cup) maple syrup

100g (¼lb) dairy-free butter

2 star anise

2 small green cardamom pods, bruised

½ tsp ground cinnamon

squeeze of lemon juice

4 ripe nectarines, halved horizontally and stoned

1 x 320g (11oz) sheet puff pastry (vegan-friendly)

I will grant you that the use of star anise and cinnamon does give this tarte tatin a little nod in the direction of the festive holiday season, but that's neurogastronomy for you. We associate star anise and cinnamon so heavily with Christmas that it's to be expected and indeed celebrated, but they are still wondrous spices in their own right and they make this version of tarte tatin deliciously fit for any month of the year, come snow or shine!

❋ Preheat the oven to 190°C (375°F).

Melt the maple syrup and dairy-free butter in an ovenproof nonstick frying pan. About 23cm diameter is a good size. Add the spices and lemon juice and continue to cook on a medium heat for about 4–5 minutes until it all starts to caramelise. You will get a toffee apple aroma from it. Add the nectarine halves, cut side down or whichever way you prefer your tart to look when it comes out. I prefer to lay the cut side down to start. Remember you will be turning it over at the end.

Carefully apply a little pressure to push the nectarine pieces into the mixture without squashing them. Cook gently until they start to become fully tender and are taking on some of the caramelised colour of the sauce (approximately 10–15 minutes). Remove the pan from the heat.

Trim the pastry to approximately 2cm wider than the pan and carefully lay it over the contents, tucking it in all round the inside with a wooden spoon so you don't touch the very hot caramel sauce. Some of the caramel will inevitably bubble up over the edge as you tuck it down, but you want that to happen.

Bake in the oven for 30–35 minutes or until the pastry is crisp and golden in colour. Remove from the oven and allow to stand for 2–3 minutes before very carefully (using oven gloves) placing a serving plate upside down on the pan and turning quickly over to release the tart on to the plate, now with the fruit side up.

Serve still hot and accompanied by whatever you fancy, or simply on its own.

Strawberry and Tarragon Sorbet

Serves 6

200g (1 cup) caster sugar

200ml (¾ cup) water

6 sprigs of fresh tarragon

800g (1½lb) fresh strawberries, hulled and halved

zest of ½ lemon

juice of ½ lemon

pinch of sea salt

Well, what can I say? I said earlier in this book that there was a time I used to run a mile from tarragon – and here I am, putting it in desserts. I absolutely love this sorbet. It may well be my favourite. A good strawberry sorbet is a delicious thing anyway, but the tarragon adds a slightly mysterious soft note, complementing the strawberries without ever overpowering them. At first read, it sounds like it shouldn't or couldn't work, but something happens between the two otherwise independent flavours to make them marry. Must be love.

❋ Make the syrup by combining the caster sugar, water and three of the tarragon sprigs in a saucepan. Heat through to dissolve the sugar, then remove from the heat and set aside to cool, leaving the tarragon in while it does.

Combine the strawberries with the lemon zest, lemon juice, the remaining three tarragon sprigs and a pinch of sea salt in a large bowl. Place the bowl over a large saucepan of simmering water and gently allow the strawberries to slowly cook in their own juice until broken down, stirring occasionally to turn them over evenly. This will take about 30 minutes.

Once ready, remove the tarragon and pour the mixture into a food processor and combine with the syrup. Blend until smooth. Taste for sweetness and acidity and correct if necessary – a squeeze of lemon for acidity or a pinch of sugar for sweetness.

Churn in an ice cream maker according to the manufacturer's instructions until fully chilled and smooth, then freeze. You can pass the sorbet mixture through a nylon sieve if you like, before churning, to make it extra smooth, but I like the texture as it is.

If churning by hand, place the sorbet mixture in the freezer, removing every hour or so to churn it before returning it to the freezer – repeat this 2–3 times until it is frozen.

You could serve the sorbet garnished with a fresh sprig of tarragon on the side, which would give the game away, of course – or not...and leave them guessing.

Some Important Plant Compounds and Their Role in Health Maintenance

This is a list of some of the plant compounds that have important roles in health maintenance – if you are following a plant-based diet, it is good to know how you may be benefiting! This is a useful reference when you are dipping into different sections and need a gentle reminder, or if you would like to consume more superfoods.

Anthocyanins (procyanidins) – all red/purple fruits and vegetables, including grapes, also red wine. Anthocyanins belong to the large flavonoid group, and are characterised by their red, purple and blue colours. They are well absorbed from dietary sources and are good antioxidants (free radical quenchers and anti-inflammatory agents). In nutritional medicine, they are used to combat arthritis and degenerative conditions of the arteries and connective tissues, and are considered to be highly protective components of foods. The high content in black grapes and red wine (where the flavonoids are retained) may confer protection from heart disease, as anthocyanins can inhibit platelet clotting, and their antioxidant actions can stop the oxidation of LDL cholesterol.

Beta-carotene – orange fruits and vegetables including carrots, sweet potatoes, squashes, apricots, mangoes, peaches, also red peppers, spinach, kale and broccoli. Beta-carotene is a very good antioxidant, and the precursor of vitamin A, and is typically orange-red in colour. Foods that are rich in beta-carotene are carrots (5–8mg in 100g), sweet potatoes, squashes, spinach, kale, apricots, mangoes, peaches, red peppers and broccoli – although the absorption from leafy greens is poor, when compared with mangoes. This is because of the different ways in which plants store carotenoids.

Betaine – beetroot, wheat and spinach. Betaine is the most important dietary source of methyl groups. It is found in beetroot, wheat and in lesser amounts in spinach. Methyl groups are essential for health (the nervous and immune systems, the coronary and vascular systems, the kidneys and the liver), and they must be obtained from dietary sources (they are also found in choline, methionine, vitamin B6 and folic acid). Betaine reduces the risk of coronary heart disease and Alzheimer's disease, and it is credited with antidepressant properties. It has been likened to a B vitamin.

Carotenoids – carrots, squashes, oranges, tomatoes, kale, spinach, red peppers. Carotenoids are the compounds that give rise to the yellow, orange, pink and red colours in some fruits and vegetables such as carrots, squashes and apricots. They are all good antioxidants, they can protect against macular degeneration and coronary artery disease, and many have an anti-cancer action. It is suggested that if they are taken as supplements, they should be accompanied by vitamin C. Examples are beta-carotene (carrots and squashes), cryptoxanthin (oranges), lycopene (tomatoes), lutein (kale) and zeaxanthin (kale, spinach, red peppers).

Flavonoids – skins and seeds of many fruits and vegetables, including grape skins, also turmeric, red wine. Flavonoids are a large and important group of compounds found in plants that are important in health maintenance. They are found in a very wide range of fruits and vegetables, and especially the skins and seeds, where they form part of the plant's defence system, but which are so often discarded! As a group, they have a wide range of health benefits – many are powerful antioxidants and antimicrobials; some are anti-inflammatory, anti-allergic and supportive of the immune system. Flavonoids often have striking colours – from the yellow curcumin in turmeric to the red, blue and purple anthocyanins in grape skins and red wine.

Genistein – soya beans. Genistein is an isoflavonoid found in soya beans. It has been shown to inhibit the proliferation of cancer cells (*in vitro*) and its potential therapeutic indications include heart disease, osteoporosis and menopause. It is sometimes described as a phytoestrogen, but does not produce estrogenic effects.

Lutein – spinach, kale, green and yellow peppers. Lutein is a yellow carotenoid, related to zeazanthin, with good antioxidant properties, and has been credited with anti-cancer potential. It is found in good levels in spinach and kale, and also in mature green and yellow bell peppers.

Lycopene – tomatoes. Lycopene is an important antioxidant that is found in tomatoes; it has anti-cancer and heart-protective potential.

Omega 3 – fish oil, seaweeds, walnuts, flax seeds, chia seeds, hemp seeds, beans, winter squash, broccoli rabe, kale, cauliflower, berries, mangoes, melons. Omega 3 is very important for cardiovascular and brain health, and is found in abundance in oily fish but also

seaweeds – sources of two important fatty acids: EPA (eicosapentaenoic acid) and DHA (docosahexaenoic acid). In plants we find Omega 3 alpha-linolenic acid (ALA) which can be used by the body to make EPA and DHA, but an excess of Omega 6 can inhibit this conversion. Plant sources of Omega 3 are nuts and seeds, especially walnuts, flax seeds, chia seeds and hemp seeds, and also beans, winter squash, spinach, broccoli rabe, kale, cauliflower and some fruits including berries, mangoes and melons.

Quercitin – onions and apples. Quercitin is a flavonoid and is considered to be a potent cardioprotective substance. It is not well absorbed in the gut, but is found in other tissues elsewhere in the body. The most important dietary sources are onions and apples.

Sterols – rice bran, sesame seeds, sunflower seeds, avocados. Sterols are plant compounds with anti-inflammatory actions and which may offer protection against stress on the immune system. The best plant dietary sources are rice bran, sesame seeds, sunflower seeds and avocados.

Zeaxanthin – spinach, kale, red peppers, paprika, sweetcorn. Zeaxanthin is a carotenoid related to lutein, and is found in kale, spinach (green leafy vegetables), red peppers, paprika and sweetcorn; it is a retinal antioxidant associated with protection against macular degeneration. It may also protect against coronary artery disease and ageing.

Bibliography and Further Reading

Carluccio, S.A. and Contaldo, G. (2011) *Two Greedy Italians*. London: Quadrille Publishing.

Clayton, P. (2004) *Health Defence*, 2nd Edition. Aylesbury: Accelerated Learning Systems.

Clayton, P. and Rose, C. (2013) *Inflamm-Ageing*. Aylesbury: Accelerated Learning Systems.

David, E. (1999) *Italian Food*. London: Penguin Classics.

Fearnley-Whittingstall, H. (2014) *Light and Easy: Healthy Recipes for Every Day*. London: Bloomsbury.

Gayler, P. (2003) *A Passion for Vegetables*. London: Kyle Cathie.

Hemphill, I. and Hemphill, E. (2003) *Herbaceous: A Cook's Guide to Culinary Herbs*. London: Conran Octopus.

Khan, Y. (2016) *The Saffron Tales: Recipes from the Persian Kitchen*. London: Bloomsbury.

Kime, T. (2005) *Exploring Taste and Flavour: The Art of Combining Hot, Sour, Salty and Sweet in 150 Recipes*. London: Kyle Cathie.

Lawless, A. (2009) *Artisan Perfumery or Being Led by the Nose*. Stroud: Boronia Souk.

McGee, H. (2004) *McGee on Food and Cooking: An Encyclopedia of Kitchen Science, History and Culture*. London: Hodder and Stoughton.

McGee, H. (n.d.) Curious Cook website. Available at http://curiouscook.typepad.com/site/about-harold-mcgee.html (accessed 29 June 2017).

Ottolenghi, Y. (2010) *Plenty*. London: Ebury Press.

Rhind, J.P. (2013) *Fragrance and Wellbeing: Plant Aromatics and Their Influence on the Psyche*. London: Singing Dragon.

Segnit, N. (2010) *The Flavour Thesaurus*. London: Bloomsbury.

Shepherd, G.M. (2012) *Neurogastronomy: How the Brain Creates Flavour and Why It Matters*. New York, NY: Columbia University Press.

Simas, T., Ficek, M., Diaz-Guilera, A., Obrador, P. and Rodriguez, P.R. (2017) Food-bridging: A new network construction to unveil the principles of cooking. *Physics and Society*, 14 April 2017. Available at https://arxiv.org/pdf/1704.03330.pdf (accessed 12 May 2017).

Slater, N. (2003) *Toast*. London: Harper Perennial.

Stevenson, R.J. (2009) *The Psychology of Flavour*. Oxford: Oxford University Press.

Resources

SALT

Seasoning is hugely important, both in its use and the quality of what you use. You want every ingredient you use to be at its best in these recipes, so why opt for lesser products? Sea salts have soft, forgiving flavours which complement good food – and do try flavoured variants such as smoked, seaweed, chipotle, rosemary and wild garlic, and regional salts such as Cornish, Isle of Skye and Guérande.

Maldon Crystal Salt Company
  www.maldonsalt.co.uk

Cornish Sea Salt Company
  www.cornishseasalt.co.uk

Falksalt
  www.falksalt.com

Isle of Skye Sea Salt Company
  www.isleofskyeseasalt.co.uk

PEPPER

If salt is important, then quality peppercorns are also fundamental ingredients in your kitchen. We have all too often regarded pepper as a common table seasoning, when it is in fact a genuine 'prince among spices'. Good peppercorns, in all their varieties, can elevate simple dishes and add depth and complexity to flavour. Make tellicherry peppercorns your 'standard', and make good use of varieties such as Indonesian long pepper, Keralan green pepper and Kampot rouge – these have such unique, individual flavour profiles to offer, which are worlds apart from the tragic pepper that many of us grew up with!

Peppermongers
  www.salthouseandpeppermongers.com

The Pepper Project (Kampot peppers from Cambodia)
  www.pepperproject.org

HERBS AND SPICES

Spices should also be of the highest quality and not kept too long – otherwise, they are just not worth using. Like seasoning, you will not be doing any justice to the flavours in a recipe if you are adding old or flat spices. So, buy regularly and replace often! Most spices are relatively inexpensive, so keep them for 6–9 months and then discard. Inevitably, you want vibrant spices that deliver their wonderful aromas and flavours to enhance the dish you are making, so if a spice is racking up the months, then plan to make something with it! Old paprika adds nothing to a dish (trust Greg – he has lots of old paprika) and even saffron has a best-before date – perish the thought!

Herbs, Spices and Much More
Cultural ingredients from around the world
http://theasiancookshop.co.uk

HERBAL TEAS

Regular consumption of organic herbal teas can be a delicious way to augment your daily intake of plant antioxidants and anti-inflammatory compounds. Try a variety – from the earthy, fragrant ginger and turmeric teas to the fresh, clean, green matcha varieties – and it will rapidly become a delightful daily ritual.

Pukka Herbal Teas
www.pukkaherbs.com

OILS

Throughout this book we have recommended the use of extra virgin olive oil and rapeseed oils. Flavoured oils can add a new dimension to dishes. Try infused rapeseed oils – there is a big range to choose from. We like the lemongrass and oregano variants!

Supernature (cold-pressed rapeseed oils)
www.supernature.uk.com

PASTA AND ITALIAN INGREDIENTS

All the pasta in this book is the dried variety, and we strongly recommend – no, we insist – on the traditional 'bronze die' type. Bronze dies are 'stamps' which the pasta dough is pressed through – giving the extruded pasta a roughened, porous surface which improves the cooking process, and which sauces can stick to – resulting in an improved flavour and texture. You can find cheaper products made with Teflon-lined equipment, but they do not compare in terms of quality and flavour.

Nife is Life
www.nifeislife.com

Delicatezza the Italian Pantry
www.delicatezza.co.uk

Afterword

A Reflection on Food and Friendship

Jennifer: I am so very lucky to have a career that reflects some of my passions – food, flavour and scent – and along the way I have gained valuable experience in research and development, quality assurance, then as an aromatherapist, a lecturer in higher education, and now in mentoring and writing. The initial proposal for this book was written shortly after my decision to become vegan, when I was finding my way around a new way of cooking and eating, all the while realising that although I knew rather a lot about the scents, chemistry and therapeutic uses of aromatic herbs and spices, I needed to focus on their flavours. And so I had the idea for a new book which I was going to call 'The Aromatic Vegan' – all about the use of herbs and spices in plant-based cuisine. But on reflection, I realised that what I was aiming to do was much bigger than that – I wanted to write a book that would change the way we think about flavour, and specifically in relation to vegan cooking! I had 'discovered' neurogastronomy and had begun to realise how this had the potential to transform the way we cook and eat. I also knew that although I could write about ingredients, I did not have skill or expertise in recipe development...but I knew people who did...

Greg and Alison were our neighbours for several years. A mutual love of cats and dogs, music and good food and wine naturally led to a rewarding and enduring friendship. This was cemented over many evenings sitting at their table, enjoying delicious food and listening to everything from jazz (when eating) to 1970s rock and country (as the night wore on), with our furry families in attendance. When I became vegan, they embarked with enormous enthusiasm on a culinary adventure – exploring how flavour theory could reveal a new approach to plant-based cooking. Greg is a 'natural' when it comes to creating dishes – and a combination of his talent, experience and curiosity (and Alison's formidable palate) led to the creation of entire menus with ingredients exclusively from the plant kingdom. The result of our endeavours is a collection of neurogastromony-inspired recipes that cook and eat very well indeed. Some may have songs written for them – I have a Recipe Collection with a soundtrack! This book is our way of sharing our mutual passion for quality ingredients, cooking, flavour creation, eating, all seasoned with tales of our travels and experiences. I am so excited to have achieved our aim of raising the bar in plant-based cuisine, and I express my heartfelt gratitude to Greg and Alison.

Cook with all of your heart.

reg: I have two enduring passions in my life. Food and music. Both of which have sustained me well throughout a career spent, so far, almost entirely within challenging 'customer-facing' roles.

I look back however and realise I have always sought to 'look after' people and their expectations, and that fundamentally I like to please the people that I like.

Therefore, when Jen's decision to change her lifestyle meant that cooking vegetarian for everyone changed to cooking vegan for all, I couldn't resist taking on the challenge.

It was an opportunity to explore further my love and knowledge of ingredients from around the world, and use them in context with Jen's examination of how and why we perceive them through our senses. My journey of exploration, explanation and plant-based recipe development began.

As I hope you will, I have learned a great deal about the worth and value of many ingredients I hitherto took for granted, and gained an ever-evolving understanding of what plant-based food has to offer. The experience has encouraged me to utilise *all* of my senses while I cook and has undoubtedly contributed to a great appreciation as to the 'what and why' of the music I play while cooking or eating.

Food simply loves music... When I recall with utter adoration my experience of the opera *Tosca* in the magnificent Arena di Verona in Italy, it comes in complete unison with the memory of the wonderful food we had there in the surrounding trattorias too. Similarly, I will forever associate the voice of Billie Holiday with celebrating my engagement in Paris. It was just an inconspicuous side-street bistro that we found, but the simple French dishes we enjoyed so much there were doubtlessly elevated by the music we listened to that night. I could have easily added a playlist to the recipes here such is the effect learning more about neurogastronomy has had in my kitchen. Indeed, many of the recipes here have personal attachment, described in their introductions, which serve to exemplify the broad reach of neurogastronomy – Spaghetti with Roasted 'San Marzano' Tomato Sauce on page 221 to name but one.

I consider myself very lucky – cooking and music have been my great escapes and I now find myself working harder than ever to put cooking at the very core of what I do.

It has been an enormous learning experience and joy to do this. Driven by my desire to please, I wanted to create plant-based dishes that were every bit as delicious to eat as any other. I have discovered things I didn't know, eaten things in ways I hadn't before and, from my own slightly distant stance, elevated plant-based food to a position of equal affection at my table. Having completed the book, I want everyone to be equally delighted when they choose a plant-based recipe... whether today, tomorrow or every day...and, of course, to understand why!

Cook happy.

Acknowledgements

We would like to thank the following individuals and organisations for sharing their time, wisdom and expertise with us.

Alison Law for your uncompromising palate, for help and guidance, and your love, empathy, generosity and friendship.

Derek Rhind for being on the journey (all the way), and for your love, companionship, insight, encouragement and support – and for believing in us...

Harry the chilled black cat with a wicked sense of humour (and saboteur of vegetable plots), and Leeloo and Gertie the Tibetan 'Little People' – you are our furry families. Thank you for lighting up our lives, bringing an inner glow, and making us smile and laugh and cry, and teaching us all about unconditional love and living 'in the moment'.

Lynn at Supernature, Tom at Peppermongers and everyone at Maldon Salt and L'Aquila for kindly supporting us with sample products to assist in recipe development.

Heather Anderson and Pete Ritchie at Whitmuir the Organic Place for sharing their experience and knowledge about the benefits of growing and eating organic produce.

Jessica Kingsley, James Cherry and the team at Singing Dragon for making this dream come true.

Jennifer would like to thank Greg for the beautiful images, and for all that preparation, cooking and styling.

And a word from Greg...

Special thanks to my good friend Matthew Roberts of www.matthewrobertsphotographer. co.uk for his expert advice and guidance.

Finally – I could not have undertaken this project without two very special people and I would like to thank them both. Without Jennifer's invitation to work with her and her trust and belief in me, I could not have started this. I will be forever grateful to her for involving me in this book. Without my wife Alison's love and constant support and encouragement I could not have fulfilled this and I thank her for ever. Together forever like the penguins.

Thank you – it's been an education and a joy!

Index